Praise for *Grading for Equity*

We don't usually think of grading when talking about equity, but in Grading for Equity: What It Is, Why It Matters, and How It Can Transform Schools and Classrooms, *Joe Feldman helps us see why grading is an integral part of an equity agenda. He shows us how we can use grading to help students become the leaders of their own learning and lift the veil on how to succeed. He reminds us that authentic assessment and transparent grading are essential parts of a culturally responsive classroom. This must-have book will help teachers learn to implement improved, equity-focused grading for impact.*

—**Zaretta Hammond,** Education Consultant and
Author of *Culturally Responsive Teaching and the Brain*
St. Mary's College's Kalmanovitz School of Education

This book will stop educators who want to improve their practices with underserved students right in their tracks. Feldman offers an insightful invitation to teachers who dare change the ways in which we have been taught to grade students' products. He demonstrates how our grading practices are grossly under-substantiated and too often unquestioned, and he challenges educators to build equitable assessment tools and mechanisms to support learning and development of all students. Grading for Equity *penetrates macro-level grading policies to transform micro-level teaching practices that embrace the cultural and the contextual. A must read for justice-centered educators.*

—**Rich Milner**, Co–Author of *"These Kids are Out of Control"* and
Cornelius Vanderbilt Professor of Education
Peabody College, Vanderbilt University

Wow, Wow Wow!!! This book hooked me as a not-to-be-missed read right from the Prologue. Joe Feldman makes a strong case for shared grading practices to overcome the inequity of traditional grading, with solid reasoning, well-chosen research evidence, and perhaps most significantly, the powerful and frequent use of teacher voice. The chapters' organizing structure encourages thoughtful and reflective reading, and will be particularly beneficial for book study within PLCs. . . . The main message of the book for me is summed up in this quote, 'We teachers cannot continue to sacrifice the integrity and reliability of our grades at the altar of professional autonomy.

—**Ken O'Connor,** Author and Consultant
How to Grade for Learning

There is growing awareness within the industry of education that traditional grading practices have become a barrier to meaningful student learning. One dilemma is that there is a lack of resources to support educators who want to adopt new grading practices that are both accurate and equitable. Joe Feldman addresses this need with his book, Grading for Equity. *Joe skillfully makes a compelling argument for change and offers specific ways educators can make profound differences to their grading practices. Students become intrinsically motivated to learn when their grades accurately measure where they are in the learning process. Students who typically give up any hope of success can now approach learning with a positive growth mindset. Grading for Equity will provide clarity and tools for an individual instructor or as a book study for an entire organization.*

—Jeffrey Tooker, Deputy Superintendent of Educational Services
Placer Union High School District

Joe Feldman peels back the curtain and shows the many flaws of our traditional grading system. His arguments are convincing - and the alternatives he proposes are both practical and powerful. Reading this book will make you re-think the way you assess students and will inspire you to enact a system that encourages revision and redemption instead of compliance and corruption.

—Denise Pope, Senior Lecturer,
Stanford Graduate School of Education
and Co-Founder, Challenge Success

Grading for Equity

This book is dedicated to Nikole, Olivia, and Ellis, for their love, courage, and joy.

Grading for Equity

What It Is, Why It Matters, and How It Can Transform Schools and Classrooms

Joe Feldman

CORWIN
A SAGE Publishing Company

FOR INFORMATION:

Corwin

A SAGE Company

2455 Teller Road

Thousand Oaks, California 91320

(800) 233-9936

www.corwin.com

SAGE Publications Ltd.

1 Oliver's Yard

55 City Road

London EC1Y 1SP

United Kingdom

SAGE Publications India Pvt. Ltd.

B 1/I 1 Mohan Cooperative Industrial Area

Mathura Road, New Delhi 110 044

India

SAGE Publications Asia-Pacific Pte. Ltd.

3 Church Street

#10-04 Samsung Hub

Singapore 049483

Program Director and Publisher: Dan Alpert

Associate Editor: Lucas Schleicher

Editorial Assistant: Mia Rodriguez

Production Editor: Amy Schroller

Copy Editor: Diane DiMura

Typesetter: C&M Digitals (P) Ltd.

Proofreader: Jennifer Grubba

Indexer: Judy Hunt

Cover Designer: Karine Hovsepian

Marketing Manager: Maura Sullivan

Printed in the United States of America.

ISBN 978-1-5063-9157-1

This book is printed on acid-free paper.

21 22 20

Contents

Acknowledgments

First and foremost, I am indebted to the hundreds of educators who I have worked alongside, struggled with, and learned from as we endeavored to implement more equitable grading practices. Some of the sites of those teachers and administrators are Centennial College Preparatory Academy Middle School and Aspire Pacific Academy Middle/High School (both charter schools) in Huntington Park, California; San Leandro High School, Bancroft Middle School, and Muir Middle School in San Leandro California; Sobrato High School in Morgan Hill, California; Placer Union High School District in Auburn, California; Georgetown Day School in Washington, DC, Phillips Andover Academy in Andover, Massachusetts, and SEED Charter High School in Baltimore, Maryland. Although I like to think that my questions have deepened the thinking of these consummate professional educators, their questions and experiences with more equitable grading practices have taught me much more.

I am deeply grateful that these sites permitted me to listen to their students, whose experiences and unfiltered opinions about grading helped all of the adults, myself included, to recognize the profound impact of our decisions about grading, and never to minimize that impact just because teenagers put on a good front.

A special thank you to Wendy Gudalewicz, my former boss in New Haven Unified School District, who charged me with improving some of the most intractable and inequitable elements of our schools—tracking and grading—and providing me with the freedom and support to begin this journey.

Thanks to Zaretta Hammond, who was the first to urge me to write this book (Heck, you *demanded* it). You were the spark in this long endeavor, and I have so appreciated your guidance, generosity, and encouragement. Thanks also to Shane Safir for your thought partnership and support.

To Dan Alpert, my editor—thanks for your flexibility, assistance, and cheerleading throughout this process. Your deep commitment to the urgency of this book has made this a perfect fit.

I also appreciate two people who assisted me with my arguments for particular grading practices and enabled me to sound much smarter than I am: Tom Denton for his math expertise, and Nathan Moore, M. D. for his OxyContin analogy.

As always, my family has shown unflagging support, with special thanks to Mom. My deepest gratitude goes to Nikole, my wife and partner in life, who not only provided invaluable feedback on a number of sections and iterations of this book, but who made this possible—whether sponsoring a writing mini-retreat, holding down the fort, putting kids to bed, or being willing to hear me talk (yet again) about my writing. I am better because of you.

Publisher's Acknowledgments

Corwin gratefully acknowledges the contributions of the following reviewers:

Waldo Alvarado
Director of Equity & Diversity
Reading School District
Reading, PA

Janice Bradley
Assistant Director, Utah Education
Policy Center
University of Utah
Salt Lake City, UT

Amy B. Colton
Executive Director and Senior Consultant
Learning Forward
Ann Arbor, MI

Patti Hendricks
Language Arts Teacher
Sunset Ridge Middle School
West Jordan, UT

Melissa Miller
Science/Math Educator
Randall G Lynch Middle School
Farmington, AR

Renee Nealon
Elementary School Teacher
McDowell Elementary
Petaluma, CA

About the Author

Joe Feldman has worked in education at the local and national levels for over twenty years in both charter and district school contexts, and as a teacher, principal, and district administrator. He began his career as a high school English and American history teacher in Atlanta Public Schools and was the founding principal of a charter high school in Washington, DC. He has been the Director of Charter Schools for New York City Department of Education, the Director of K–12 Instruction in Union City, California, and was a Fellow to the Chief of Staff for U.S. Secretary of Education Richard Riley. Joe is currently CEO of Crescendo Education Group (crescendoedgroup.org), a consulting organization that partners with schools and districts to help teachers use improved and more equitable grading and assessment practices. Joe graduated from Stanford, Harvard Graduate School of Education, and NYU Law School. He is the author of several articles on grading, assessment, and equity, and the author of *Teaching Without Bells: What We Can Learn from Powerful Practice in Small Schools* (Paradigm). He lives in Oakland, California with his wife and two children.

Prologue

Mallory's Dilemma

The data couldn't be possible. Actually, it *shouldn't* be possible.

Mallory had just completed her first year as principal of Centennial College Prep Middle School, a new public charter school in Huntington Park, California. As a young, white woman leading a school that served nearly all Latino students, many living below the poverty line, Mallory had approached her job humbly, not immediately pushing initiatives and changing policies to align to her own personal vision (what she called the "new sheriff in town approach"). Instead, her priority was to first understand her school community: its context, history, strengths, and needs. She had watched, listened, and built relationships with her faculty, students, and their families. She had visited classrooms, reviewed teachers' lesson plans, and studied the school's statistics: attendance percentages, disciplinary referrals, and test scores.

Whether the data she reviewed was "hard" data like test scores or "soft" data like her observations of teacher–student dynamics in classrooms, Mallory kept a sharp lookout for how the school could be made more equitable. Mallory's vision was that students should have equal opportunities for success regardless of their ethnicity, first language, gender, income, or special needs. She paid attention to patterns of unequal achievement or opportunity in her school. For example, were boys being referred more frequently to the office? Were poorer students showing a common weakness on a strand of skills on the writing assessment? Did students who received special education services have a higher rate of absenteeism?

But that wasn't all. To Mallory, one of the most important indications of a high-quality, equitable school is that students are successful regardless of their teacher.

One teacher's students shouldn't learn different material or be less prepared for the next grade than another teacher's students. Fortunately, based on her classroom visits and other data, Mallory found that although teachers approached their work in ways that reflected their individual backgrounds and personalities, students' learning experiences were generally consistent across classrooms. Students in the same course taught by two different teachers—such as Ms. Thompson's and Ms. Richardson's sixth-grade English classes—were learning the same skills, reading the same books and essays, getting the same homework, receiving similar support, and taking the same tests. Mallory was confident that regardless of their sixth-grade teacher, students would be similarly prepared for seventh-grade English.

Since teachers were aligned with what and how they were teaching, and because the school didn't track students or create unbalanced classes where one sixth-grade English class would be stronger than the others, Mallory reasoned that by all accounts the performance of students should be comparable across teachers of the same course. In other words, the rate of As, Bs, Cs, Ds, and Fs in any course should be relatively similar for each teacher of that course. But that wasn't happening. Strange things were showing up in the data.

Take, for example, her school's sixth-grade math and English classes, each taught by three different teachers:

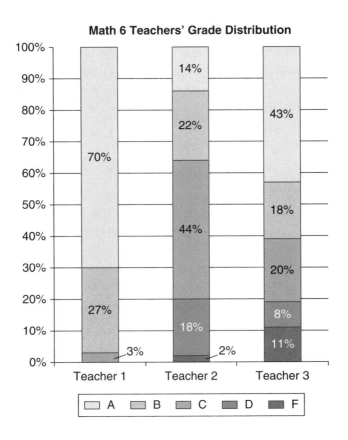

Math 6 Teachers' Grade Distribution

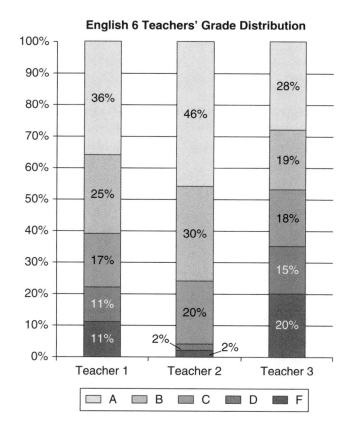

English 6 Teachers' Grade Distribution

If you were a student in two of the three teachers' math classes you had about a 20 percent chance of getting a D or F, but if you were in the third teacher's math class, you had 0 percent chance of getting a D or F. In the English classes, taught by three different teachers including Ms. Richardson and Ms. Thompson, the range of D and F rates—4 percent, 22 percent, and 35 percent—was even more dramatic. Mallory double-checked the grade data, then double-checked that students in the classes weren't significantly different—in other words, one teacher's students as a group didn't have lower standardized test scores or higher rates of absences. No, the groups of students were similar; the only difference among the classes seemed to be the chances of receiving a particular grade.

Mallory put on her detective hat and considered, investigated, and then rejected several explanations: No substantive differences in instruction. Teachers were using the same curriculum with the same tests and even scored those tests as a team to ensure fairness and uniform evaluation. Mallory scoured students' previous test scores and grades, with no indication of drastically different profiles of the classes as a whole. No substantive difference in the classroom physically—it wasn't as if one classroom had a broken thermostat or was closer to a noisy playground. What was even odder was that students with identical standardized test scores received different grades depending on their teacher. The teachers were teaching similarly, the students were demonstrating similar achievement, but the grades showed inconsistency. This data seemed unexplainable, impossible, and grossly inequitable.

On a lark, Mallory looked at the syllabus for each class—each teacher of a course had created her own personalized version—and it shocked her. Each teacher's syllabus began with a similar introduction to the course content and description of important materials for the class, but then it was as if each teacher was in an entirely different school:

- One teacher accepted no homework after the attendance bell rang, some deducted points if homework was late (although the amount deducted ranged from a few points to two letter grades' worth), and another accepted work beyond the due date up until the end of the quarter, with no penalty.

- One teacher gave each daily homework assignment a grade of 10 percent or 100 percent based on how much of the homework was completed and correct, and allowed students who had received 10 percent up to one week to correct mistakes. Another gave full credit for an assignment if the student showed effort to complete it, regardless of whether answers were correct.

- One teacher reduced points on an assignment if the student didn't completely and correctly write her or his first and last name, along with the title of the assignment. Another subtracted points if an assignment was submitted on notebook paper that had ripped holes or ripped edges.

- Most teachers organized their gradebook by grouping types of assignments into categories (Homework, Classwork, Tests, etc.), and weighted each category to denote its importance (Homework = 30% of the grade; Tests = 70%). However, no teacher had the same weightings for any categories. For example, the weight of tests ranged from 40 percent to 70 percent of a student's grade.

- Some teachers had only three categories of assignments (Tests, Classwork, and Homework), while others included categories that seemed more subjective, such as Citizenship, Participation, and Effort. There was no explanation in the syllabus of how these subjective categories were calculated or on what they were based.

- Other teachers didn't use percentage weights at all, but assigned different point values to different assignments. For example, Homework assignments might be 5 to 10 points each, with tests worth 100 points.

Teachers' different grading policies made it possible for two students with the same academic performance to receive different grades. What particularly confused and concerned Mallory was that some teachers were grading students on criteria that seemed to have nothing to do with their academic achievement—such as whether their paper had intact holes or had the proper heading—and others were basing parts of students' grades entirely on subjective criteria, such as effort, that were susceptible to teachers' implicit biases. This grade data that couldn't be possible suddenly was.

A few days later, something happened that changed Mallory's confusion to concern. Maria, a shy but earnest eighth grader, came to her office nearly in tears. Last year as a seventh grader, she had received a B in math, her most challenging subject, but this year was barely passing with a D. What was really frustrating Maria was that even though she often handed in homework assignments late or incomplete—she had after-school responsibilities at home in addition to dance class three times a week—she consistently performed well on every exam. She obviously had learned the math and had shown it when it mattered most, and though last year this type of performance had earned her a B, her teacher this year gave zeros for late or incomplete homework, resulting in her D. Maria was feeling a crisis of confidence: Other students copied to get their homework in on time for the homework points, which Maria had resisted, but would she have no other choice? Had last year's teacher lied to her about her math skills? Was she not as good at math as she thought? Or was this year's teacher out to get her?

To Mallory, no longer were her teachers' inconsistent policies a theoretical dilemma. The school had spent months of planning and coordination to make sure teachers in the math department were using sequenced curriculum and that each teacher was preparing students to be ready for the next year—called "vertical alignment." Yet teachers' different approaches to grading was undermining all of it, sending confusing messages about learning and impacting students' grades and promotion rates, their beliefs about school, and even their self-image.

Mallory had to talk to her teachers about what was happening. The prior year, she had broached many conversations—some quite difficult and uncomfortable—with her teachers about curriculum, teaching strategies, job responsibilities, even evaluation. Surely, she assumed, they would be as astonished as she was when they saw the data and would reconsider how they graded.

But now came her second shock: When she began a discussion of grades with her teachers, it was like poking a hornet's nest. Nothing prepared her for the volatility of conversations about teachers' grading practices. Many of her teachers, previously open to exploring new ideas about nearly every aspect of their work, reacted with defensiveness and adamant justification. Teachers with higher failure rates argued proudly that their grading reflected higher standards, that they were the "real teachers." A teacher with low failure rates explained that he was the only teacher who cared enough to give students retakes and second chances. One teacher simply refused to discuss the topic, citing her state's Education Code that protected teachers from administrators' pressure to change or overwrite grades. One teacher began to cry, confessing that she had never received any training or support on how to grade and feared that she was grading students unfairly. Conversations about grading weren't like conversations about classroom management or assessment design, which teachers approached with openness and in deference to research. Instead, teachers talked about grading in a language of morals about the "real world" and beliefs about students; grading seemed to tap directly into the deepest sense of who teachers were in their classroom.

When she talked about these grading problems with principals of other schools, Mallory was surprised and dismayed to learn that grading varied by teacher in *every* school. This phenomenon was widespread, even the norm. Teachers thoughtfully and intentionally were creating policies that they believed, in their most thoughtful professional judgment, would promote learning. Yet they were doing so independently and often contradicting each other, yielding in each school a patchwork of well-intentioned but ultimately idiosyncratic approaches to evaluating and reporting student performance. Even when a department or a group of teachers made agreements—for example, to have homework count for no more than 40 percent of a grade—teachers' other unique policies and practices, such as whether homework would be accepted after the due date, made their attempts at consistency seem half-hearted and ineffectual.

What's more, even though every principal had the same problems and frustrations with inconsistent grading, no one had any success in addressing it. Other principals had tried to raise the topic of grading and had met the same kind of resistance Mallory had experienced, sometimes even with vitriol and formal allegations of attempted infringement upon teachers' academic freedom.

Mallory wondered: Was inconsistent grading an unavoidable part of schools, like the annoying bells between classes, the complaints about cafeteria food, the awkward physical education outfits, and weak turnout at Open House? Was it an inevitable side effect of teacher creativity, ownership, and initiative? Were teachers' different ways of evaluating and reporting student performance a hallmark of teachers' professionalism or an undermining of that professionalism? And did principals' avoidance of addressing the variance and inconsistency of grading represent support of their teachers, a détente between teachers and administrators, or an unspoken compromise that ignored the damaging impact on children, particularly those who are most vulnerable?

My Own Journey: Frustrations and Hope

In over twenty years of working in schools as a teacher, principal, and district administrator, I've known lots of "Mallory"s. In fact, as a principal I was a "Mallory." Grading among my teachers—my professional, awesome, hardworking, ethical, deeply committed and emotionally invested teachers—was inconsistent. Though as a professional learning community of educators we tackled the challenging topics of relevant curriculum design, high-quality instructional practices, writing across the curriculum, our racial disparities in achievement and discipline, and, occasionally, our obligation to stand against the historically and culturally hegemonic function of American schools, we couldn't mention grading. Years later, as a district administrator responsible for supporting and coaching principals, I could never convince my principals, much less equip them, to find the language, strategies, or courage to address teachers' grading practices.

I could not agree more with Jeffrey Erickson (2010) who calls grading the "third rail" of schools. On one hand, like a train's third rail, grades provide power and legitimacy to teaching and learning. Grades are the main criteria in nearly every decision that schools make about students. Here are some examples:

- course assignment (eligibility for advanced, honors, or AP classes)

- graduation (completion of course requirements)

- academic awards (valedictorian, summa cum laude)

- extracurricular activities (athletics, clubs)

- promotion (able to progress to next grade level or sequenced course)

- retention (repeating a course or grade level)

- additional supports (mandatory tutoring or remediation)

- additional opportunities (special field trips)

- scholarships

- college admission

Grades inform decisions outside the educational world as well. Potential employers consider grades when hiring, and GPAs are often required for youth work permits and reductions in car insurance, which means students' grades can affect family income and expenses. And those are just the decisions made by institutions. Caregivers and families often provide rewards and privileges (including praise) or enforce punishments and restrictions (including shame) based on grades.

But like a train's third rail, grades are so powerful and important to classrooms and schools that no one dares touch them. As Mallory experienced, the questioning of grading practices by administrators, caregivers, students, and even teachers can invoke anxiety, insecurity, pride, obstinacy, and conflict. And so most of us avoid the topic altogether.

It wasn't until I read a few articles—including "The Case Against the Zero" by Doug Reeves (2004), "The Case Against Percentage Grades" by Thomas Guskey (2013), and *A Repair Kit for Grading* by Ken O'Connor (2010)—that I began to see that teachers use grading for many different, and contradictory, purposes:

1. To communicate the achievement status of students to parents or guardians and others

2. To provide information that students can use for self-evaluation

3. To select, identify, or group students for certain educational paths or programs

4. To provide incentives for students to learn

5. To inform instructional decisions

6. To provide evidence of students' lack of effort or inappropriate responsibility

No wonder that grading practices vary so widely. The teacher who grades to sort students into programs will use grading practices incompatible with the teacher who grades to incentivize students to learn.

And beyond the variation in grading among teachers, I found that many grading practices themselves had deep flaws. For example, I learned that the calculations that we commonly use to derive grades—and often embedded in our grading software—are mathematically unsound.

Secondly, I learned that many of us evaluate students on criteria that are nonacademic and highly susceptible to bias. For example, a teacher who evaluates a student's effort as part of a grade likely applies a culturally narrow definition of what effort looks like.

Thirdly, teachers often use grades for behavior modification, offering the reward or punishment of points and use (or threaten to use) the zero or F to motivate students even though the "motivational F" is largely a myth; research is clear that low grades, or the threat of low grades, do nothing for the student who has low confidence in their academic abilities or limited experience with academic success—the majority of students who receive Fs.

I also learned that our grading often creates "collateral consequences" that contradict our intentions. For example, we lament our students' rampant cheating and copying of homework. Yet when we take a no-excuses approach to late work in the name of preparing students for real-world skills and subtract points or even refuse to accept the work, we incentivize students to complete work on time by hook or by crook and disincentivize real learning. Some common grading practices encourage the very behaviors we want to stop.

As I continued to research and learn more, I realized that the inaccuracy of grades seemed to be only a symptom of a deeper problem. Although I had previously attributed schools' achievement and opportunity gaps of race and income entirely to unaddressed needs in our instruction and curriculum, limited cultural understanding, or a weakness in resolve, I came to realize that our common grading practices make us active accomplices in perpetuating these gaps. The ways we grade disproportionately favor students with privilege and harm students with less privilege: students of color, from low-income families, who receive special education services, and English learners. For example, we teachers often assign students a zero in the gradebook if homework isn't handed in by the deadline. However, we don't account for all the reasons that a student wouldn't turn something in on time. One reason, of course, might be laziness or disinterest—certainly not legitimate reasons. Perhaps a student has after-school classes or sports, which could make it harder to turn in work on time, but arguably this is a self-inflicted wound. But what if a student's circumstances are beyond her control? What if there isn't a space at home that is quiet enough, or well-lit enough, or not distraction-free enough for a child to complete homework? What if a student's caregiver is away at a job (or second job, or third job), so that she isn't around to provide support? What if the parent or caregiver isn't formally educated enough or doesn't speak enough English to help the child complete the homework? What if the child has home responsibilities (caring for an older relative or younger siblings) or has her own job in order to contribute to the family income? What if the student who has few supports simply doesn't know the answers to the homework? What option is there <u>but</u> to submit the work incomplete or late? Clearly, we don't want to grade students based on their environment or situations beyond their control, but unfortunately, when we use grading practices such as penalizing students for late work, that is often what we do.

It was a very depressing and discouraging awakening.

To my relief, I also learned that grading, if done differently, can be accurate, not infected with bias, and can intrinsically motivate students to learn. Grades can clearly and more objectively describe what students know and can do. Grading practices can encourage students not to cheat but to learn, to persevere when they fail and not lose hope, and to take more ownership and agency for their achievement. And the power of these approaches can be especially transformative for struggling students—the students who have been beaten down year after year by a punishing grading system of negative feedback and unredeemable failure.

Yet despite my own research and revelations, knowing how to make grading more accurate and equitable was only the very first step. The real challenge was to understand how teachers could learn, understand, and then implement improved grading. I had to not just touch but embrace the third rail of grading; I had to get others to embrace it with me.

It didn't work out so well at first. When I discussed these practices with teachers, I was constantly met with the same arguments: Our current grading system prepares students for the real world and if we alter it we're doing our students a disservice; "smart kids" can handle changes to grading and can be internally motivated but "remedial" or "regular" students need external motivation; these changes just inflate grades; students will just game the system. Conversations were intellectual jousts that didn't really change what teachers believed or did. Grading was so deeply intertwined with teachers' belief systems and their daily practices that it wasn't as simple as just explaining and justifying the practices. I realized that for teachers to become convinced of the effectiveness and the equitable impact of different grading practices, they had to try them out. Through a combination of persuasion, promises, and appeals, I found some teachers willing to test out these new grading practices.

Amazingly, it worked.

Teachers who tried these grading practices were surprised and sometimes shocked by the results. The practices seemed to do the impossible: decrease student failures, reduce grade inflation, and reduce achievement gaps—all at the *same time*. Here were the results in one high school:

High School Teacher Cohort: Percentage of D or F Grades Awarded 2015–2016 (before grading initiative) vs. 2016–2017 (1st year of grading initiative)[1]				
	2015–2016 SEM. 2	2016–2017 SEM. 2	PERCENTAGE POINT CHANGE	PERCENTAGE DIFFERENCE
Percentage of D or F Grades Awarded	23%	17%	−6	**26% decrease**

In the 2015–2016 school year, 23 percent of the grades that the teachers assigned were Ds or Fs, and fell by over one-quarter, to 17 percent of the grades in 2016–2017. Although this decrease may seem small (and is still too high), because these high school teachers had student loads of 125 to 150 each and assigned thousands of grades every semester, this decrease in D and F grades represents *hundreds* of fewer failed grades, meaning fewer remedial "seats" and therefore less money needed for remedial classes, to say nothing of the long-term impact on graduation rates. What was even more energizing was that the grading practices had a greater (and statistically significant) impact on groups who had been historically underserved in schools. From the same high school:

High School Teacher Cohort: Percentage of D or F Grades Awarded 2015–2016 (before grading initiative) vs. 2016–2017 (1st year of grading initiative)				
	2015–2016 SEM. 2	ACHIEVEMENT GAP 2015–2016	2016–2017 SEM. 2	ACHIEVEMENT GAP 2016–2017
FRPL* Students	27%	8% points	19%	3% points
Non-FRPL Students	19%		16%	

* Free and Reduced Price Lunch

---

[1]The results in these figures on pages xxvi–xxviii were generated by Leading Edge Advisors, an independent evaluation firm.

With these more equitable practices, the rate of Ds and Fs the teachers assigned to students who qualified for free or reduced-price lunch, a proxy for low-income, decreased from 27 percent to 19 percent, while the percentage of Ds and Fs assigned to students who came from higher income families (who therefore did not qualify for free or reduced-price lunch) decreased much less, from 19 percent to 16 percent. The rate of Ds and Fs decreased more sharply for low-income students, meaning that the school decreased their D and F achievement gap between these groups of students from 8 percent to 3 percent.

Here are results at a middle school, where teachers' changes reduced grade inflation *and* failing grades, and narrowed the achievement gaps of income and race:

Middle School Teacher Cohort 2015–2016 (before grading initiative) vs. 2016–2017 (1st year of grading initiative)				
Percentage of A Grades Awarded				
	2015–2016 SEM. 2	**ACHIEVEMENT GAP 2015–2016**	**2016–2017 SEM. 2**	**ACHIEVEMENT**
FRPL Students	36%		31%	
		14% points		9% points
Non-FRPL Students	50%		40%	

Percentage of D or F Grades Awarded				
	2015–2016 SEM. 2	**ACHIEVEMENT GAP 2015–2016**	**2016–17 SEM. 2**	**ACHIEVEMENT GAP 2016–2017**
African American Students	25%		14%	
		8% points		1% point
White Students	17%		13%	

When teachers used these more equitable grading practices, the disparity in the percent of As assigned to students who qualified for free or reduced price lunch compared to the percent of As assigned to students who did not qualify for free or reduced price lunch decreased by over one-third, and the disparity in the percent of Ds and Fs assigned to African American students compared to white students, which had been eight percentage points, was virtually eliminated.

Of course, it is notoriously difficult to tie changes in student achievement to a specific change in a teacher's practice; student performance and teacher effectiveness are influenced by so many variables inside and outside the school. When teachers at this middle school confidently explained that a primary cause of these changes in student achievement was their improvements to grading and assessment, I wasn't satisfied. I first asked what might be *incorrect* explanations others might give if they saw this data. They quickly responded: "That we lowered our standards; that we were too soft; that we were pressured to give passing grades." One teacher added, almost adamantly, "Actually, we *raised* our standards. Students no longer can get good grades with fluff assignments."

I believed the teachers, but wasn't yet convinced. I was worried that the practices might yield grades that were improved, but weren't more valid. To determine whether the grades were more valid—that they more accurately and consistently described student achievement—we compared teachers' classroom grades to students' standardized test scores. We found that teachers' grades had an increased correlation to standardized test scores. Not only were grades less inflated or deflated, they were also more *accurate*:

State Test Score Results vs. Sem. 2 Grades Assigned Spring 2016 (before grading initiative) vs. Spring 2017 (1st year of grading initiative)				
	SPRING 2016 SEM. 2	SPRING 2017 SEM. 2	PERCENTAGE POINT CHANGE	PERCENTAGE DIFFERENCE
Percentage of Students for Whom State Exam ELA Score **MATCHES** Teacher-Assigned English Sem. 2 Grade (ex.: 3 = B, 2 = C, etc.)	34%	48%	+14	**41% Increase**
Percentage of Students for Whom State Exam Math Score **MATCHES** Teacher-Assigned Math Sem. 2 Grade (ex.: 3 = B, 2 = C, etc.)	21%	38%	+17	**80% Increase**

Although in 2016, before teachers used more equitable grading practices, only about one-third of semester 2 English grades matched standardized test scores in English, after teachers used the practices in 2017 nearly half of teachers' English grades matched the test scores, and the percent of semester 2 math grades that matched standardized test scores in math nearly doubled. And even though there are plenty of reasons to be skeptical of standardized tests, we'd prefer teachers' grades to be more correlated with external test results than less correlated.

Beyond the quantitative data, the impact of these more equitable grading practices on the day-to-day work of teachers and students was even more transformational. Students were less stressed, and grateful to not have everything "count" in their grade; to have flexibility to turn in assignments after a deadline; and to be allowed to retake exams. Teachers felt the emphasis in their classrooms had shifted from meeting due dates and earning points to *learning*. Students completed assignments because they found that doing so improved their performance on assessments, not because of the homework or classwork points they could earn or lose.

What's more, teachers felt empowered by this work. Prior to this work, the ways their students behaved—what motivated them, whether they cheated or not, how much they understood or cared about their grade—had seemed to the teachers to be fixed and often chalked up to "that's how kids are these days." But the teachers who tried these practices found that they could actually change students' attitudes and behaviors. Students who had seemed unmotivated and even resistant to learning became more engaged. Relationships between students and teachers—which had been based on compliance and a system of extrinsic threats and rewards—were now partnerships based on trust, transparency, and, perhaps most importantly, hope. Students persevered when they struggled, took initiative, stopped cheating, and wanted to learn even after the test—all because of changes to how teachers graded. After using these new more equitable practices, these once skeptical teachers had the passion of religious converts. Cathy, a middle school history and English teacher, was typical in her reaction:

"I have a different outlook now on how I want to grade. Last year it was almost punishment: 'Oh, you didn't do the work, now you have a bad grade.' Doing this work really changed my perspective. This helped me realize that the main purpose of grading is to see how much the students know, to assess their learning instead of assessing their efforts; do they really understand the work, as opposed to did they do all of the assignments."

Plus, this work to improve grading didn't just change how teachers graded. It changed their beliefs about themselves, about teaching and learning, and about their students. They discovered that they didn't need to give points for assignments to make students value and complete the work. They found that they were just as respected, and more trusted and appreciated, by their students when they changed their grading. Most powerfully, they learned that by changing how they graded, their students—whether elementary children, middle school tweens, or high school teenagers, and whether overachieving or struggling and resistant—would take ownership and responsibility over their learning, would be intrinsically motivated to succeed, and would be excited about learning and their own progress.

Over the past several years, we have seen these benefits of equitable grading in many school types and environments: at large comprehensive district-run schools, charter schools, and independent schools; at schools with only white students and those with only students of color; at schools nestled in urban centers and located in suburbs; and at schools with students who enter with skills far below grade level and at Phillips Andover Academy, one of the most elite boarding schools in the country. But regardless of the school's context or its student population, this work was hard. Examining our grading practices can challenge our deepest beliefs about what we know (or think we know) about our teaching, our students, and ourselves. Lucy, an eighteen-year veteran high school English teacher, best expressed the difficulty of considering changes to longstanding grading practices, and why the experience can be so transformational:

> "This challenges what I've learned to do as a teacher in terms of what I think students need to know, what they need to show back to me, and how to grade them. This feels really important, messy, and really uncomfortable. It is 'Oh my gosh, look what I've been doing!' I don't blame myself because I didn't know any better. I did what was done to me. But now I'm in a place that I feel really strongly that I can't do that anymore. I can't use grading as a way to discipline kids any more. I look at what I have been doing and I have to do things differently."

Lucy's description captures it all: Examining grading is "important, messy, and uncomfortable." It can be difficult to amass the energy and resolve, particularly with all the mandates and sky-high expectations placed on teachers, to make grading more accurate and equitable. But it is some of the most important and rewarding work we can do. We know that students' family income, whether they have a stable, safe home (or even a home at all), their caregivers' education background, their race, and other elements outside teachers' control all have a huge influence on achievement, but at the end of the day, it's their grades—our description of students' academic performance—that opens doors or closes them. We can learn a new curriculum or a new instructional strategy, but if our grading doesn't change, nothing for our students, particularly those most vulnerable, will really change, and the achievement and opportunity gaps will remain.

It's time to embrace the third rail.

PART I

Foundations

"The reliability of the school's estimate of the accomplishment and progress of pupils is of large practical importance. For, after all, the marks or grades attached to a pupil's work are the tangible measure of the result of his attainments and constitute the chief basis for the determination of essential administrative problems of the school, such as transfer promotion, retardation, elimination and admission to higher institutions; to say nothing of the problem of the influence of these marks or grades upon the moral attitude of the pupil toward the school, education, and even life."

(Starch & Elliott, 1912, p. 442)

CHAPTER 1

What Makes Grading So Difficult to Talk About (and Even Harder to Change)?

In this chapter, we will answer the following questions:

1. What are common struggles for principals and teachers regarding grading?

2. What makes it hard for us to critically examine traditional grading practices?

3. How can educators and noneducators benefit from this book, and what is the best way to approach its content and organization?

W e teachers deeply love our work, we love our students (at least, most of them), and love working with our colleagues (at least, most of them). What fulfills us is the relationships we build with our students and the profound impact and influence we have on them. Any given day we may provide a learning experience that fundamentally alters a student's life trajectory: an intellectual awakening, a deeper understanding of who she is and what she can become, a kindling of a passion, a realization of her voice.

And yet, teaching has never been so challenging and so embattled. Our students, who are increasingly diverse, with greater percentages of students whose first language is not English, and whose families live below the poverty line, need us to occupy so many roles beyond teacher: nurse, mentor, social worker, therapist, parent, cheerleader, tutor, and college advisor. We are responsible to adhere to regulations, laws, and directives under layers of bureaucracies. We often feel buffeted by ever-shifting political winds, pawns in complex political games in which people outside our schools argue over competing values and philosophies that affect what we do inside our classrooms: how and whether to teach certain topics (the perspectives of the Civil War, the genocide of Native Americans, evolution, global warming), read certain authors (J. D. Salinger, Toni Morrison), prepare for standardized exams (SBAC. PARCC, state graduation or end-of-course tests), and use certain materials (state-adopted textbooks, iPads and apps, laptops, smart boards). Solidarity and organizing among us seem less possible because of the waning influence and presence of teacher unions and the fragmentation of how we are trained: alternative certification programs, residencies, university programs, and fast-track programs that even threaten the very concept of teaching as a "profession." Even the idea of a "school system" seems to be shifting beneath our feet into a "system of schools," where cities agnostically support a portfolio of traditional public schools, charter schools, home schools, distance learning centers, and even private schools via vouchers and "educational savings accounts." Salaries are rising but are still well below that of other professionals, and often are alone insufficient to support a family. Too many of us work within schools and communities where violence is a fact of life, adding to our own stress as well as our students'. We are guinea pigs in experiments testing how best to evaluate and motivate us, and we are judged by criteria that suggests ignorance—or worse, dismissal—of the challenges of our students and the complexity of our work. It is no surprise that as many as one out of three teachers report experiencing high levels of occupational stress (Brackett & Floman, 2013). An obvious result is high turnover, a "revolving door" of teachers, particularly in schools that serve low-income communities, where teachers stay just long enough to hone their skills before leaving and being replaced by brand new teachers.

Amid all of these pressures and expectations, with administrators and policymakers defining nearly every aspect of a teacher's practice, we have one remaining "island of autonomy": our grades. Grades are entirely within our control—the declaration of our professional judgment of student performance and the most concrete symbol of our authority and expertise.

The teacher's authorship over the grade has even been enshrined into a number of states' education codes and regulations, ensuring that the grade a teacher assigns may not be overwritten by an administrator (e.g., Maine §4708, Texas §28.0214) and even protecting the teacher from external pressures to change the grade. Take, for example, Georgia's Grade Integrity Act (§ 20-2-989.20), which states

> No classroom teacher shall be required, coerced, intimidated, or disciplined in any manner by the local board of education, superintendent, or any local school administrator to change the grade of a student.

And even when the sanctity of a teacher's grade is not so formally codified, administrators know that they tread on thin ice when they talk to teachers about their grading, potentially inviting formal complaints, union grievances, and even lawsuits. Grading is arguably the only aspect of schools in which the power dynamic between the teacher and her supervisor is inverted!

The topic of grading is so hallowed that it inhibits conversations even among colleagues. Only after much tiptoeing and reassurances that there will be no compromise to professional autonomy, teachers of the same grade or subject may manage to agree on broad common agreements: The final exam in every course will be worth 10 percent of the grade, or homework can be worth no more than 50 percent of a student's total grade. Rarely, though, are there honest conversations where grading is examined, researched, and deliberated. As a result of having virtually no safe forum to discuss grading practices, each teacher remains in her own echo chamber, validated by little except inertia and the vague sense that students seem to be getting the grade they deserve.

The irony in our vigorous defense of our grading is that most teachers detest the act of grading. It's unpleasant, time consuming, and anxiety provoking (Thorndike, 2005, as cited by Randall & Engelhard, 2010, p. 1376). In each marking period, teachers on average assess dozens of assignments per student and spend approximately twenty hours per week on "non-instructional school activities of which evaluating student work is a large part" (National Center for Education Statistics, 2007, as cited by Brackett, Floman, Ashton-James, Cherkasskiya, & Salovey, 2013). Teachers often agonize over what grade to assign, are uncomfortable with how much grades matter, and face constant arguments, bargaining, and pleading by students and caregivers over grades. The grading and reporting of student progress, according to Linn and Miller (2005) is "one of the more frustrating aspects of teaching" (as cited in Randall & Engelhard, 2010, p. 1376). If grading is so important to our work, whether we like it or not, why is the topic so avoided, so threatening, so intimidating?

Grading as Identity

Maybe we struggle with discussing grading because we have very little experience doing so. Grading and measurement is rarely if ever included in teacher preparation programs or in-school professional development. As a result, the majority of teachers are left on their own to decide how to grade and why and are unaware of the research on effective grading practices. Daniele, a middle school education specialist of eight years, confessed, "I couldn't even tell you exactly what I thought about grading. I just had undefined notions of what grading is and what it should be like and held onto that." It's completely understandable that most teachers replicate the grading systems they experienced as students or follow the grading practices of their school colleagues (Guskey, 2009).

Despite this complete lack of training and support with how to grade, teachers' grading policies and practices aren't arbitrary. We apply our professional expertise and experiences and carefully deliberate over what assignments and behaviors we include in the grade and what we exclude, the relative weight of those assignments and behaviors, and the magnitude of consequences, rewards, incentives, and disincentives. And yet, each teacher makes very different choices. If we choose to award points to students for being on time, raising their hands to contribute ideas, for working collaboratively, or for turning in work by the deadline, we believe that these skills are important in life and that a grade should reflect performance in these skills. If we instead prioritize that students learn the academic content, perhaps we deemphasize or exclude those "soft skills" from the grade. If we want students to learn responsibility, we allocate a large portion of the grade to students' homework. If we believe that our grades are an important way to distinguish the top students, we grade on a curve. Teachers can even disagree on what makes a grade "fair." Most teachers believe that students who try should not fail regardless of whether they actually learn (Brookhart et al., 2016), but other teachers believe the opposite: that fairness is honestly reporting academic performance regardless of effort. Because each teacher's grading system is virtually unregulated and unconstrained, a teacher's grading policies and practices reveal how she defines and envisions her relationship to students, what she predicts best prepares them for success, her beliefs about students, and her self-concept as a teacher. That's why challenges to our grading practices don't just offend our professional judgment; they can invoke an emotional and psychological threat.

If the grading practices in this book are, in fact, more equitable and effective than what most of us currently do, the implications are profound and disturbing: we may have perpetuated inequities in our classrooms and schools for years without realizing it. Our use of inaccurate and inequitable grading may have barred students from getting into the college they wanted, kept them out of honors classes, and prevented them from graduating. As Jillian, a twelve-year math and science middle school teacher courageously shared with me, "As I'm learning these improved grading practices, I'm thinking about how many students I may have hurt in the past, and I don't want to go there."

As I researched and learned more about the equitable practices in this book, I had the same experience as Jillian: feelings of guilt, shame, and anger. How could I have not seen the faults in our traditional system, the ways many of our current grading and assessment practices harm the most vulnerable students? Throughout my teaching career, I created the best curriculum I could, built the most positive relationships with students possible, but were my efforts compromised, or even undermined, when I graded? That can't be, can it?

Though grades are so much a part of schools, they are never included in analyses of education inequity, much less included in strategies to address the inequities. Can something so prominent in our schools be so innocent in the promulgation of disparate achievement? Are we, by using, supporting, and not interrogating traditional grading practices, accessories to the inequities in our schools? Do we really believe that, despite initiative after initiative to improve the disparity in student achievement, our faulty grading system isn't somehow contributing to the intractability of the achievement and opportunity gaps over multiple generations? How can we, as professionals, caregivers, and moral citizens, continue to avoid a critical examination of our legacy of grading?

Grading and Our "Web of Belief"

I want to show one more explanation for why it can be so difficult to examine grading.

Think about the hostile reaction to Galileo's assertion of a universe with the sun at the center instead of the Earth, the fierce debate over global warming, or the intense doubt that women had the capacity to vote. Why can it be so difficult to encounter evidence and ideas that contradict what we already know, or think we know? Why do we, like Jillian, when confronted with clear and convincing evidence that contradicts our current understanding, not "want to go there"?

Forty years ago, the philosopher W. V. Quine (1978) explained that we each have a "web of belief"—a complex system of what we hold to be true in the world based on our experiences and prior understanding, with a "web" of interconnected and mutually supportive ideas. Each of us has a web of belief about students and grading. For example, when I believe that it is a good practice to include extra credit in a grade, that belief is connected to my beliefs about whether extra credit makes a grade more accurate ("It does because it reflects a student's engagement and effort."), how students are best motivated ("Students will do more work and learn more if extra credit is offered."), and whether extra credit makes a grade more equitable ("Extra credit provides multiple ways for students to succeed.").

According to Quine, when we learn information and evidence that contradicts part of our belief system—that extra credit actually makes grades less accurate, less motivational, and more inequitable (see chapter 9)—we are faced with two options: Dismiss the evidence or accept it. We can dismiss the new information by disqualifying the speaker's credibility (Joe Feldman is at best, naïve, and at worst, a buffoon.), by ignoring it (Skip chapter 9 or close this book and return it to the shelf.), or by finding the evidence incongruent with our own experiences ("I have used extra credit and I am fully confident that there is no better system despite any contradictory evidence."). If we can dismiss the new information, our web of belief remains intact and undisturbed.

If, on the other hand, we accept that the new information is true, Quine claims that we will adjust our web of belief as little as possible, maintaining all of our other related beliefs. If the evidence against offering extra credit convinces us, we might constrain the disruptive influence of that evidence on our web of belief by limiting the circumstances in which the new evidence holds true: Maybe we make a small concession: that extra credit is inappropriate for already motivated students, but for struggling students it is still effective. We tweak our belief about extra credit just a little, but keep intact our overall belief about extra credit being beneficial. We do not have to adjust our other beliefs connected to our belief about extra credit, such as what motivates students generally or what makes a grading practice equitable. We maintain the "inertia" of our belief—that extra credit is good; it's just not helpful in a specific circumstance. The web is adjusted only slightly.

With each new piece of evidence and information that contradicts a belief, we have to make more significant changes to our expanded web of belief, each time rejecting the new information or accepting it while limiting its validity so that it impacts our web as little as possible. Quine describes this dynamic as the "conservatism" of our web of belief:

> *Conservatism is rather effortless on the whole, having inertia in its favor. But it is sound strategy too, since at each step it sacrifices as little as possible of the evidential support, whatever that may have been, that our overall system of beliefs has hitherto been enjoying. The truth may indeed be radically remote from our present system of beliefs, so that we may need a long series of conservative steps to attain what might have been attained in one rash leap. The longer the leap, however, the more serious an angular error in the direction. For a leap in the dark the likelihood of a happy landing is severely limited. Conservatism holds out the advantages of limited liability and a maximum of live options for each next move. (pp. 67–68)*

As you progress through this book, be aware of how you are reacting to new information. In the face of persuasive and nearly incontrovertible evidence that our current grading practices are harmful and ineffective and that other practices are more accurate, equitable, and motivational, you may dismiss or marginalize that evidence. It will not be easy to concede that what we have believed to be true may actually not be true. As Quine predicts, it may not be a "happy landing," but as teachers we must always be open to new ideas, knowing that we can always improve, that we can always do better by our students. Maybe that is enough for us to take a "leap in the dark."

When the concepts in this book challenge you in uncomfortable ways, stay open to new evidence and possibilities, imagine what could be, and be less conservative in your web of belief. Consider equitable approaches to grading that you may have previously believed were impossible:

> *"I can't believe that!" said Alice.*
>
> *"Can't you?" the Queen said in a pitying tone. "Try again: draw a long breath, and shut your eyes."*
>
> *Alice laughed. "There's no use trying," she said: "one can't believe impossible things."*

"I dare say you haven't had much practice," said the Queen. "When I was your age I always did it for half-an-hour a day. Why, sometimes I've believed as many as six impossible things before breakfast." (Carroll, Ch. 5)

What you are doing may seem like Alice's challenge, but you are actually not being asked to believe in impossible things. The practices in this book are supported by research and, perhaps more convincingly, they have been used by teachers all over the country across a broad range of students. To change one's grading practices is not simple, psychologically or logistically, for teachers or their students. But these changes lead to higher academic achievement and less stressful classrooms, and they support all students, particularly those who have languished and failed in our current system. These practices give us, and them, hope.

Who Is This Book For?

First and foremost, this book is for teachers. They are the professionals most responsible and most intimately involved with grading our students, and therefore are in the most powerful position to make grading practices more equitable. As a former (and therefore, lifelong) teacher, I know that most of our work as teachers in a school is isolated—we work in separate rooms, teach different courses, rarely share the same groups of students, and have very different daily teaching schedules (and "prep" periods)—which means very few opportunities to chat with each other, much less to engage each other in deep pedagogical discourse. I write this book to support a critically important conversation that helps teachers to be more informed and conscious of the impact of our traditional grading practices, and that prepares them with the understanding and strategies to implement more equitable practices.

This book is also for those accountable for the grades students receive—school and district administrators, board members, and other officials. This book will give you a clearer sense of the urgency to improve traditional grading and can inform your vision about how more equitable grading will improve passing rates, reduce grade inflation, strengthen instruction, and even save money. Improved grading can be a lever for systemwide efforts to promote more equitable opportunities and outcomes for students, particularly those most historically disadvantaged. In your non-teaching role, you can encourage, normalize, support, and demand a critical conversation about grades, and to provide the inspiration, the incentives, the resources, and the "cover" to those who are part of that conversation. Considering the amount of professional development we provide teachers on curriculum design and instructional planning, how can we not invest resources in improving how teachers grade?

For parents and caregivers, conversations about children's grades are so important and yet often intimidating. By strengthening your understanding of grading, you become more qualified to be true partners in your child's education. Perhaps you can apply some gentle pressure on schools, and then partner with them, to improve their grading. This book also can be informative and empowering to students and their advocates, to pull back the curtain on a system that directly and profoundly affects them. Rather than be only the recipients of grades, students can be active in a community-wide discussion about how to grade more equitably.

Ultimately, no matter your role, background, or viewpoint, I write this book as a dialogue between you and me. You come to this book with a set of expectations, skepticism, pressures, experiences, and hopes, as do I. This work of examining and reimagining grading is personal and interpersonal, so my tone in this book is more familiar than formal, more curious than prescriptive, more suggestive than demanding, more forgiving than accusatory. I do this not only to make the ideas in the book less threatening, but to model the stance that I've found most helpful when discussing these ideas. In addition, to help you navigate the content, I begin each chapter with a preview of the main concepts and close each chapter with a summary of key points and reflective questions. These questions will help you construct meaning from these new ideas, to reflect on your own beliefs and experiences, and to imagine doing things differently.

Blending the Technical and Theoretical

This book will address both the technical *how* of grading practices and the *why* behind those practices—the concrete steps teachers can use immediately as well as the underlying ideas to create and tailor grading practices that fit unique classrooms and contexts.

The Technical Guide

- What are more equitable grading practices, and how are they specifically implemented in a classroom?

- What changes do more equitable grading practices require in terms of time, messaging, assessment design, and gradebook software?

- What are successful, concrete examples of those practices?

- What are teachers' common struggles and successes when they implement the more equitable grading practices?

The Theoretical Exploration

- What is the history and evolution of our current grading practices, what were their purposes, and how does their continued use thwart high-quality instruction and perpetuate inequities?

- How does our current research-based understanding of equity, motivation, adolescent psychology, and teaching and learning inform more equitable grading practices?

- What messages do our current grading practices send to our students, and how could more equitable grading send messages that are more aligned to what we believe about teaching, learning, and the potential of our students, particularly for those who have struggled in our schools?

- How do more equitable grading practices improve our assessments, curriculum design, and instructional decisions?

A risk of blending theory and practice is that I will satisfy no one: To those readers who simply want to be told the *how*, they may become impatient with the theory and research citations, and for those who desire research and theory, they may find the description of practices to be insufficiently substantiated. Perhaps, though, this reflects the complexity of teaching—we always want more examples, and we always want more research—and yet our students are there right now, in front of us, waiting.

How Is This Book Organized?

This book has three overarching sections. Part I, "Foundations," lays out the context for addressing the inequities of traditional grading. Part II, "The Case for Change," is an examination of our inherited grading practices and how, in the present day, their continued use undermines our contemporary teaching and learning practices and beliefs. By continuing to use these grading practices, we inadvertently perpetuate debunked ideas and inequities of the early twentieth century. Part II also proposes an alternate, more equitable, vision for grading.

Part III, "Equitable Grading Practices," describes the five sets of practices that can lead us to this vision:

- **Practices That Are Accurate and Mathematically Sound**: Using algorithms that allow and support student growth rather than consigning students to failure. Examples: Using a 0–4 instead of a 0–100 point scale; not giving zeros.

- **Practices That Value Knowledge, Not Environment or Behavior**: Evaluating students only on their level of content mastery. Examples: Not grading subjectively interpreted behaviors such as a student's "effort" or "growth," or on completion of homework; grading students' knowledge of content based on multiple sources of information.

- **Practices That Support Hope and a Growth Mindset**: Encouraging mistakes as part of the learning process. Examples: Allowing test or project retakes; replacing previous scores with current scores (rather than averaging).

- **Practices That Lift the Veil on How to Succeed**: Making grades simpler and more transparent. Examples: Creating rubrics; using simplified grade calculations.

- **Practices That Build "Soft Skills" and Motivate Students Without Grading Them**: Supporting intrinsic motivation and self-regulation rather than relying on an extrinsic point system. Examples: Using peer or self-evaluation and reflection; employing a more expansive menu of feedback strategies.

There is a near consensus among researchers, teachers who I have worked with, and their students that the equitable grading practices in this book improve learning, decrease failure rates and grade inflation, make classrooms more caring and less stressful, strengthen relationships between teachers and students, and build students' responsibility and character. In addition, we have seen benefits of more equitable grading in many different school types and contexts: with large comprehensive district schools, charter schools, and independent schools; with schools with entirely white student populations and at schools where there are only students of color; and with schools where students enroll with skills far below grade level and where students enroll with skills far above grade level, such as Phillips Andover Academy, one of the most elite schools in the country.

But because our traditional and inequitable system of grading has been hardwired into our conception of schools, and because of the conservatism of our "web of belief," in this book I will do everything I can to help you feel more confident disturbing your web: research studies, emotional appeals, analogies to the worlds outside of schools, teacher and student perspectives, moral demands, and specific models and tools. Each set of practices will include supporting research and successful examples from teachers which will be either included in this book or available at the link **www.gradingforequity.org**, along with how to address common concerns—instructional, philosophical, and technological—so that you can implement the practices more confidently and successfully. In addition, throughout this book are the voices of researchers, teachers, administrators, and students whose experiences or ideas provide important perspective and embolden us to challenge traditional grading, to not feel so alone in our risk-taking. All of the teachers' voices include first names and subject area, and the students' voices are cited using pseudonyms.

This book is best read from beginning to end, as each chapter builds somewhat on previously addressed ideas, but I invite the reader to jump around based on your interests or needs. Like our students, each of us enters new content from a slightly different perspective with a different learning trajectory. Perhaps you're most interested in how we came to have this particular grading system and why it's so inequitable, or maybe you've already tried some of the practices and want to learn some additional approaches. In Part III in particular, you may find yourself jumping from practice to practice, because even though the practices are categorized into different elements of equitable grading, they overlap and implicate each other. For example, when you consider using summative assessments as the primary consideration of a grade, you'll need to consider offering retakes, which means that you'll rethink the design of your assessments, which will mean that you may want to score them on a 0–4 instead of a 0–100 scale. You may even find that you need to search out other books and articles on grading or related topics—assessment, for example—so I have cited supporting research and publications throughout the text and included a full bibliography.

A Final Word

As we prepare for our journey, let's be ready to suspend what we think we know about grading, teaching, learning, and even students. As we'll learn in chapter 2, we have been brought up in a grading system that is virtually unchanged in over a century and was premised on turn-of-the-twentieth-century beliefs about the role of schools and who they're for, how to motivate people, and what effective teaching and learning look like. We have been unwitting victims of this system as students, and unwitting promoters of this system as teachers (and even as caregivers). For many of us, the system worked just fine, or at least we believe that it did, but in fact the traditional system of evaluating students and reporting information about them has been part of the inequities, unfairness, and injustices built into our schools. When this book challenges you, try to put aside your devil's advocate stance—why these practices can't possibly work—and try an "angel's advocate" stance: Envision the possibilities and potential for teachers and students if we were to grade differently—more fairly, accurately, and equitably. As radical and revolutionary as some of these ideas might seem, they really aren't; they're based on research, common sense, and most importantly, successful implementation in classrooms. In fact, the more you critically examine how we commonly grade, the stranger, more counterproductive, and more absurd our current practices will reveal themselves to be. As we learn new ideas, let us be open, humble, honest, and forgive ourselves if we weren't aware that things could be different. Perhaps we've never had a reason, an opportunity, or a mechanism to question grading. Now is our chance.

Jessica, a middle school math teacher who changed her grading to be more equitable and accurate after ten years of using traditional grading practices, described what many teachers experience when they examine their grading:

"My grading practices had pretty much been the same over time. I knew something needed to change, but I didn't have an idea of where to start, or what needed to be changed. I was seeing that a lot of my students who I knew were strong in content—I could tell they knew what they were doing—had grades that weren't necessarily reflective of their abilities. I was surprised at their grades; how was this possible?

"Then I started learning more about grading, and I started to feel really bad for my previous students. What if by giving them Fs I have totally ruined things for them and they think they don't have any ability . . .? I had known all these years that I needed to do something differently but just didn't know how, I didn't know what. I appreciate that I had the chance to change. I feel bad that it happened 10 years after I started teaching, but I am glad that it happened now."

Finally, with the stubborn persistence of the achievement gap, we can no longer implement equitable practices in some areas of our schools—responsive classrooms, alternative disciplinary procedures, diverse curriculum—but meanwhile preserve our inequitable grading. Although a handful of authors have addressed grading, there hasn't been discussion of grading through an equity lens—how grading is a critical element to affirmatively promote equity, to stop rewarding students because of their wealth, privilege, environment, or caregivers' education and to prevent us from punishing students for their poverty, gaps in education, or environment. Traditional grading practices perpetuate our achievement and opportunity gaps and improved grading practices promote objective assessment of academic mastery, transparent expectations, growth mindsets, a focus on learning instead of points, and student agency—all key ingredients to serve diverse learners and create culturally responsive classrooms.

I'm not sure if seeing the inequities in our 100-year old grading practices is like Plato coming out of the cave or ingesting *The Matrix* blue pill instead of the red one, but I guarantee you will think differently after you read this book. You will also likely feel the range of emotions Jessica felt—confusion, guilt, relief, optimism. At its core, this book will help you to examine your experiences and to learn how to approach grading with greater hope, empathy, and belief in the capacity of students, *all* of them. That's what grading for equity is all about.

Summary of Concepts

1. Grading is a critically important element of schooling, but is so challenging to discuss because it is so interwoven with teachers' conceptions of learning, motivation, and themselves.

2. We have never had the opportunity, resources, and support to examine our traditional grading practices, and so we must forgive ourselves for inadvertently perpetuating outdated and even harmful practices.

3. When we learn new, more effective, and more equitable grading practices, it will challenge what Quine calls our "web of belief."

4. This book offers both the theory and the practices of improved, equitable grading, and while its content is particularly focused on teachers, it can equip school and district administrators, parents or caregivers, students, and their advocates to be more informed policymakers and school community members.

Questions to Consider

1. What are some deep beliefs you have about teenagers? What motivates and demotivates them? Are they more concerned with learning or their grade?

2. What is your vision for grading? What do you wish grading could be for students, particularly for the most vulnerable populations? What do you wish grading could be for you? In which ways do current grading practices meet those expectations, and in which ways do they not?

3. What brings you to this book? What are your goals for reading it? How will the way you read it help or hinder you from realizing those goals?

4. It's helpful to have someone with whom you can discuss the ideas in this book. Who would be the right person or group to read this with you? How will you construct meaning from what you read, either alone or with others?

5. For teachers: Which of your grading practices do you believe best support learning? Why? Which of your grading practices are you most open to reconsidering? Why?

CHAPTER 2

A Brief History of Grading

In this chapter, we will answer the following questions:

1. What were significant societal trends and beliefs in the United States during the first half of the twentieth century, and how were they manifested in schools?

2. What were the original purposes and designs of our current grading practices?

> *Grading remains a central feature of nearly every student's [and teacher's, and parent's] school experience. As such, it can be easy to perceive them as both fixed and inevitable—without origin or evolution. An effect of this is that despite their limitations, grades are often accepted quite uncritically by all parties involved. (Schneider & Hutt, 2014)*

Grading is part of the "grammar of schools" (Tyack & Cuban, 1995), a concept so embedded in our idea of what a school is that it seems silly to question it. What seems more foundational to everyone's school experience than getting grades?

Of course, the ways we grade weren't handed down from heaven, but they have an origin and an evolution. It turns out that our current grading practices were designed over 100 years ago, responding to the needs of the United States in the early twentieth century, and intending to solve problems of that context. Because grading practices have changed very little in a century, as a first step toward more informed decisions about grading, we must examine and excavate the history of grading. Of all possible approaches to grading, why do we have the ones we have?

What were the larger ideas in the American *gestalt* of the early twentieth century, and how were schools, and their grading practices, a manifestation of those ideas? What were needs and "problems" that schools generally, and grades specifically, were intended to solve? Who defined those needs and problems, and what were deemed appropriate solutions? This informed understanding will challenge us with a crucial question: If any of those century-old ideas and beliefs are no longer accepted, should we continue to use grading practices on which they were based?

The Twentieth Century Context

Teachers have always given feedback to students about their learning, all the way back to Socrates and his pupil Plato (as well as God to Abraham). But the introduction of our current grading system is a relatively recent phenomenon, borne out of a particular American political, economic, and social context. While what follows is not intended to be a definitive history of grading and the broader history of schools, if we're going to understand our grading, question it, and find ways to improve it, particularly for vulnerable student populations, we need a basic understanding of its genealogy and its evolution. That understanding begins with contextualizing grading within changes in American K–12 schools in the last century.

We'll begin our history at the end of the 1800s. Prior to that, in the first half of the nineteenth century, the family was primarily responsible for educating children, with schools serving a relatively small role. Relatively few children attended any formalized school—around half of white children ages fifteen to nineteen, and far fewer children of color for both legal and nonlegal reasons—and the school year averaged only seventy-eight days (Snyder, 1993). In each school (which sometimes was simply a single room), students of different ages learned side by side with age-appropriate curricula that often consisted of whatever books or other materials were available. The teacher herself—and she almost always was a woman—may or may not have received formal training, and if she had it was in "normal" training at the high school level. This model accommodated a nation organized around agricultural economies, independent proprietorship, and rural populations (Tyack, 1974).

In the early decades of the twentieth century, the country experienced radical social, economic, political, and scientific changes that demanded changes to its schools:

1. *The rise of manufacturing.* While in the early 1800s, most people earned a living through agriculture or as craftsmen, by the turn of the twentieth century, American productivity exploded and factories became the primary employers. In 1860, the United States lagged behind England, France, and Germany in its industrial output, but by 1900, it led the world and produced nearly as much value as those three countries combined (Tyack, 1974). Owners of factories needed workers, and they put pressure on school boards and city leaders to create schools that prepared their future employees. There was also a cultural

veneration for the power and productivity of factories, which persuaded policymakers to incorporate characteristics of industry—specialization, chain of command, timed routines, and efficiencies—into public institutions, including schools.

2. *Progressive educators.* John Dewey and others envisioned that the realization of our still emerging democracy depended on an education that was "universal," that integrated students from all backgrounds, that provided opportunities to elevate one's social and economic position, and that supported one's moral development. While many Progressives advocated for making school attendance compulsory and more standardized—a "common school" in which all students would be offered the same curriculum—others believed that differentiated education would address and accommodate the specialization of work in factories. In the end, although Dewey's vision of schools-as-democratic-engine provided overarching rhetoric about schools, it was often eclipsed by the vision of schools-as-training-ground. Bowles and Gintis (1976) write,

> In the end, the role of education as capitalist expansion and the integration of new workers into the wage-labor system came to dominate the potential role of schooling as the great equalizer and the instrument of full human development. (p. 181)

3. *Migration and immigration.* The lure of cities' manufacturing jobs and the modernized services (including water and sewage), along with a stronger railroad system, pulled people from their rural towns to the urban cities. While in 1820 there were only four U.S. cities of populations over 25,000 people, four decades later, thirty-five cities had populations of over 25,000, with nine cities of over 100,000 (Tyack, 1974). In addition, a massive wave of immigrants from Western Europe, and then Eastern Europe, came to the United States for jobs, and at the same time, cheap U.S. grain imports drove them out of employment in their home countries. By 1910, 40 percent of the entire U.S. population had foreign-born parents (Bowles, 1976), and at around the same time, 58 percent of students had fathers who were born outside the United States, from over fifty countries (Tyack, 1974). Clearly, the radical changes in the student population couldn't help but profoundly affect schools.

4. *Intelligence testing and categorization.* By the turn of the twentieth century, scientists had been exploring and theorizing about "natural intelligence"—the idea that one's mental ability was innate, immutable, and could be quantified by a range of assessments including those based on phrenology, the study of how a person's intellect and other characteristics are correlated to the physical shape of the skull. The use of intelligence testing, stemming from Alfred Binet's tests in the early 1900s, expanded dramatically in World War I when there was a need to quickly assign roles to the millions of enlisting servicemen. Scores on these tests soon became viewed as a reliable description of one's intellectual capacity,

character, and disposition, and provided seemingly scientific explanations and justification for racist beliefs. When African Americans and immigrants groups from southeastern Europe and the Mediterranean scored lower, their scores were ascribed to weaknesses in intellectual capacity, character, and upbringing among the groups, rather than to the cultural biases of the tests or to the idea that those trends reflected gross social inequities associated with poverty or oppression. Higher scores among white, wealthy Protestants and lower scores among immigrant groups and African Americans were used both to affirm the idea of the United States as a meritocracy and to reinforce the validity of the existing hierarchy.

5. *Behaviorism.* The first half of the twentieth century saw the popularity of behaviorism—the strand of psychology that argues that all human and animal behavior is the result of external physics stimuli, responses, learning histories, and reinforcements. It drew on Pavlov's findings from the 1890's that external stimuli could cause a reflexive effect: Dogs salivate when they see food, but if you introduce the stimulus of ringing a bell each time you show food, the dogs will be conditioned to salivate when you just ring the bell. John Watson built on Pavlov's ideas to argue that, similar to animals, humans are profoundly affected by their environment. Watson's most famous experiment, although it would be prohibited today, was with nine-month-old "Little Albert" in 1920. Every time little Albert was presented with a white rat, Watson would loudly bang an iron rod, scaring the infant and making him cry. Although Little Albert had not been initially afraid of the white rat, after multiple presentations of banging the rod when showing the rat, Watson "taught" Little Albert to be scared and cry when he saw the rat. B. F. Skinner took behaviorism one step further and identified "operant conditioning." With his "Skinner box" experiments in the 1920s and 1930s, in which he taught rats to pull a lever by giving them food, he argued that one could increase or decrease a subject's voluntary behaviors through associated stimuli. This theory of learning—that humans could be taught to act in certain ways through extrinsic reinforcement or consequences—became wildly popular in schools and factories.

Impact on Schools

These five trends powerfully influenced twentieth century schools and their grading systems. The migration to cities (whether from rural areas or other countries) along with compulsory education laws resulted in a huge increase in the student population. High school enrollment alone grew from approximately 203,000 in 1890 to 1.6 million in 1918 and created a need not only to increase the number of schools but to change the number of students each school could accommodate. On average over this period, over one new high school was built every day, and each was built to serve hundreds, and even thousands, of students across multiple neighborhoods (Tyack, 1974).

Now that schools served many more students with a much wider diversity of backgrounds, languages, ethnicities, and incomes, there were two fundamental shifts in the purposes and design of schools. First, whereas schools had always been responsible for acculturating students, the one-room schools had served a relatively homogenous group of students from families deeply rooted in the community. Now, schools were expected to "Americanize" the diverse, unruly mass of immigrants, rural transplants, and the poor by preparing them with the discipline and habits that factories prized in its assembly-line laborers. In a document signed by seventy-seven college presidents and city and school superintendents of schools in 1874, the authors endorsed that schools should teach obedience and very specific skills:

> *Great stress is laid upon (1) punctuality, (2) regularity, (3) attention, and (4) silence, as habits necessary through life for successful combination with one's fellow-men in an industrial and commercial civilization. (Harris & Doty as cited in Tyack, 1974, p. 50)*

Behaviorism made this expectation possible; with the right combination of reinforcement and consequences, any student could learn to act in desired ways.

Secondly, charged with preparing students to meet the needs of the industrial and commercial world, schools could do so most efficiently if they matched each student with the appropriate curriculum based on the student's ability—the Progressives' vision of schools-as-training-ground. Equipping each student with the skills most appropriate to their intellectual ability would create the smoothest and most successful transition into the work world, and this would lead to economic success for the country. The Director of Bureau of Research and Guidance, in Oakland, California, for example, believed it was critically important to "find the natural ability of the pupil and place him where he belongs" (Dickson, 1922). If a student did not possess the intellectual capacity to succeed in a more rigorous academic track, then to not match that student with a vocational track would be a waste of school resources and would frustrate the child, perhaps leading to dropping out and depriving the commercial world of the student's contribution. To help schools efficiently place each student "where he belongs," a group of psychologists adapted the scales of the U.S. Army's IQ test, used to screen enrollees for officer training, to place students into different tracks—a use that spread like wildfire. In 1919, 400,000 copies of the "National Intelligence Test" were sold within the first six months on the market, and by 1920–1921, approximately two million children were tested (Tyack, 1974). By 1932, of the 150 American cities with populations over 100,000, 75 percent of them used IQ tests to assign students into schools' ability tracks. Detroit, for example, divided its students citywide into the top 20 percent, middle 60 percent, and bottom 20 percent of scorers and placed students of each group into different course sequences (Tyack, 1974).

Tracking students to situate them for specific roles in the economic hierarchy helped to replicate the existing social and racial hierarchy, and to provide "scientific" justification for doing so. For example, when IQ scores among African American students trended significantly lower than white students, educators who controlled schools and policies, usually white and from the established upper class, attributed these trends to generalized weaknesses in African American students' character and family upbringing, rather than recognizing the disparity as a result of biased testing and institutional racism. Schools assigned African Americans, immigrants, and lower-income student groups to lower tracks that would teach them behaviors and skills that essentially consigned them to reap fewer opportunities and a smaller share of the American Dream. Elwood Cubberly (1909), a prominent educator and scholar during the turn of the century and dean of the Stanford School of Education for nearly two decades, wrote that urban schools should "give up the exceedingly democratic idea that all are equal, and that our society is devoid of classes" (pp. 56–57). Some went even further. In 1924, Frank Freeman, a writer for *Educational Review*, wrote:

> It is the business of the school to help the child to acquire such an attitude toward the inequalities of life, whether in accomplishment or in reward, that he may adjust himself to its conditions with the least possible friction. (as cited in Bowles & Gintis, p. 102)

Dewey, who saw the institutional problems in society as being more about income inequality rather than race, recognized how deeply flawed this strategy was, not only for educators' reverence for testing but also as it undermined schools' democratizing function. He derisively asserted that

> Our mechanical, industrialized civilization is concerned with averages, with percents. . . . [W]e welcome a procedure which under the title of science sinks the individual in a numerical class; judges him with reference to capacity to fit into a limited number of vocations ranked according to present business standards; assigns him to a predestined niche and thereby does whatever education can do to perpetuate the present order. (Dewey, 1922/1983, p. 297)

It's also important to keep in mind that schools' new commitment to evaluating students and sorting them occurred alongside a legal sorting out of many African American students, who were constitutionally mandated to attend separate and unequal schools.

It's easy to see how these ideas—schools as sorting and acculturating mechanisms in service to efficient and appropriate preparation for workforce employment—remain pervasive 100 years later. Tracking in our schools persists despite evidence of uneven pedagogical benefit and its discriminatory result. Students of low income, black and brown ethnicity, and those with special education needs are disproportionately placed in vocational and lower track classes, and those classes have been consistently found to have lower academic expectations and more traditional and less engaging pedagogy. In addition, the largest industries (currently, computer technology) constantly exert pressure on schools to provide more appropriately trained employees for entry and lower-skilled positions. Schools continue to serve as assimilating and socializing agents, and though twenty-first century industries often demand more advanced skills than the assembly-line factory owners a century ago, in many classrooms, we continue to place a premium on punctuality, quiet attention, and following directions, the same behaviors desired of students over a century ago.

Grading in the Twentieth Century

With our understanding of how American schools in the early twentieth century reflected the zeitgeist of the country, let's look specifically at the evolution of grading in K–12 education and how it reflected and facilitated schooling.[1]

As we mentioned earlier, prior to the turn of the century, before the large influx of families to urban centers and the rise of large schools to accommodate their children, the one-room school served few students and the teacher was a familiar member of the tight-knit community. It therefore should come as no surprise that communicating student progress looked very different than today. In most cases, the teacher would present oral reports or written narratives to families, perhaps during a visit to a student's home, to describe how students were performing in certain skills like penmanship, reading, or arithmetic (Guskey & Bailey, 2001). These reports helped to determine areas for the teacher's further instruction for the student, readiness for apprenticeships, or eligibility for higher education (Craig, 2011).

With compulsory education laws, larger schools, and the emphasis on efficiency, schools had to develop more succinct and simplified descriptions of student progress. No longer could educators use the clumsy "unscientific" narrative reporting—it was time consuming and too unstandardized. Instead, there was pressure to identify a standardized system of communicating student achievement, not only for bureaucratic ease within the school for sorting purposes, but also for external audiences—colleges or employers. Letter grades (A–F) had already been in place in some colleges and universities since the early 1900s to signify a student's achievement in a course relative to others in the course—called "norm-referenced grading"—and secondary schools began to use the letters well (Cronbach, 1975, cited in Schneider, 2014). Because, as the thinking went, intelligence is distributed across a population with a normal distribution (more familiarly known as a "bell curve") just like height or weight, then grades are more objective when they reflect that curve within any population. Schools therefore superimposed the normal distribution across a student group and labeled them by letter according to that distribution. By the mid-1900s, a majority of secondary schools used A–F grading and assigned grades according to the normal curve distribution.

---

[1]"The roots of grading in higher education can be traced back hundreds of years. In the sixteenth century, Cambridge University developed a three-tier grading system with 25 percent of the grades at the top, 50 percent in the middle, and 25 percent at the bottom (Winter, 1993). Working from European models, American universities invented systems for ranking and categorizing students based both on academic performance and on progress, conduct, attentiveness, interest, effort, and regular attendance at class and chapel" (Brookhart, 2016, p. 831).

Though our twenty-first century schools may have little apparent resemblance to schools of the twentieth century—the desks arranged for collaboration (rather than bolted to the floor), the laptops and iPads (rather than books), and the smart boards and PowerPoint presentations (rather than chalkboards)—the grading systems invented during that time continue to exist almost unchanged today: Students receive a letter grade in each class that represents their performance. In many classrooms, those grades are assigned with the normal curve in mind, and these grades are used to sort students into different racks and opportunities. In the next chapter, we'll hold century-old grading practices, driven by century-old beliefs and interests, up against our contemporary approaches and understanding: Is our best thinking about effective teaching and learning thwarted by our century-old grading?

Summary of Concepts

1. In the first half of the twentieth century, our country experienced radical social, economic, political, and scientific changes that included the rise of manufacturing, mass emigration from foreign countries and rural communities to cities, progressive educational theory, intelligence testing, and behaviorism. All of these shifts influenced the transformation of American schools during this period.

2. Schools during this time were expected to assimilate large numbers of students into "American" culture, specifically to make them ready to be employed by factories. This meant that there was a priority placed on both teaching students certain behaviors suited for factory labor and to replicate the ethos of industry: efficiency and productivity.

3. While grading had previously existed as a teacher's narrative of student progress, twentieth century schools adopted single letter grading (A, B, C, D, F) and the use of the "curve" to more efficiently describe and communicate student performance, and to sort students easily.

Questions to Consider

1. How do schools in the first half of the twenty-first century—their design, their purpose, their student—compare to schools in the first half of the twentieth century?

2. How do you see the ideas and beliefs of the early twentieth century manifesting themselves through your school's communication, curriculum, instruction, policies, and grading?

PART II

The Case for Change

How Traditional Grading Thwarts Effective and Equitable Teaching and Learning

"[A grade is] an inadequate report of an inaccurate judgment by a biased and variable judge of the extent to which a student has attained an undefined level of mastery of an unknown proportion of an indefinite material."

Dressel (1983), *Grades: One more tilt at the windmill*

How Traditional Grading Stifles Risk-Taking and Supports the "Commodity of Grades"

In this chapter, we will answer the following questions:

1. How does our use of traditional and inequitable grading practices send mixed messages to our students about the role of mistakes in learning?

2. How does the element of trust in the student–teacher relationship influence a student's approach to the learning process, particularly for historically underserved student populations, and how does our traditional grading affect that trust?

3. How do "points" in grading, often used to incentivize compliance, divert a student's focus away from intrinsic motivation to learn and instead toward the teacher's extrinsic rewards?

As we learned in the previous chapter, schools in the twentieth century were designed within larger societal beliefs that student achievement occurs on a curve, students are effectively motivated through extrinsic reinforcement and consequences, and a key purpose of schools is to sort students. In this chapter, we'll see how a century of learning and research, tectonic shifts in student demographics, and our more informed sense of justice and opportunity have fundamentally changed our thinking about schools and the children we serve in them. In contrast to those early twentieth century beliefs, we now know that when students experience differentiated and culturally responsive supports and challenges, only the slimmest subset of children are incapable of meeting our academic standards, and each student can choose for herself a future path among many attainable opportunities. With these new understandings, our contemporary teaching is so much more student centered, collaborative, and differentiated than a century ago, technology has redefined how students access information and demonstrate their learning, and we try to respond to the diversity of student ethnicities, religions, languages, gender identities, families, and histories.

INDUSTRIAL REVOLUTION BELIEFS	21ST CENTURY BELIEFS
Student achievement occurs on a curve, and only a subset of students is capable of meeting academic standards.	All students are capable of meeting academic standards.
Schools are expected to sort students.	Schools should not be in the business of sorting students.
Extrinsic motivation is the most effective means of influencing behaviors, which include behaviors associated with learning.	Extrinsic motivation is NOT the most effective means of influencing behaviors associated with learning and higher-order thinking; intrinsic motivation is superior.

And yet, twenty-first century classrooms continue to use the grading systems of the early twentieth century even though, as Marzano (2000) writes, there is "no meaningful research reports to support it." In the next two chapters, we explore four ways in which, despite our most informed ideas and socially conscious intentions, our continued use of traditional grading practices contradicts and even undermines effective and equitable teaching and learning, particularly for students historically underserved. As we'll see, traditional grading:

- Stifles risk-taking and trust between the teacher and student

- Supports the "commodity of grades"

- Hides information, invites biases, and provides misleading information

- Demotivates and disempowers students

Risk-Taking, Trust, and the Teacher–Student Relationship

Let's begin by examining the critical ingredients of an effective teacher–student relationship, and how many of our current grading practices undermine that relationship through constant judgments of students.

No matter the qualifications or experience of the teacher, successful learning depends on a successful student–teacher relationship. More colloquially, there is a saying among teachers that "Students don't care how much you know until they know how much you care." Research across the fields of sociology, psychology, and communications shows that students are motivated, engaged, and have higher achievement when they have supportive classroom climates anchored by positive relationships with their teacher.[1] John Hattie (2008, 2012), in his exhaustive study of over 900 meta-analyses of over 50,000 education research articles (which included 240 million students), found that a positive teacher–student relationship had one of the most powerful influences (or "effect size") on student achievement. This powerful relationship begins with a teacher's positive behavior toward a student, and the student reciprocates. Nearly three decades ago, Lisa Delpit (2006), a researcher on cultural-responsive teaching and MacArthur "Genius" Fellow, called for teachers to be "warm demanders" and to "expect a great deal of their students, convince them of their own brilliance, and help them to reach their potential in a disciplined and structured environment." A decade later, Nell Noddings (1996, 2015) emphasized "care" in teacher–student relationships: a blend of academic expectations, consistent support, and mutual understanding.

It is the teacher's "burden of proof"—to use a legal term—to convince students that they are cared for in this academic and interpersonal way. When students know that their teacher believes in them, treats them fairly, listens and responds to their needs, and respects them, they are more willing to work hard, to persevere through challenge, to be open to new ideas, and to believe in their own potential (Wentzel, 1997). With this knowledge, the student decides whether to trust the teacher, to assume the risk of making herself vulnerable to someone who could do her harm (Pianta, 1999). How does a student decide whether to trust or not to trust the teacher with that vulnerability? She evaluates the teacher's behavior when her weaknesses are exposed: "If I make a mistake or reveal that I don't know something, what will I gain or lose? If I disclose a weakness—academic or otherwise—will the teacher respond with understanding, care, and support, or with ridicule, punishment, and indifference?" (Ennis & McCauley, 2002). Particularly for students in communities whose experiences with schools (and other institutions of power) have led to distrust of those in power over them, there is a caution, even a survival mandate, against showing vulnerability. For example, African Americans have lower general trust than most other racial and ethnic groups, especially relative to white Americans (Yeager et al., 2013). For these students and others historically underserved and previously

---

[1]Brock, L. L., Nishida, T. K., Chiong, C., Grimm, K. J., & Rimm-Kaufman, S. E. (2008). Children's perceptions of the classroom environment and social and academic performance: A longitudinal analysis of the contribution of the Responsive Classroom approach. *Journal of School Psychology, 46*, 129–149; Pianta, R., Belsky, J., Vandergrift, N., Houts, R., & Morrison, F. (2008). Classroom effects on children's achievement trajectories in elementary school. *American Educational Research Journal, 45*, 365–397; Reyes, M. R., Brackett, M. A., Rivers, S. E., White, M., & Salovey, P. (2012). Classroom emotional climate, student engagement, and academic achievement. *Journal of Educational Psychology, 104*(3), 700; Wentzel, K. R. (1997). Student motivation in middle school: The role of perceived pedagogical caring. *Journal of Educational Psychology, 89*, 411–419.

treated with indifference or hostility, convincing them to trust and show their weaknesses—academic and otherwise—is much more difficult and all the more critical to effective teaching and learning (Heath & McLaughlin, 1993).

For their part, teachers know that gaining a student's trust requires careful responses to mistakes and vulnerabilities. Teachers recognize that mistakes are not only important to learning but learning cannot occur *without* mistakes, whether studying the Pythagorean theorem, the proper method to analyze a primary document, time management, conducting a lab experiment, or hitting a ball, and therefore teachers expect, and the best ones *demand*, that their students make mistakes, because those mistakes create opportunities for students to grow from their misconceptions and misunderstandings. Teachers actually *depend* on students taking risks and revealing mistakes in order to help them—teachers can't correct mistakes or misconceptions that students don't reveal—but this mechanism only works if students trust the teacher enough to reveal mistakes. Therefore, they try to create classrooms where risks are encouraged and mistakes are normal, expected, and valuable.

The problem is that our traditional grading practices send the opposite message: Mistakes are unwanted, unhelpful, and punished.

To understand how, let's start with the obvious: Students take tests to show what they know, and their scores and grades reflect how much they've learned. If students make mistakes, they lose points. This is perfectly reasonable *at the end* of the learning process. Unfortunately, in most classrooms teachers penalize students for mistakes they make *during* the learning process, for assignments that prepare them for the test. Students lose points for errors (and for answers they don't complete) on homework, classwork, and on any task that the teacher designs to help students learn content. Those scores are entered into the gradebook and included in the overall calculation of a student's grade. With this grading approach, student mistakes are penalized during the very stage of learning when students *should* be making mistakes. If mistakes on any work—homework assignments, tests, quizzes, in-class worksheets, discussions—are always penalized with a score that is incorporated into a grade no matter whether those mistakes occur at the beginning, middle, or end of learning, then the message is that mistakes aren't ever acceptable, much less desired, and they certainly aren't ever valuable. Students will be discouraged, not encouraged, to take risks and be vulnerable.

Even worse, traditional grading that penalizes students for mistakes often isn't just limited to a student's academic work. Teachers often assign grades based on mistakes in students' behaviors as well: downgrading a score if an assignment is late, subtracting points from a daily participation grade if a student is tardy to class, or lowering a group's grade if the group becomes too noisy while they work. In this environment, *every* mistake is penalized and incorporated into the final grade. Even if just a few points are docked for forgetting to bring a notebook to class or losing a few points for not heading a paper correctly, the message is clear: All mistakes result in penalties. While some might argue that this is simply accountability—"I asked the students to do something, so it *has* to count"—it's missing the forest for the trees. The more assignments and behaviors a teacher grades, the less willing a student will be to reveal her weaknesses and vulnerability. With no zones of learning that are "grade free," it becomes nearly impossible to build an effective teacher–student relationship and positive learning environment in which students try new things, venture into unfamiliar learning territory, or feel comfortable making errors, and grow. When everything a student does is graded, and every mistake counts against her grade, that student can perceive that to receive a good grade she has to be perfect all of the time. Students don't feel trust in their teachers, only the pressure to conceal weaknesses and avoid errors.

One might respond: If the student's answer is correct during the learning phase, heads her paper as instructed, submits assignments on time, shouldn't she be recognized for that success? The problem is that if teachers raise grades for correct answers or for following directions during the learning phase, students will realize that they will also be punished in their grade for the wrong answer or missing directions. The result will be the same: less trust and risk-taking. As we'll learn in Part III, a teacher can respond to productive student behaviors in ways other than through grade-based feedback.

Viewed through this lens, we might be more empathetic and charitable toward student behaviors we often characterize as "lazy" or "refusing to learn," but which might in fact be reasonable reactions to the traditional grading policies that constantly penalize mistakes. For example, when students skip a class they may be doing so because they are unprepared or not confident that they can perform mistake free. This decision to not attend a class, instead of being immature and irresponsible, may instead be rational and self-preserving: It's safer psychologically to fail for not showing up than to be penalized and feel shame for giving incorrect answers that reveal weakness and vulnerability.

Another logical yet unintended consequence from penalizing all mistakes is that students are incentivized to copy and cheat. I have interviewed hundreds of students, and I have yet to find one that hasn't copied homework. When I ask them why, they often share that they were doing whatever they could to avoid losing points for mistakes. The risk of a student getting caught copying is likely less than the certainty that incorrect or incomplete responses will lower a grade. If imperfections on homework will negatively impact the grade, and the student isn't confident that she will get all the answers right or will complete it, the decision to copy seems more of a survival tactic than a moral failure.

A final point: Some teachers try to address the problems that arise from punishing mistakes by awarding points for homework *completion*, not whether the student answers questions correctly. The thinking often is "To show my students I value the attempt, not the result, during this learning phase, I assign a grade to students simply for trying and sharing their mistakes. With this policy, I reward and encourage students to take risks, make errors acceptable, and make my classroom a more mistake-friendly place." However, this only works for the students who know enough (or feel sufficiently confident that they know enough) to put something on paper: the academically weaker student faces a penalty for not completing the assignment even though they may have tried but did not have enough skill or content knowledge to give an *incorrect* answer. The teacher's well-intentioned strategy doesn't create a safer environment to make mistakes among the least confident, academically weakest, or most time-crunched students, and still provides an incentive to cheat if the student doesn't know the answers or have enough time.

The message when everything is included in the grade is clear: You are always being judged and must show your absolute best performance in every respect—academic and nonacademic—every day. If you make a mistake, or even are just having a bad day, it's going to count against you. There is no room for error, no safe place to make mistakes. Death (or an academic "death" of an F) by a thousand cuts.

Boud (1995) hones in on how profoundly a classroom of constant evaluations can affect our students, often without us even realizing it:

> We [teachers] judge too much and too powerfully, not realising the extent to which students experience our power over them. Learning is an act which necessarily leaves us vulnerable: we open ourselves to changes in the ways we see the world, not knowing where we shall end up. We might find a secure spot or be exposed. Rarely are we confident about what we know during the early stages (which include most of the time we are being taught)—the very stages at which we are most likely to receive the comments from a teacher. We know how little we know and we fear the depths of our ignorance. To have someone come along and tell us that, for example, what we are doing is all wrong or that we will never do it well or that we haven't read the book when we thought we had, is a direct attack on us when we are least able to cope with it. In treating students in such ways, and, indeed, with some students by using far less direct forms, we go beyond the realm of valid statements into the world of abusive language. It abuses them in the sense of taking undue advantage of them by virtue of our position, of betraying them. It does not seem abusive to us, but to those on the receiving end, it is profoundly so. (pp. 5–6)

Most of us entered teaching to build meaningful relationships with young people, to engender in them a sense of trust and safety by accepting mistakes along a path to proficiency, but our traditional grading encourages us to judge nearly everything a student does or doesn't do, and we create pressure-cooker classrooms where no mistake goes unpenalized. Effective teacher–student relationships require students' confidence that the classroom is a space to take risks without penalty, to disclose weaknesses without being judged, to simply feel safe knowing that they don't have to perform perfectly day in and day out. Our traditional practice of grading *everything* students do inadvertently creates distrust, shame, and deceit—undermining the teacher–student relationship qualities that support learning.

The "Commodity of Grades" and Extrinsic Motivation

In the early elementary grades, school is purely about learning. When asked to perform a learning task, my first-grade son and his classmates are full of energetic curiosity. They learn because learning is exciting. His teachers' feedback on their work or behavior is almost entirely verbal—through encouragement, supportive correction, and reflection—with occasional stickers or stamps. For the first few years of school, students are taught that success at learning is its own reward.

In the second half of elementary school, a shift occurs in how learning is defined: Teachers begin attaching learning to points, categorizing and tracking achievement or behavior numerically. Here is a point system that a fifth-grade teacher in a Northern California elementary school published to her students and their families (a different kind of educator quote in that it is a common example of what *not* to do):

> "We have a point system for behavior and homework. Students are divided into five teams, which will change each six weeks. Students earn points for their team each day in the following ways:
>
> 10 points—all team members have all homework all day
>
> 3 points—all team members display excellent behavior all day, earning no behavior cards [for violations of behavior rules]
>
> 2 points—class receives unasked-for praise from an adult in the building
>
> 10 points awarded each week for organization. Teams will lose points throughout the week if members are unorganized."

This point system is not unique. Across fifth-grade classrooms everywhere (and sometimes fourth- and third-grade classrooms), in addition to receiving points for correct answers, students are introduced to the idea of earning points for turning in completed homework, cleaning up their work station, bringing their notebook and pencil to class, having a quiet and attentive table group, and lining up quietly for recess. They lose points for talking while the teacher is explaining directions, coming late to class, not pushing in their chairs, or forgetting to write their name at the top of their homework. Each student has her own "account" of points which the teacher adds to or subtracts from. The teacher motivates students to behave in desired ways by creating a "currency" of points and awarding or withdrawing currency based on students' actions.

By middle and high school, the currency of points to motivate students has become a full-blown economic system of incentives and penalties. Teachers assign "denominations" of points to academic work based on the importance of the task;

for example, homework assignments are 5 points each, quizzes are worth 50 points, and tests are worth 100 points. (It's worth noting that teachers don't usually decide point values of each category in a quantifiable relationship to each other, even though it might seem so. For instance, in the above example, it's not likely that the value of ten homework assignments is equal to the value of one quiz and that the value of two quizzes is equal to the value of one test.)

Once these point values are established, teachers enter the points earned or lost into their gradebook software, sometimes inputting multiple entries for each student because several tasks with points attached were awarded in a single class. By the end of a marking term, teachers' gradebooks are filled with dozens of point entries, rendering the final grade a relatively straightforward ratio calculation: the total points a student earned divided by the total points offered. With all the points assigned to behaviors and academic performance, the sum total that a student can earn in a single course during a grading term can be in the hundreds or even thousands. Keeping track of these points and entering them into the grade book for so many students can eat up hours each week for a teacher, but in many classrooms and schools, teachers feel that it's worth it. Point economies are believed to be a vital incentive and feedback mechanism to help students successfully meet classroom expectations. When students get 5 points for turning in an assignment on time, they immediately and unambiguously know that they are meeting the teacher's expectations, and when they see a "-5" on their group's project submission, they know they were talking too much. Students learn appropriate academic and behavior habits, which also helps create a well-managed classroom.

Using points to motivate students is to assume that extrinsic motivation—rewards and consequences provided by the teacher—is the most effective way to promote learning. Behaviorists like Skinner taught us this in the early twentieth century, and this apparent truism became embedded in our schools of that era. But our understanding of motivation has evolved significantly in the last 100 years: research has shown that *extrinsic motivation is not an effective motivation strategy for authentic learning*. While extrinsic motivation yields benefits for menial and repetitive tasks—such as offering prizes for stuffing the most envelopes, or those that Skinner and factories were focused on incentivizing—extrinsic rewards and consequences have been found to be wholly ineffective to engage people in tasks that require higher-order and creative thinking, the goal of modern schools. Daniel Pink (2011), in his best-selling book, *Drive, the Surprising Truth About What Motivates Us*, reviewed over fifty years of research on motivation, and found "one of the sturdiest findings in social science":

> [E]xtrinsic rewards can be effective for algorithmic tasks—those that depend on following an existing formula to its logical conclusion. But for more right-brain undertakings—those that demand flexible problem-solving, inventiveness, or conceptual understanding—contingent rewards can be dangerous . . . For artists, scientists, inventors, school-children, and the rest of us, intrinsic motivation—the drive to do something because it is interesting, challenging, and absorbing—is

essential for high levels of creativity. But the "if-then" motivators that are the staple of most businesses [and schools!] often stifle, rather than stir, creative thinking. As the economy moves toward more right-brain, conceptual work—this might be the most alarming gap between what science knows and what business [and school] does. (pp. 44–45)

We face a sobering admission: Five-year-old children don't come into school looking for points (even those who know their numbers), which means that if we believe that our middle school and high school students are motivated extrinsically, it is because *we have taught them to be*, in no small part through our widespread use of points. In essence when we award points, we teach students that the satisfaction, even joy, of learning is not valued or even expected. As Kohn (1993) writes,

When we repeatedly promise rewards to children for acting responsibly, or to students for making an effort to learn something new, or to employees for doing quality work, we are assuming that they could not or would not choose to act this way on their own. If the capacity for responsible action, the natural love of learning, and the desire to do good work are already part of who we are, then the tacit assumption to the contrary can fairly be described as dehumanizing. (p. 26)

Like the cheating we inadvertently cause when we punish mistakes, teachers' use of points inadvertently pulls students (and their teachers) farther away from a focus on learning. Rather than teach students to be curious about the academic content, to care about their progress as a learner, to invest in the health of the classroom community, and to co-construct productive relationships with their peers or teacher, we teach them to care about points. We take children who come to school with innate interest in learning and growing, and we teach them that those things are only a means to the ultimate end: lots of points.

It's depressingly clear how well we've taught them this concept. Every classroom task, no matter how focused on content and learning, becomes infiltrated and infected with the question: "How many points is this worth?" Students bargain and haggle over points, plead not to lose points, and propose supplemental tasks for points ("Can I erase the white board for 10 points?"). The teacher is essentially the Federal Reserve of the classroom who can "print" more currency and inject more points into the classroom economy when needed. Especially toward the end of a term, teachers feel pressure to create more point-generating opportunities—perhaps a menu of extra credit assignments in the final weeks of the semester—so that students have a last chance to boost their grade. Many teachers feel trapped by their own sophisticated incentive system, with no choice but to support students' constant quest for points. The measure of learning, contrary to the curiosity and joy that students enter school with, becomes a race to earn the most points.

We preach the gospel of learning, but we make students genuflect to the altar of points.

Another unintended negative consequence is that the use of point systems makes students more dependent on the teacher and less independent learners. Because the teacher essentially "owns" all points and determines how many points students receive or are withheld from them, she holds all the power in the classroom. By creating a point system, a teacher's relationship with students—one which we learned should be built on trust, mutual understanding, high expectations, and support—is reduced to a transactional one that feels artificial, tedious, even demeaning: Students' actions are valued only inasmuch as they earn points, and a teacher is important only inasmuch as she provides those points. When we rely on extrinsic motivation but a student is not motivated by the specific reward (the student who couldn't care less if she gets the five points for turning in homework), we assume a character weakness—laziness or a lack of responsibility—or missing elements in her home environment or upbringing, rather than recognize the ineffectiveness of extrinsic rewards to motivate learning.

Perhaps most disturbingly, extrinsic motivation systems are often endorsed as particularly appropriate, even necessary, to manage students who are from low-income families, have struggled academically, or who have historically been underserved. Many educators, whether limited by unconsciously racist assumptions or guided by theories of a "culture of poverty" (Payne, 1998), too often apply a "deficit lens" to African American, Latino, and low-income students, believing that those groups of children require and even hunger for immediate, concrete rewards and extrinsic incentive systems—that their environment simply does not support, and they cannot handle intrinsic motivation. It is an offensive belief that fueled our application of extrinsic motivation to the immigrants and poor in our twentieth century schools and factories, but which has no basis in fact unless we have taught students to respond to extrinsic motivation. Rather than expect of them the same capacity of intrinsic motivation that we would more readily expect in students who have stronger academic backgrounds or who are from higher-income families, we perpetuate the idea that "those" students won't work unless we bribe them with points: "I want them to contribute to the class discussions by asking questions, so each time she asks a question I'll award her points."

It's a tempting incentive strategy to use points to manage behavior, whether it's to get our students to complete the homework or to be respectful, particularly when it gives us immediate results—the students are quieter during our lecture when we threaten to take away points. But it only creates the illusion of engagement and motivation: When we institute point systems, we are making an assumption that students won't join us in our classroom activities, won't invest and participate in their learning, and won't see the joy and value in the struggle of learning unless we explicitly reward them.

> *Using only extrinsic incentives to inspire learning is a form of educational engineering that implicitly views students as inferior, inert, and in need of motivation. Such an orientation dims our awareness of learners' own determination and promotes their dependency. (Ginsberg, 2015, p. 12)*

Teachers may bemoan that students care only about points, that learning has become commodified, and wish they had more trusting relationships with their students. Our approach to grading may be to blame. In the next chapter, we'll focus squarely on how grades are traditionally calculated and understand how those practices make our grades confusing, biased, and unreliable.

Summary of Concepts

1. Mistakes are necessary for any learning to happen, and yet traditional grading treats mistakes as unwanted, unhelpful, and deserving of penalty.

2. In traditional grading, teachers judge nearly every action of a student throughout the learning process, weakening trust in the student–teacher relationship and inhibiting students from disclosing weaknesses or incentivizing dishonest means to conceal weaknesses.

3. Teachers use "points" in grading based on the traditional belief that points motivate students to learn, even though "one of the sturdiest findings in social science" is that extrinsic motivation for learning is ineffective and even harmful.

Questions to Consider

1. How have different supervisors (or those whose opinions you care about) responded to your mistakes? How have helpful responses impacted you and your effectiveness? How have unhelpful responses impacted you and your effectiveness?

2. Recall something you learned to do outside of the school context. What motivated you to learn and to continue learning when you struggled?

3. *For Teachers*: Some teachers think, "If I motivate students to learn with points now, they'll realize success and become internally motivated." If you believe this, how could you test this theory?

4. *For Teachers*: How effective are the use of points for students who are the least motivated and engaged? How might the use of points—the addition and subtraction throughout a student's day—affect those students' relationships with adults and their self-concept about whether school is "for" them?

Traditional Grading Hides Information, Invites Biases, and Provides Misleading Information

In this chapter, we will answer the following questions:

1. What are the mathematical weaknesses of our traditional grading calculations, and how do those render our grades less transparent, and less valid?

2. What are ways in which our traditional grading practices attract and incorporate our implicit biases, and how do our inherited practices thereby disproportionately harm our historically underserved students?

3. How does our inherited approach to grading collapse so many varied aspects of a student's performance that our "omnibus" grades often become confusing and nearly meaningless?

4. What "grade hacks" do teachers use to thoughtfully counteract the weaknesses of our traditional grade calculations, and how do these adjustments inadvertently make our grades even less reliable?

A teacher collects an extraordinary amount of information about her students during a grading term. She knows each student's academic performance: the scores earned on each assignment, quiz, test, and project. She knows each student's nonacademic strengths and weaknesses: how that student communicates and collaborates (or doesn't) with peers, her level of responsibility, creativity, tardiness, and attitude. She also knows the trajectory and trends of each student's performance during the term: how each grew or regressed, where each struggled and succeeded. It is not unusual for a teacher to have several dozen, even hundreds, of pieces of data about each student entered into her electronic gradebook, and she collects it because knowing as much as she can about her students is critical to the work of teaching.

And yet with all of this information about of her students, when it comes to report card time, how does she distill and communicate the student's performance over a term? With a single letter: A, B, C, D, or F. Teachers may have the option of adding a plus or a minus to the letter, and some schools allow teachers to enter descriptive comments either from a drop-down menu or within a certain character limit. But overall, teachers use a letter to describe the entirety of a student's performance, a practice that is a direct descendant of the early twentieth century's emphasis on efficient communication and sorting. A century later, teachers continue to be forced to collapse the entire diverse information they know about students into those same five letters. If we weren't so accustomed to the A–F scale, educators and noneducators alike might call such a task absurd, even impossible.

This constraint on teachers of reporting student performance with a single letter grade results in several negative consequences—some planned, some unanticipated. Because these consequences are quite complex and require us to excavate letter grades—one of the most defining elements of our schools—we'll need to slow down a bit and examine their impact in bite-size chunks.

Traditional Grading Evaluates Both a Student's Content Knowledge as Well as Their Behaviors, and Invites Subjectivity and Bias

With all of the information teachers collect on their students over a term, they have to find ways to organize that data. Most teachers group the information into categories, such as Homework, Tests, Quizzes, Class Activities, Projects, and Participation. From my review of hundreds of middle and high school teachers' syllabi, including my own when I taught high school, teachers generally include the following student information in each category:

CATEGORY	TYPES OF INFORMATION
Homework	Performance on worksheets, end-of-chapter questions, problem sets, and test review sheets. Includes extra credit assignments and returning parent-signed syllabus or other paperwork.

CATEGORY	TYPES OF INFORMATION
Tests and Projects	Performance on mid-terms, group presentations or performances, chapter or unit tests, and research papers
Classwork and Class Activities	Performance on in-class assignments, labs, discussions, peer editing, group work, and whole class activities
Participation and Effort	Performance on weekly notebook checks, preparation (e.g., bringing all materials to class), engagement, asking questions, showing proper conduct, demonstrating respect for classmates or for teacher, following classroom rules, punctuality to class, showing positive attitude, and responding appropriately to feedback

We can see that each category captures a range of information about students. The Tests and Projects category might describe what the student has learned about the academic content of the class—whether she has learned to use the FOIL method to multiply binomials or understands the water cycle or can analyze and critique a rhetorical argument. Evaluating this type of student performance is relatively objective and straightforward: A student either knows the water cycle or she doesn't. By contrast, categories like Class Activities and Participation are more subjective and undefined. Although some subjectivity may exist in evaluating academic categories like Tests and Projects, it is nothing compared to the significant subjectivity of evaluating these nonacademic categories. What is the right way for students to behave in a class? What does it mean to show sufficient "respect"? How much listening is good enough? Each teacher likely has her own unique definition and criteria of how these categories are evaluated and entered into the grade.

And not only does each teacher define these student behaviors individually and subjectively, but each teacher measures a student's demonstration of those behaviors through a deeply flawed lens: the teacher's observations of a student's behaviors. As the teacher, if I don't see a student talking during group work, did I look at the wrong time or was the student not contributing to the activity? Though the Class Activities and Participation types of categories may be designed to build important citizenship skills and encourage learning behaviors, each teacher identifies what student behaviors are appropriate and decides how much a student met those behaviors, based not just on what she observes but on *how she interprets what she observes*. When a student interrupts another student, is that disrespect or engagement? Is a student who doodles on her paper being off-task or a signal of her focus? When we grade behaviors based on our subjective interpretation of those behaviors it isn't just unavoidable imprecision; it's a recipe for inequity.

Let's better understand why.

Implicit Bias and Traditional Grading

When we observe someone, we bring to that observation a set of assumptions and beliefs that color our interpretation of that person's action. Most of the time, those assumptions are subconscious and ingrained in us from an early age, a phenomenon called "implicit bias." No one is immune to implicit biases; they are both pervasive and robust (see, e.g., Greenwald, McGhee, & Schwartz, 1998; Kang & Lane, 2010; Nosek et al., 2007). Because the implicit associations we hold arise outside of conscious awareness, these biases may not necessarily align with our explicit beliefs (Greenwald & Krieger, 2006; Reskin, 2005). In other words, even with our self-assured and avowed commitments to impartiality and fairness, we are susceptible to acting according to these unconscious biases (Rachlinski, Johnson, Wistrich, & Guthrie, 2009).

Much has been written in the last several years about the disproportionate impact of implicit bias in schools, particularly because the teaching population is predominantly (over 80%) white while the majority of students are students of color, overwhelmingly so in urban areas (Staats, 2014). Researchers such as Gershenson, Holt, and Papageorge (2015) have found that non-black teachers have lower expectations for black students than do black teachers.[1] Teachers' implicit biases and subjective interpretations of students' behaviors influence how teachers respond in terms of both discipline and instruction. For example, black students are disproportionately punished throughout preschool, elementary, middle, and high school, often in the absence of violent behavior (Vavrus & Cole, 2002, cited by Staats, 2014). There is evidence that implicit bias leads to an "adultification" of black children, in which actions of black boys are more likely to be interpreted as threatening than other students, and black girls are assumed to be less innocent and needing less protection and support than white girls (Epstein, Blake, & González, 2017). Teachers' implicit biases also have been identified as a cause for the overreferral of black and brown students for special education services (Codrington & Fairchild, 2009). In 2013, compared to white, Asian, and Hispanic/Latino students, black students were nearly 1½ times as likely to receive special education services, and over twice as likely to receive services for emotional disturbance and intellectual disabilities (U.S. Department of Education, 2015).

Researchers have found that when implicit bias is operating, teachers interpret African American students through a faulty, culturally biased lens:

> *Culture-based misunderstandings between students and teachers can lead to students being disciplined unnecessarily for perceived unruliness even when their actions were not intended to be inappropriate. . . . [F]or Black students, these*

---

[1] "[R]elative to teachers of the same race and sex as the student, other-race teachers were 12 percentage points less likely to expect black students to complete a four-year college degree" (p. 18).

disconnects are particularly perplexing when teachers sanction them for behavior that may be accepted or even rewarded in their home life. In sum, influenced by implicit biases, practitioners' misunderstanding of the intent behind student actions can lead to the disproportionate administration of school discipline by race. (Staats, 2014, pp. 8–9)

White teachers can misinterpret African-American students' behaviors, incorrectly believing them to be signs of disrespect or stemming from some evil intent or judging it to be inappropriate because the teacher comes from a different cultural background in which that behavior is less familiar or accepted. Teachers may not recognize how important and valuable certain behaviors are to historically under-served or oppressed populations, for cultural identity and even cultural survival.

This extended excerpt from Staats (2014) provides some concrete examples:

Several examples illustrate this contrast between "mainstream sociocultural norms" and "culturally influenced" student behavior (C. Weinstein, et al., 2003, pp. 269–270). A lively debate may be interpreted as aggressive and contentious rather than simply verbal sparring common among African American teenagers (C. S. Weinstein, et al., 2004). Differences in discourse models can also signal cultural mismatch. Overlapping speech, such as the active "call-response" partici-patory pattern familiar to African American students, may be perceived as disrup-tive and/or rude when contrasted with the more "passive-receptive" approach that is likely to be more typical to White teachers' expectations (Monroe, 2005; C. S. Weinstein et al., 2004). In other cases, play fighting may be mistakenly regarded as genuine aggression (Monroe, 2005). For Black females in particular, what may be perceived as loud and defiant behavior may actually be the manifestation of important survival qualities that have historically reflected resilience in the face of racism, sexism, and classism (Morris, 2013). (p. 9)

Additionally, the U.S. Departments of Justice and Education have found that implicit bias results in disproportionate consequences when the school authority relies on a "subjective exercise of unguided discretion" (Lhamon & Samuels, 2014). Even distinct from the disciplinary context, the classroom is unfortunately filled with subjective exercises of unguided discretion—micro-events such as whether to allow a student to use the bathroom pass, how to encourage (or whether to ignore) the student reluctant to participate in an activity, or to redirect behavior perceived as "off task."

Most importantly for our work, there is no more "subjective exercise of unguided discretion" than how a teacher grades (or awards or subtracts points) for student behaviors.

Can we simply stop our implicit biases? Probably not. Americans—regardless of race—hold an anti-black/pro-white implicit bias (Staats, 2014), a legacy of our country's shameful and inescapable history of enslavement, colonization, and discrimination, and that is constantly reinforced through discriminatory legal and regulatory decisions, stereotyping media, and people's individual and communal aggressions. According to Gershenson, Holt, and Papageorge (2015), when our biases lead our most vulnerable students to feel that they or their actions are stigmatized, it can significantly harm their likelihood of academic success:

> *First, the perception that teachers have low expectations may exacerbate the harmful effects of stereotype threat, whereby low expectations either cause emotional responses that directly harm performance or cause students to disidentify with educational environments (Steele, 1997). Second, stigmatized students may modify their expectations, and in turn their behavior, to conform to teachers' negative biases (Ferguson, 2003). In each of the first two cases, teachers' stigmatization of information-poor racial minority students could create a feedback loop that functions like a self-fulfilling prophecy (Burgess & Greaves, 2013; Loury, 2009). Finally, teachers who stigmatize certain types of students may modify how they teach, evaluate, and advise them, again leading to poor educational outcomes for stigmatized students (Ferguson, 2003). All three scenarios potentially perpetuate sociodemographic gaps in educational attainment. (p. 5)*

If we can't stop our implicit racial biases, can teachers, particularly those of us who are white teachers, limit the opportunities to perpetuate inequities through our racial biases? One important strategy is to remain vigilantly aware of our biases. In 2014, the U.S. Departments of Education and Justice, based on research findings, released a joint policy guidance package to schools and districts, specifically encouraging programs to "enhance staff awareness of their implicit or unconscious biases and the harms associated with using or failing to counter racial and ethnic stereotypes" (Lhamon & Samuels, 2014). But we can't just be aware of our biases. If we truly want to limit our implicit biases from operating, we have to reconsider policies that invite them to operate, that allow a "subjective exercise of unbridled discretion."

How do traditional grading policies invite our implicit biases? Research has found that in classrooms taught by white teachers, black students "are typically rated as poorer classroom citizens"—meaning the kinds of behaviors often included in Participation and Effort categories—than their white peers (Downey & Pribesh, 2004). When we create a Participation or Effort category that is populated nearly entirely by subjective judgments of students' behaviors, we are inviting our biases to infect our judgments, particularly when we're white and our students are black or brown. We are exposing our students of color (and importantly, ourselves) to the same unfair and inequitable consequences that we see in student discipline and special education referrals. It's a symptom of the same disease.

While subjective criteria for grading can impact any student, this insight may help to explain part of our country's achievement gap: African American and Latino students' behaviors are evaluated by subjective criteria in Participation-like grading categories infected with implicit biases which, because the evaluation of these behaviors is included in a grade, lowers students' grades regardless of a students' academic performance. But this is only the tip of the iceberg of why the single-letter grade constraint bequeathed to us by the Industrial Revolution is so harmful to our students.

The "Omnibus" Grade: A Barrel-ful of Information in a Thimble-Size Container

While teachers a generation or two ago entered grades into paper grid-lined gradebooks and crunched computations on their calculators, teachers today rely on powerful and sophisticated grading software to conduct the mathematical formulae used to render the grade. Too often, I've heard teachers cede ownership of their grades to the software: "The grade is how the software calculated it," or "The grade is what the numbers say." Even though the software performs complex calculations so teachers don't have to, it's critically important to understand how those computations function. We know that formulas represent choices, and we need to critically examine how those formulas work and what those choices represent. Only then can we be empowered to decide whether we accept those choices or want to make different ones. Even though this next section may start to feel technical, it's actually empowering to understand what's going on "beneath the hood" of our grading software.

As explained earlier, traditional grading includes multiple categories of a student's performance. However, not all categories are equally important. For example, how well a student does on homework might be more important than her Participation but less important than her scores on tests. Common grading software allows teachers to assign percentage "weights" to each category to indicate its relative importance in the course. Below is a typical teacher's approach:

CATEGORY	WEIGHT
Homework	30%
Tests and Projects	40%
Class Activities	20%
Participation	10%

In this example, the teacher assigns relative weights of the categories to convey that certain kinds of student work or activities (in this example, tests, projects, and homework) are more important than others (quizzes, class activities, and participation).

Why are percentages so important to teachers' grading? Not only is the teacher trying to achieve optimal accuracy of the final grade—what is most important in the class receives the most value—but she wants to make it clear to students what the course is about, to provide a "recipe" for achievement. The teacher hopes that the students, knowing the weights of the categories, will allocate attention in roughly the same ratios. Teachers do this to be more transparent and precise—transparent in that the student can understand a pathway to success in the class, and precise so a student's grade most accurately reflects her performance.

However, these categories are all ultimately combined into a single-letter grade—our inheritance from the Industrial Revolution. We distill a barrel-ful of information into a thimble-size container of a single letter. All the disparate information of a student's performance—test scores, her respect of classmates, extra credit, homework completion, and everything else—is collapsed into a single "omnibus" grade, sometimes called, much less charitably, a "hodgepodge" grade. (Brookhart, 1991)

Considering it's how most teachers have constructed grades for the past century, is there a downside? Even if the omnibus grade is not very specific, is it basically accurate? Even though it may not be ideal, does it tell us essentially what we need to know about our students?

A Tale of Two Students: Tangela and Isabel

Let's better understand the omnibus grade by considering two hypothetical students:

- **Tangela, "The Teacher's Dream":** She is a kind and helpful student, a great teammate and friend to her classmates. She is the first to volunteer and is a leader during group work. However, she struggles academically. Most of the time she completes her homework (although often not entirely correctly). When it comes to summative assessments (tests and projects), she performs poorly.

- **Isabel, "The Teacher's Nightmare":** She is a reluctant participant, generally has an unpleasant attitude toward the teacher and the class, and submits homework that is incomplete. However, she pays attention (even though it often doesn't seem like it), and clearly understands the content being taught in the class; she consistently does very well on tests and projects.

Tangela-type students pull teachers' heartstrings; she is the kind of person we want more of in the world, perhaps not as our doctor or electrician but certainly as a dinner companion and next door neighbor (bless her heart). Isabel-type students give teachers headaches and heartburn. She isn't enjoyable to have in the classroom, and she knows the content of the course despite not doing much of the assigned work, which can truly frustrate teachers. True, she may be doing a lot of thinking and learning, but she's not learning in the ways teachers prefer.

Let's assume that both Tangela and Isabel are in the same class and their teacher calculates grades using the categories of Homework, Tests and Projects, Class Activities, and Participation. Let's assign each student some percentage scores in each category (note that this is not the *weight* of each category, but the students' percentage *scores* in each category):

	TANGELA	ISABEL
Homework	80%	60%
Tests and Projects	60%	90%
Class Activities	90%	70%
Participation	100%	60%

In categories reflecting soft skills and behaviors, Tangela does well, but not so well on tests. Isabel is the opposite. For example, across all of the homework assignments, Tangela has scored an average of 80 percent[2] and Isabel earned only a 60 percent average on her homework assignments (most likely because they were incomplete or perhaps even unsubmitted).

As explained earlier, in our traditional grading system, a student earns a score within a category based on all the assignments in that category, and then the scores of those categories are weighted. Let's apply our previous hypothetical teacher's weighted categories:

CATEGORY	WEIGHT
Homework	30%
Tests and Projects	40%
Class Activities	20%
Participation	10%

Applied to Tangela, her 100 percent average for Participation will receive a weight of only 10 percent of her grade, which is weighted less than the 60 percent average she earned on her Tests and Projects category, worth 40 percent of her grade. This weighting reflects the teacher's opinion that these larger assessments are more important than participation.

While most teachers, in order to be transparent, include in their course syllabus a description of their category weights, they hardly ever explain how the category weights are mathematically calculated to render a final grade. If our hypothetical teacher did, it would look something like the formula shown on the following page.

---

[2]Another equivalent way of understanding an 80 percent score in a category is that if we add up all the points Tangela earned on homework assignments and divide by the homework points possible, we'd see she earned 80 percent of the possible points.

(Your Homework Score × Homework Category weight of 30 percent)

+

(Your Tests & Project Score × Tests & Projects Category weight of 40 percent)

+

(Your Class Activities Score × Class Activities Category weight of 20 percent)

+

(Your Participation Score × Participation Category weight of 10 percent)

=

"Weighted Contribution" or Your Total Weighted Percentage

(In other words, Your Final Grade)

This is the formula by which the majority of middle school and high school teachers calculate grades (or more technically, how grading programs calculate grades). While the formula certainly seems precise, it seems a far cry from transparent. It's likely that most teachers have no idea that their grades are computed with this complexity. If the formula confuses us, imagine how confusing it is for students and parents, particularly those who have less educational background. It's hard to see how this kind of a formula gives students any feeling of ownership or control. Though teachers claim that providing students with percentages for each category is to provide them with a roadmap to success, it seems more a maze than a roadmap.

But perhaps we can stomach the opacity of an intricate and confusing grading formula if its complexity reveals accurate information. After all, there are lots of systems in schools that are complex and difficult for students, caregivers, and teachers to understand. Since a teacher carefully collects lots of data about a student—dozens and sometimes hundreds of pieces of information—and assigns each to a deliberately weighted category, our most important question is this: Does this current approach to how we calculate grades, despite its complexity, yield an accurate grade?

To find out, let's apply our category weights to both Tangela's and Isabel's scores in the charts that follow.

With this intricate system, used in nearly every secondary school classroom and designed to convey each student's performance with perfect accuracy, Tangela and Isabel receive the identical final score: a 76 percent, which in most schools equates to a solid C, a passing grade for the course.

	CATEGORY WEIGHT	TANGELA'S CATEGORY SCORE	TANGELA'S WEIGHTED CONTRIBUTION
Homework	30%	80%	.24
Tests and Projects	40%	60%	.24
Class Activities	20%	90%	.18
Participation	10%	100%	.10
Total Weighted Percentage			76%

	CATEGORY WEIGHT	ISABEL'S CATEGORY SCORE	ISABEL'S WEIGHTED CONTRIBUTION
Homework	30%	60%	.18
Tests and Projects	40%	95%	.38
Class Activities	20%	70%	.14
Participation	10%	60%	.06
Total Weighted Percentage			76%

But clearly, *nothing about their performance is the same.* The teacher's laborious attention to data, paired with her sincere intent to convey clear information, has been undermined by her grading system, a system that collects and categorizes and collapses every bit of a student's performance in the class and at the same time makes the overall description of that performance indiscernible. Our grading system can't render accurate grades when two students with entirely different academic and behavior performance profiles receive the same grade.

Omnibus grading can even confuse grades on individual assignments. Take, for example, a common late policy in classrooms: If a student turns in an assignment late, points are subtracted. Tangela, who turns in an assignment right on time but gets several problems incorrect, and Isabel, who gets every problem correct but submits the assignment late, can both earn the same grade.

This irony—reporting two students so different as Tangela and Isabel as having identical achievement—has serious consequences. It conceals critical information about students and leads to decisions that harm them.

- When Tangela's caregivers, and Tangela herself, receive her report card, they aren't concerned about her academic progress and take no steps to assist her. She's passing the course comfortably although, unbeknown to her, she has very weak (D-) proficiency in the content.

- When the school principal or counselor reviews report cards to identify the students who need additional support, Tangela—who clearly needs additional academic support—isn't identified because of her passing grade, and therefore doesn't receive the help she needs. She may be promoted to the next grade or a higher academic track, qualify for extracurricular activities, and even receive awards and privileges, but is unprepared for the next level of a course. Tangela's grades tell her, her family, and her teachers that she is academically ready for a course for which she's not ready. She might graduate, be accepted to college, and receive scholarships based on those grades.

- The next year, when Tangela begins the next grade level of this subject (or a four-year college), she is woefully unprepared for and overwhelmed by the content. She's shocked and dispirited when she feels lost and has so much difficulty in the class. She wonders, "I did fine last year. Why is this subject so hard for me now?"

- Isabel, on the other hand, is harmed in a different way. She knows, based on her scores, that she knows the course content, yet still she has earned only a C. Her teacher wants her to express a more positive attitude in the class and clearly expects her to complete homework more consistently—although Isabel is in fact doing what she needs to learn the material and show mastery. Isabel learns that this course (and perhaps school overall) isn't really about what you know, but whether you do what the teacher wants—how much you "play the game" of school. She becomes less invested and engaged, realizing that the school doesn't value what she knows and how she learns even when she proves she has learned the content. Instead, learning is only recognized if she does all the tasks assigned—even if the tasks don't help her learn. If the teacher thinks that Isabel's attitude in class is negative now, it's about to get a whole lot worse!

In our example, if homework and participation were weighted even more heavily, Isabel would receive an even lower grade, possibly a failing one, even though she demonstrated knowledge of the content according to the summative assessments. Isabel might be assigned to tutoring she doesn't need, or worse, to *repeat the course*, even though she already learned the content. And Tangela would have a higher grade—perhaps a B, making her eligible for certain opportunities and privileges— rewarding her not for learning content, only for compliance. This isn't to say that Tangela's behaviors—following directions, leading her group, doing her best to complete assignments—aren't important. In fact, they are critical to success. Isabel needs support to learn how to be part of a team, to be respectful, and to choose her battles wisely. However, our grading formula hides who each student is, bluntly showing Isabel and Tangela to be essentially the same C student, and thereby providing information that is inaccurate, uninformative, and plainly misleading.

The result in our schools is that students like Tangela who are weak on content but follow directions can receive grades that inflate—and therefore misrepresent—their proficiency in the course content. Students like Isabel get grades that show they're not academically prepared because they aren't behaving in ways that teachers request or not fulfilling all of the classroom rules, and so they are excluded from extracurriculars, must attend tutoring, and are less eligible for awards.

The omnibus grade that includes so many diverse aspects of student performance conceals important information and really tells us very little about our students. When we use our traditional methods of calculating grades, though we seek precision and transparency, information about students becomes only more vague, hidden, and misleading.

Grade Hacks

While many teachers may not understand how the mathematics of multiple categories creates faulty grades, teachers are aware of the weaknesses of the single-letter omnibus grading system. They see that Tangela and Isabel receive the same grade and they know that something's wrong. They look at the software's final grades for their students at the end of a grading term and do "gut checks" for every student: "Is a C grade the right grade for Tangela?" Some simply shrug their shoulders, perhaps consoling themselves that "numbers don't lie," and any calculation done by a computer must be correct. However, most teachers who notice these problems are more dissatisfied and uneasy, or more confident and empowered, and create what I call "grade hacks." These grade hacks allow the teacher to manipulate the online grading program so that the calculations of the software render grades that "match" the students. In other words, the teachers see results that they don't like, so they retroactively make changes to earlier assignments or tests so that computations render grades that are what the teachers believe they should be—so that Tangela and Isabel get the grades they're supposed to get—*despite* the software's original calculation.

Teachers use a variety of grade hacks to correct the inaccuracies of the omnibus grade. Here are a few:

Some Grade Hacks	
• Drop lowest score	• Assign non-academic tasks
• Selectively average scores	• "Curve up" scores
• Create extra credit assignments	• "Bump up" for effort or growth

And when all these grade hacks fail, many teachers make what I call "End-of-Term Fudge." No, it's not a tasty dessert when grades are finally submitted at the end of a term. Before teachers submit their grades to be printed on report cards, they look at the final computed scores for each student and make sure they agree with those scores. For example, "According to the grading program, Justin got a 89.4 percent. Do I think he deserves a B+?" If the minimum percentage for an A- is 90 percent, and Justin has a 89.4 percent (a B+), the teacher who believes he deserves an A- will review his scores and look for how she can add a few insignificant points to a few assignments so that Justin's final computed average becomes an 89.5 percent, which the grading software will round up to a 90 percent, which is an A-. The teacher will fudge points, making slight adjustments to scores until Justin gets the grade the teacher believes he has earned. Problem solved.

Let that sink in: Teachers—educational professionals with graduate training, expertise in their subject area, and years of teaching experience—are often reduced to tweaking points and outfoxing a grading program to make sure that students get the grades they deserve. The software generates inaccurate grades, but fortunately we have teachers' creativity, ingenuity, and professional dedication to make grades accurate despite the limitations of that faulty grading software. Teachers create different categories, weights of those categories, and grade hacks to overcome the inaccuracies caused by collapsing diverse information into a single grade. The system ultimately works, right?

Wrong. The problem is that each teacher solves for weaknesses in our software and our dysfunctional omnibus grade design in unique ways, guided by individual beliefs about what motivates students and what aspects of a course are most important, different levels of technical knowhow and comfort with the grading software, and diverse ideas about what students need to learn and how.

This only makes the situation more damaging to students and even to the integrity of our schools. We saw how two hypothetical students—Tangela and Isabel—had very different performances in a class but received the same grade. Let's try a new thought experiment: Let's clone Tangela and put her in two different classrooms of the same course. In other words, two different teachers teach the same course and one of our Tangelas is in each of them. Let's assume that both teachers have the same categories that comprise their grade, but each teacher makes an independent yet deliberate choice about category weights. With different philosophies of what matters most in a course, one of the teachers, Ms. Jones, assigns the category weights we've used earlier, but the other teacher, Ms. Lopez, emphasizes academic achievement far more than all other categories.

Let's assume that our two hypothetical teachers use the same curriculum and use the same instructional methods—in other words, everything else about the classrooms we'll hold constant except the grading category weights. Our Tangelas perform identically in the two teachers' classrooms (after all, they're clones). Look what happens when our Tangelas earn identical scores in each category but their teachers weight those categories differently:

Ms. Jones			
	MS. JONES'S CATEGORY WEIGHT	TANGELA'S CATEGORY SCORE	TANGELA'S WEIGHTED CONTRIBUTION
Homework	30%	80%	.24
Tests and Projects	40%	60%	.24
Class Activities	20%	90%	.18
Participation	10%	100%	.10
Total Weighted Percentage			76%

Ms. Lopez			
	MS. LOPEZ'S CATEGORY WEIGHT	TANGELA'S CATEGORY SCORE	TANGELA'S WEIGHTED CONTRIBUTION
Homework	5%	80%	.04
Tests and Projects	85%	60%	.51
Class Activities	5%	90%	.05
Participation	5%	100%	.05
Total Weighted Percentage			65%

In Ms. Jones's class, Tangela receives a C, but in Ms. Lopez's class, Tangela receives a D. Same student, same course, different grades. If our confidence in the accuracy and validity of grades weren't already shaken by knowing that Isabel and Tangela, two students with very *different performance* in the same classroom can receive the *same grade*, now we see that students with *identical performance* in two different classes can receive *different grades* based on teachers' grading policies.

What if we cloned Isabel, who is far from the model student in terms of her compliance but who has mastered the content of the course? Her experiences with Ms. Lopez and Ms. Jones would be reversed:

Ms. Jones	MS. JONES' CATEGORY WEIGHT	ISABEL'S CATEGORY SCORE	ISABEL'S WEIGHTED CONTRIBUTION
Homework	30%	60%	.18
Tests and Projects	40%	95%	.38
Class Activities	20%	70%	.14
Participation	10%	60%	.06
Total Weighted Percentage			76%

Ms. Lopez	MS. LOPEZ'S CATEGORY WEIGHT	ISABEL'S CATEGORY SCORE	ISABEL'S WEIGHTED CONTRIBUTION
Homework	5%	60%	.03
Tests and Projects	85%	95%	.81
Class Activities	5%	70%	.4
Participation	5%	60%	.03
Total Weighted Percentage			91%

In Ms. Lopez's class, because content mastery demonstrated through tests and projects is weighted at 85 percent, Isabel's grade would not be lowered significantly by her late homework and disrespectful behavior (subjectively interpreted, as we learned earlier in this chapter). While in Ms. Jones's class she'd earn a 76 percent, a C, in Ms. Lopez's class Isabel would earn a 91 percent—an A!

What's more disturbing is that there are a nearly infinite number of variances among teachers' grading policies. Take, for example, a late assignment policy. Some teachers choose to subtract points if an assignment is late, some refuse to accept it at all which results in a zero, and others accept it with no penalty. The same performance on the same assignment could receive a different number of points, or grade, depending on the teacher's late policy. Teachers even have unique definitions of what constitutes "late"!

Now imagine the full range of students—many have some Tangela characteristics as well as Isabel in each of them. Then consider the number of teachers in a school, each with her own category weights and day-to-day grading policies and multiply that by the number of assignments in each class and we get a glimpse into the magnitude of the problem and how indefensible our traditional, omnibus grading is. Faced with the constraints of using a single letter, teachers are forced to make creative adjustments and adaptations, making grades idiosyncratic and, therefore, unreliable.

The Impact of Variable and Unreliable Grading

Imagine the difficulty for students when every teacher has her own category weights, policies for late work, retakes, and other grading policies: The student has to keep track of the distinct requirements and rewards of each teacher and must make adjustments in each class each day. One ninth grader said it best:

"Every teacher has their own way of grading, which I think is confusing to the students. When you first change classes, you don't know how that teacher's going to grade the homework so you don't really know how to do it. Some teachers, they don't grade it at all. They just look through it and say, 'Oh, you tried: 100%.' And then other teachers are just, 'No, you have to get this answer exactly right, or you're not getting the points.' It's really confusing because you don't know how it's going to be. My sister's a teacher, so I try and talk to her about this kind of stuff all the time, and she's usually confused by it a lot too, and she's 28 . . ."

Even though this student closed her thought in a particularly endearing way, her experience is sobering. Teachers' variable grading practices create in students an uncertainty and confusion about the very element of school—grades—that have the most far-reaching consequences for them and embody the power of school authorities. Particularly for students with weaker educational backgrounds, keeping track of each teacher's uniquely complex grading policies and category weights is one more huge challenge tacked on to the challenges of learning the academic content.

As the above quote reflects, at least, the frustrated students can be consoled knowing that teachers may be just as perplexed and frustrated about the varied ways to grade. When Tangela is promoted to the next grade level of the subject, her weak content knowledge is quickly apparent, and her new teacher can't understand how she made it this far in the subject area without being proficient in the content. Out of curiosity, her new teacher might research the history of Tangela's performance in that subject, and would be astonished that her previous teacher awarded her a C even though she clearly wasn't ready to move on to the next grade level in that content. The teacher's surprise may become irritation and anger when she concludes that her colleague either has much lower expectations for students or "passed the buck" to the next year to address Tangela's gaps in content. In either case, the previous teacher's grade has made Tangela's current teacher's job much harder, and perhaps set up Tangela to struggle, even to fail. Isabel, who receives lower grades than those around her even though she knows more, perhaps even failed and has to repeat a class in which she has learned the content. She is even more resistant to the rules this year than last year—she is justifiably frustrated that she has to sit through and demonstrate, *again*, knowledge of content she already knows. Perhaps her teacher wonders what Isabel's previous teacher did to make Isabel so resistant to the subject, a subject in which Isabel shows capacity. Because of inconsistent grading practices, teachers receive misplaced students from other teachers—students who aren't ready for a course or who already know enough to move on and become behavior problems—and can become more distrustful, even suspicious and disdainful, of their fellow educators, accusing them of having the wrong expectations, of being "too easy" or "too hard."

The data from a survey of teachers at one school is common and symptomatic of what grading variance does to a professional community:

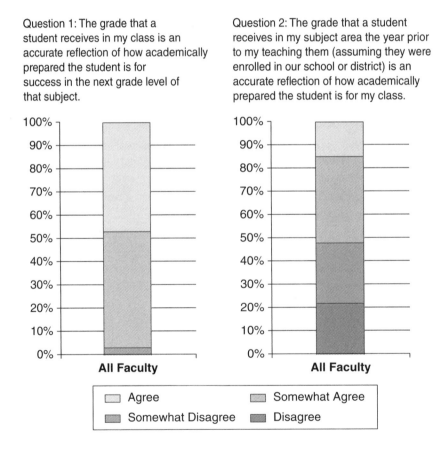

Question 1: The grade that a student receives in my class is an accurate reflection of how academically prepared the student is for success in the next grade level of that subject.

Question 2: The grade that a student receives in my subject area the year prior to my teaching them (assuming they were enrolled in our school or district) is an accurate reflection of how academically prepared the student is for my class.

Nearly each teacher at the school agrees that the grades she assigns accurately signify a student's readiness for promotion, but approximately 50 percent of the teachers at the same school disagree that their colleagues' grades accurately reflect that students are prepared for promotion. The ironic and logically impossible message is "My grades are accurate, but my colleagues' grades are incorrect." The people who arguably have the most complete information about students—their teachers—are stuck using, idiosyncratically tweaking, and hacking a grading system that makes it more difficult to communicate clear and valuable information to the people who could best use that information to help students: the other educators in the school. There are few ways to more quickly degrade trust and build provincialism in a school community than by having teachers not trust others' evaluations of students.

As mentioned earlier, these variances in grading policies aren't random; they are the result of each teacher's unique, thoughtful, and strategic way to overcome the limitations of traditional, omnibus grading. Each teacher builds her own intricate system that flows from her beliefs about learning, and when teachers have varying and contradictory approaches to grading, they end up working against each other: The teacher who is constantly penalizing students for handing in assignments late has a much harder job teaching students about deadlines because her colleague is allowing the same students to have flexible due dates. The teacher who refuses to give extra credit and wants students to do the work she assigns finds herself hounded by student requests because another teacher publishes a menu of extra credit opportunities. How can any teacher's grading practices be successful when they are undermined by other teachers' grading practices?

Furthermore, how does a student or parent community know what the school cares about and, more importantly, how can the school ever hope to teach students a coherent set of skills and content they need for success when each teacher's grading practices send different messages about what matters?

The systemic and long-term consequences for students are even more disturbing. As we know, schools, colleges, and others outside our education system rely on grades for so many high-stakes decisions about students. When grades are calculated in so many variable ways and represent student achievement so inconsistently, many of those decisions may be wrong, with awful consequences: Colleges (and the students themselves) believe that students' grades reflect preparation for postsecondary work and offer admission based in part on those grades. Students enroll in college and take on debt, assuming that their high school grades reflect their readiness for postsecondary success. However, students' scores on placement tests or low performance in introductory courses may reveal that they do not yet have the adequate academic foundation despite their prior grades. Colleges have little choice but to place them in remedial and noncredit-bearing courses, even academic probation, creating additional financial burdens and frustration for students and families.

The disturbing reality is that the constraints of our traditional grading system, combined with the most well-intentioned professional decisions of teachers to work within and compensate for those constraints, result in variance and unreliability that can threaten the very integrity of our educational institutions.

Summary of Concepts

1. The traditional use of a single-letter grade blends all the aspects of a student's academic and nonacademic performance using overly complicated and inappropriate mathematics, rendering grades inaccurate and frequently meaningless.

2. Faced with the constraints of using a single letter to report student performance, teachers are forced to make creative adjustments and adaptations, making grades idiosyncratic and, therefore, unreliable.

3. The variance and unreliability of single-letter grades frustrate students, weaken the school's professional community of teachers, and challenge the integrity of our schools.

Questions to Consider

1. What confidence or uncertainty do you have that two teachers in your school would assign the same grade to a student?

2. Are there teachers with reputations as "hard" or "easy" graders? What, specifically, defines them as that? How does this categorization make you feel? How does it make that teacher feel? How do students react?

CHAPTER 5

Traditional Grading Demotivates and Disempowers

In this chapter, we will answer the following questions:

1. What impact does being judged for every mistake, awarded points for their actions, and faced with complex and variable grading have on students' motivation to learn?

2. How do historically underserved students—those with less trust in their teachers and in the education institution—experience these effects even more dramatically?

3. In contrast to Skinner's behaviorism of the first half of the twentieth century (which our traditional grading practices draw upon), what do we currently know about student motivation and teachers' power to influence that motivation?

Our final perspective on the impact of traditional grading is how those practices harm students not because of a mathematical calculation or variances from teacher to teacher, but because of how students psychologically understand and react to their grades. Like all of us, our students want to accomplish those challenges we put in front of them, to feel confident and competent, and to be motivated for the next academic challenge. How does traditional grading support or erode these traits in our students? How does our inherited approach make those dispositions harder for students to sustain and more difficult for us to support?

Disengagement and Disempowerment

Let's take the three effects of our traditional grading that we've already examined and view them from a student's perspective:

- Teachers constantly and subjectively judge me, adding or subtracting points for everything I do: for instance, my punctuality to class, whether I meet deadlines, the way I show effort, my politeness, what I say in class and when I say it, my homework performance, and my test scores. (chapter 3)

- The mathematical formula used to calculate my grade is too complex for me to understand. (chapter 4)

- Each of my teachers grades differently, with different behaviors they care about, with different policies and different point penalties or rewards. (chapter 4)

Though we intend our grading to make our expectations transparent, clear, and reliable—to place firm ground beneath our students' feet with clear guidance for what they must do to succeed—our traditional grading practices generate tremendous uncertainty for students. It's easy to see how. First, when everything is judged and assigned a point value, students can't be realistically confident they will succeed at all the many different tasks. Second, omnibus grades are nearly impossible to understand, making students uncertain about how and whether they can be successful. Third, when each teacher has a different system of grading, students don't know whether any given teacher's system will benefit them or be fair. Imagine getting a new job and being told that you will be evaluated on every task and expectation, by different supervisors with different approaches, and that evaluation scores will be combined in complex formulae unique to each supervisor. And on top of that, you'll be responsible to understand and remember each supervisor's unique approaches, and if you forget or confuse those distinct expectations you'll be penalized. It's as if we wanted to create for our students the most stressful, disempowering, and least desirable work environments imaginable!

When our grading is so varied and complex, it's no surprise that grades can seem arbitrary and beyond a student's control, an unalterable description of what kind of student they are in the eyes of adults.

For example, though schools may claim to embrace Carol Dweck's (2006) "growth mindset"—that a student's capacity for achievement is not fixed but that every student is capable of success with support and practice—the way schools continue to grade can send the opposite message to students. We hear students say, "I'm a D student in math," and now we have some insight into why. If everything about me in a class is judged and included in a grade, and it's impossible for me to understand exactly how, or whether it's even possible, to affect my grade because of the complexity of the weights and calculations, then my grade says not what I've learned in the subject so far, but who I am. An omnibus grade captures everything I do in a class, so how could the grade not describe everything I am? These two high school students described how deeply their grades affected their self-concept:

"In sophomore year, I had straight As until the second semester when I had a C in AP World History, and right after that, I changed. I saw that even with how much effort I put in, I'm not going to get the grade I deserve in this class, so I'm not going to even try anymore. This year, I do the assignments but I don't put as much effort in. I feel like when I slipped up, I just changed." (Freddie)

"I've put in my full effort into a class and I still end up doing bad, then I think it defines me that I cannot succeed in that subject." (Sam)

These happen to be the voices of higher-achieving students. If successful students change their self-concept and become less motivated when they don't see a relationship between the work they invest and their grades, what must it be like for the struggling student who has less experience with success to begin with?

This uncertainty and stress can be even more pronounced and harmful for communities and families who have been historically underserved by schools—where there is greater poverty, more people of color, weaker educational background among both adults and children, and fewer English speakers. School, a key institution of a society that has historically not served them well, seems to have rules designed to confuse and restrict access. When grades are different for each teacher, overly complex, and based on subjective interpretations of "attitude" and "effort," it increases students' fear of failure and a historically underserved community's suspicion of whether their children will be treated fairly. With this stress and uncertainty, some students and their families choose to opt out of part or all of the system that seems to offer no clarity on how to succeed, only seemingly arbitrary judgments.

Motivating Students to Do the Wrong Thing

Carol Dweck and other sociologists have found that how students think about a goal—whether to ace a test, give a speech, make friends, or shoot a free throw—affects their motivation. For example, if a student pursues a goal and her success is based on her own evaluation ("Have I learned?" "Have I improved?") or whether she reaches some external standard, that is termed a "mastery goal." By contrast, if a student's achievement of the goal is based on demonstrating competence in others' eyes, ("Do others think I did well?") or dependent on outperforming others ("Did I do better than others on the test?"), that is a "performance goal." Mastery goals have been found to improve students' persistence (Kaplan & Midgley, 1999) and a greater sense of well-being (Kaplan & Maehr, 1999). Performance goals have been found to encourage competition ("Only a few students will earn an A.") (Elliot & Church, 1997) and make students focus on external judgment and external rewards (LaGuardia & Ryan, 2002).

What is most important about both of these types of goals is that research has found that students define these goals in large part based on their learning environment; we as teachers influence whether students see academic success as a mastery or performance goal, and we therefore influence how they behave in response to the tasks we give them, which in turns affects their likelihood of success (see, e.g., Anderman & Midgley, 1997; Roeser, Midgley, & Urdan, 1996; Ryan, Alfeld-Liro, & Pintrich, 1996; Wolters, 2004).

As if the variability of grading did not create enough stress, when we use grades to compare students either explicitly with class rankings, merit awards based on a student's achievement relative to peers or as woven into our grading through the use of the curve (or perhaps more importantly, when students *perceive* that grades are being used in this way), we encourage competition and send the message that achievement is only meaningful when it's higher than someone else's achievement. Grading is variable, mysterious, and uncertain, but now we add heat to our pressure cooker: students aren't just stumbling in the dark about how to succeed; they have to do better than everyone else who is also stumbling in the dark.

But here's where the research on performance goals gets even more interesting, or depressing, depending on how much faith you've had in traditional grading practices. Dweck and others have found that when students believe they are competing against each other—a performance goal—students motivated by the possibility of success will act in ways that improve their performance only as long as the *task seems easy*. When the task is more challenging and the student is less confident of their competence and likelihood of success, the fear of failure rears its head and the student no longer acts in ways that improve their performance— they'll give up (Barron & Harackiewicz, 2001; Grant & Dweck, 2003). In other words, when we have an environment that supports performance goal orientations, as long as a student has no difficulty with the task or is confident that she'll master it, she'll engage in productive actions that will avoid failure. Once the student doubts her own ability and becomes afraid of failure, she'll act in ways that increase the likelihood of failure.

This theory can add to our diagnosis of the underlying causes of cheating and copying. Our current grading structures orient students to see success as a performance avoidance goal—do anything, just as long as you don't lose points. If homework is easy, no problem, but if it is challenging (which most teachers hope theirs are), then the consequences of failure—a loss of points—encourages students to do whatever they can to avoid failure. As one high school student explained,

"Honestly, I sometimes just don't want to do homework. When other people do it, I'm just like, 'I need to do that. Can I see your work?' But most of the time I just don't get it, or I can't find the information to do it. That's happened a couple times where I actually can't find the information for whatever I need for my homework. And I'm freaking out and so I'm just like, 'Can you send me the homework?'" (Judy)

At its heart, this is about a student's uncertainty: If I don't know whether I'll succeed or fail compared with others, I won't do as well on the task. I don't want to fail, lose points, or get a comparatively lower grade, so I must copy.

A paragraph by Black and Wiliam (1998) perfectly summarizes how traditional and inequitable grading, in all the ways discussed above, negatively impacts how our students think about themselves as learners:

> *Where the classroom culture focuses on rewards, "gold stars," grades or place-in-the-class ranking, then pupils look for the ways to obtain the best marks rather than at the needs of their learning which these marks ought to reflect. One reported consequence is that where they have any choice, pupils avoid difficult tasks. They also spend time and energy looking for clues to the "right answer." Many are reluctant to ask questions out of fear of failure. Pupils who encounter difficulties and poor results are led to believe that they lack ability, and this belief leads them to attribute their difficulties to a defect in themselves about which they cannot do a great deal. So, they "retire hurt," avoid investing effort in learning which could only lead to disappointment, and try to build up their self-esteem in other ways. Whilst the high-achievers can do well in such a culture, the overall result is to enhance the frequency and the extent of under-achievement. (p. 142)*

So Where Do We Go From Here?

We can't deny the awful weaknesses of the century-old grading system we've inherited, and we may feel depressed and helpless, powerless to push against what seems so embedded in the work of teachers and schools. But we are only at the beginning. Now that we know how unreliable and harmful traditional grading is to our students and the work of educators, we are able and responsible to do something about it. The goal for us moving forward is absolutely critical: How can we minimize traditional grading's negative impact on learning, particularly for vulnerable student populations, and instead reimagine grading to encourage, rather than undermine, effective teaching and learning? How we can use grading to expand rather than limit educational equity and achievement in our schools?

Summary of Concepts

1. Though schools and teachers believe in Dweck's empowering concept of "growth mindset," traditional grading practices often communicate a disempowering "fixed mindset" framework for learning, add stress and uncertainty, and can result in students engaging in compensating behaviors.

2. Traditional grading practices frame grades as "performance goals" which often result in students motivated to be successful only when the task is easy, and to be motivated to avoid failure—more psychologically uncertain and stressful—when the task is challenging.

3. Our new insight into the many weaknesses and inequities of our traditional grading must galvanize us to reimagine what twenty-first century grading must be.

Questions to Consider

1. Interview some students. Are they motivated to achieve success or to avoid failure? What specific actions, policies, or words by teachers cause students to experience one type of motivation instead of the other?

2. Do you think of your tasks at work as performance or mastery goals? What affects how you define the goal? How does this affect how you pursue the task?

3. In what ways do schools and classrooms send a message of competition for achievement? How does your school's treatment of awards and honors promote or undermine a growth or fixed mindset?

CHAPTER 6

A New Vision of Grading

In this chapter, we will answer the following questions:

1. What are key qualities—or pillars—that characterize equitable grading, and why?

2. If we engage in this important work, what might we accomplish?

I f our inherited system of grading is not only outdated but interferes with what we want and believe about student learning, we need to construct a new vision for grading. What do we want grading to be, and not to be?

Based on how traditional grading undermines our best hopes, the most obvious conclusion is that we shouldn't have single-letter grades, and maybe no grades at all. They add uncertainty, hide our expectations, confuse everyone involved, fragment a school's expectations, add stress, and pull attention away from true learning. But for most of us, the reality is that grades are not going to be eliminated. Our society's understanding of school and the decisions our institutions need to make mean that we will continue to rely on grades in much the same manner as the institutions of the Industrial Revolution: as efficient ways to describe student performance.

If grades are here to stay, we want them and our grading practices to promote the best and most aspirational thinking of what our students are capable of as learners, regardless of their race, their first language, their family's income, or their previous educational experiences, and to similarly support the best of what we are capable of as educators. We want grading to be truthful, dignifying our students by telling them exactly where they are academically and what they need to be successful. We want our grading to interrupt the structures and patterns that have made the high achievement of some student groups, and the underachievement of other groups, predictable. We want our grading practices to continue to facilitate the success of those student populations who have been relatively well-served; our improved grading needs to specifically support those groups that have been historically underserved and therefore have underperformed in our schools: students of color (particularly black and brown students), students of low income, English learners, and students with special needs.

In sum, equitable grading has three pillars: *Accurate, Bias-Resistant, and Motivational.*

ACCURATE

First and foremost, we want grading to be accurate: We want our calculations to be mathematically correct and sound. But we want our grades to be more than that. We want to prevent omnibus grades that include such a diversity of information that they become misleading. We don't want to include so much information that we confuse our Tangelas—the students who work hard and follow directions but don't know the standards—with our Isabels—the students who know the standards but have weaker study habits and are less compliant. We want to make sure we don't include irrelevant information that makes our grade ambiguous, and we don't exclude information that renders our grade deficient or incomplete.

BIAS-RESISTANT

As we've seen, traditional grading promotes and reinforces a system that sorts students and replicates achievement and opportunity disparities. Our grading practices must give all students an opportunity to succeed regardless of privilege. Yet this is not enough. We are self-aware enough to know that although we are committed to creating classrooms and schools where every student can and will succeed, we unavoidably carry our conscious and unconscious biases. Therefore, our vision of grading requires grading practices that not only counteract the biases embedded in twentieth century grading but that also act as a check on those biases we each bring into classrooms. We want grades to systemically promote the success of every student, but we *need* our grades to be "inoculated," to resist infection by our own subjective biases, particularly when those biases are based on a student's race, gender, family income, first language, or special needs.

MOTIVATIONAL

Although we don't want students to be myopically focused or fixated on their grades, we certainly want grades to motivate rather than demotivate students, and to orient students to the value of learning rather than point collecting.

We know the powerful impact grades can have on adolescents' self-concept, especially as our students can be consumed by attention to their imperfections and how others perceive and judge them. Our grading practices should support a growth mindset, encouraging students to take risks and to recognize the fruits of prolonged practicing through mistakes. The way we grade should increase students' confidence so that each student feels that she is equally eligible for academic success—even predestined for that success—regardless of circumstances or educational background. We want students not to give up in the face of difficulties and low grades but to persevere, to realize that their success does not depend on others' failure. We also want our grading practices to give students valuable feedback that encourages them to build not only academic proficiency but lifelong "soft skills."

These three pillars of our vision will guide our analysis and understanding of grading practices in the next section of this book. We will organize the improved practices as falling within each of these pillars as a narrative structure, but in fact, the three pillars and the practices within them are mutually reinforcing. For example, when our grading practices more accurately describe students' academic performance, they become more bias-resistant because they exclude subjective and inchoate judgments such as "effort." Similarly, a grade that accurately describes performance and that excludes nonacademic judgments is more motivating because it gives students a clearer sense that they will be judged more fairly (engendering more trust in their teachers, and they will want to work harder).

Supporting the Pillars: Coherence

The need for equitable grades to be coherent will be addressed in subsequent writing on leading equitable grading reform in your school or district, but it's important to acknowledge and briefly describe this element of equitable grading and its importance to our vision.

It's clear that grade variability is unacceptable and inequitable, and yet a hallmark of teaching is intellectual freedom and authority over grading. These two countervailing notions make the possibility of uniform grading systems not just extremely challenging but perhaps even undesirable to some teachers. However, we teachers cannot continue to sacrifice the integrity and reliability of our grades at the altar of professional autonomy—such an argument seems to cut off our nose to spite our face. I propose that we envision grading not as *identical* from teacher to teacher with no deviation, but as coherent across teachers who share a common understanding about grading and use a common set of practices that allow reasonable wiggle room. Imagine the benefits of coherent grading practices across teachers within a grade, a department, a school, or even a district: (1) We would reduce the cognitive load on students to keep track of multiple and often contradictory approaches to grading, a particularly challenging task for students with a weaker educational background; (2) teachers would be able to depend on and trust colleagues' descriptions of student performance and readiness for the next course; and (3) people external to the school—college admissions staff, scholarship reviewers, insurance companies, parents and caregivers, employers—would have a better understanding of grades and more trust in teachers' judgments, and they therefore could make better decisions about students. In other words, rather than the variance in traditional grading contributing to teachers' isolation and the devaluing of their evaluation, coherent grading would garner stronger interpersonal trust among teachers and increase respect for their professional, expert evaluation of student performance.

This book focuses on the *why* and *what* of equitable grading; getting our grading to be coherent across classrooms and schools. The *how* to lead a transition to equitable grading for an entire school community will for now be set aside.

A Measured Vision

This vision of grading as accurate, bias-resistant, motivational, and coherent certainly doesn't suffer from low expectations. Like all visions, it is aspirational, lofty, and idealized. We know that the challenges of our students and their communities, and therefore our schools, are numerous and complicated, influenced and driven by forces historical, economic, political, and legal. More equitable grading will not solve all of the problems in our schools; the way we grade is simply one element of schools.

And yet despite these limitations we dare not underestimate how much we leverage when we tackle grading. Grading is implicated in every teaching and learning action in every classroom every day: how much any task is valued, how we describe student performance on that task, and what messages we communicate by both of these decisions. Grading is the third rail of teaching and learning. Its power courses through every part of our schools, and if we can make adjustments to how we grade to be more equitable, we can alter how our schools function. How much can improving grading fundamentally improve our schools, reduce the achievement and opportunity gaps, and change how students learn? There's no better way to find out than to get started.

Summary of Concepts

1. Our vision of equitable grading in this book has three pillars: Grades are Accurate, Bias-Resistant, and Motivational.

2. Because grading is interwoven into nearly every instructional action in a classroom, making our grading more equitable has the potential to leverage significant improvements in every aspect of teaching and learning.

Questions to Consider

1. Review your classroom's current grading policies through the pillars of our vision: How accurate are they? How bias-resistant? How motivating?

2. How much does this book's vision for equitable grading align with your own, personal vision for grading? What concerns do you have about this vision? What are your hopes? How much does this vision match against your school's overall vision? How likely is it that your school community could agree on this vision?

PART III

Equitable Grading Practices

"I've moved away of thinking of grading as a carrot or stick. Grades should be a mirror."
(Zac, High School Math Teacher)

In Part III of this book, we'll interrogate traditional grading practices and consider more equitable practices. The chapters will be grouped according to the three pillars of our vision of equitable grading:

1. They are mathematically **accurate**, validly reflecting a student's academic performance.

2. They are **bias-resistant**, preventing biased subjectivity from infecting our grades.

3. They **motivate** students to strive for academic success, persevere, accept struggles and setbacks, and to gain critical lifelong skills.

We'll start with practices that make our grades mathematically accurate, then understand grading practices that are bias-resistant, and finally address practices that are motivational. To be clear, it's not as if practices have to be implemented in this order, or that one pillar or set of practices is more important or dependent on the others. All of these more equitable practices have some combination of accuracy, bias-resistance, and motivation, but grouping them helps us digest their theory and practice in bite-size pieces. In addition, each pillar is informed by Driving Principles that will guide and ground our work. This structure should help the practices to seem less over-whelming and ultimately not as discreet and technical tools, but as interlocking and interdependent practices within a larger pedagogical ecosystem—an ecosystem that supports all students, particularly those from historically underserved groups.

PILLAR	DRIVING PRINCIPLE	CHAPTER	GRADING PRACTICES
Accurate	Our grading must use calculations that are mathematically sound, easy to understand, and correctly describe a student's level of academic performance.	7	• Avoiding zeros • Minimum grading • 0–4 scale
		8	• Weighting more recent performance • Grades based on an individual's achievement, not the group's
Bias-Resistant	Grades should be based on valid evidence of a student's content knowledge, and not based on evidence that is likely to be corrupted by a teacher's implicit bias or reflect a student's environment.	9	• Grades based on required content, not extra credit • Grades based on student work, not the timing of work • Alternative (non-grade) consequences for cheating • Excluding participation and effort
		10	• Grades based entirely on summative assessments, not formative assessments (such as homework)
Motivational	The way we grade should motivate students to achieve academic success, support a growth mindset, and give students opportunities for redemption.	11	• Minimum grading and 0–4 scale • Renaming grades • Retakes and redos
	The way we grade should be so transparent and understandable that every student can know her grade at any time and know how to get the grade she wants.	12	• Rubrics • Grades based on standards scales, not points • Standards based gradebooks
	Equitable grading distinguishes and connects the means for learning effectively the "soft skills," the practice, the mistakes, from its ends— academic success, and utilizes the broad and diverse universe of feedback and consequences, of which only one part is a grade.	13	• Emphasizing self-regulation • Creating a community of feedback • Student trackers

CHAPTER 7

Practices That Are Mathematically Accurate

- Avoiding Zeros
- Minimum Grading
- 0–4 Scale

In this chapter, we will answer the following questions:

1. What are structural weaknesses of the 0-100 scale, and how does its use create inaccuracies in our grades?

2. How does our use of the zero to indicate missing work create inaccuracies in our grades?

3. What alternative scales or strategies render our grades more mathematically sound and easy to understand?

Pillar 1: Accuracy

Driving Principle: Our grading must use calculations that are mathematically sound, easy to understand, and correctly describe a student's level of academic performance.

A good reason to start with the pillar of accuracy is that the other two pillars of our vision seem to be more weighty and complex, and implicate profound values and beliefs. We can all agree that we want every student's grade to be accurate, to truly reflect the student's academic performance. Especially when grades are considered in so many high-stakes decisions about our students, we don't want the grade to provide misleading information. Substantively, this requires us to make decisions about what data gets included or excluded in the grade—considerations we'll address in subsequent chapters. Right now, we'll stick with the purely technical and mathematical: we need to be confident that we, through our grading software and our own calculations, are mathematically accurate. In this chapter, we'll examine the mathematical weaknesses and inaccuracies of the 100-point scale and more ways to calculate a grade that more accurately describes a student's level of performance: avoiding the "zero"; minimum grading; using a 0–4 scale; and attributing more weight to a student's more recent performance.

There's a deep assumption in education that a student's academic performance can be mathematically calculated and described, and that the more precisely we quantify a student's performance, the more accurate it is. In grade books and progress reports, students' percentage grades can be calculated to the tenth, or even the hundredth place (that's the third number after the decimal point), and some schools determine valedictorians by calculating GPAs to the thousandth place. Never mind that we can't really qualitatively describe the difference between the student who earns an 87 percent and the student who earns an 88 percent, or between a student with a 3.76 GPA and another with a 3.77 GPA; we just know that the second student has somehow higher achievement than the first. Yet we say this with complete confidence and certainty: The best method to describe a student's academic achievement, in all its complexity, struggles, and uniqueness, is to calculate her performance mathematically. In part, this belief is an echo of the Industrial Revolution: We're more efficient at our sorting if we're more mathematically exact.

But behind this quest for finely tuned accuracy, there's an even deeper assumption, perhaps even a hope: The more math we use to arrive at a grade, the more objective it will be. For many of us, more math = more fair, and so we imbue our grade book with mathematical authority. We believe that the math of our grading software purges our grades of any unfairness, cleanses our grades of the potential stains of subjectivity or bias, and shields them (and us) against criticism from students, caregivers, and administrators. When asked why a student got a certain grade, we can respond simply, "That's just how the math worked out," as if the grade was out of our hands. We feel a comfort and a relief knowing that we're just entering student data; it's the grading program that awards the grades.

But as every software designer knows, every computer program has embedded within it the biases and beliefs of its programmers, and as every mathematician admits, math has its biases as well. At the end of the day, we teachers are responsible for the grades yielded by the grading program. Honestly, that's how it should be, how we'd prefer it—to preserve the exercise of our professional judgment and not relinquish that authority and expertise to computer programmers. The math calculations behind our grades are ours to understand and, if necessary, to change.

The problem is that we haven't examined the math calculations that our grading software use, and our reliance on those programs have lulled us into accepting the calculations unconditionally, ignorantly. Guskey and Jung (2016) observe that

> *Instead of looking carefully at the array of data on students' performance and making thoughtful decisions about what grade best describes what students have achieved, teachers rely on the grading program's statistical algorithms to calculate grades. In teachers' minds, these dispassionate mathematical calculations make grades fairer and more objective. Explaining grades to students, parents, or school leaders involves simply "doing the math." Doubting their own professional judgment, teachers often believe that grades calculated from statistical algorithms are more accurate and more reliable. (p. 50)*

The authors conclude, "The takeaway message for teachers is, trust your mind instead of your machine" (p. 54). If the first step of equitable grades is to ensure that they are accurate—that grades describe a student's level of academic mastery—then we must begin by asking: How are the numbers that we use to describe student performance calculated and derived to generate a student's grade, and are those calculations mathematically sound?

Building on chapter 4's initial analysis of traditional grading calculations, this chapter will examine how many of our established methods of calculating grades create inaccuracies and misleading descriptions of student performance, and what approaches can improve the accuracy of our grades. Even though we may not all have earned high grades in math, we have a responsibility to understand the math in our grades.

The Zero

A student doesn't hand in an assignment or complete an assessment. What do we enter as her score in our grade book? What does the student deserve, and what does it indicate?

Most of the time, we enter a zero. No points were earned on the assignment. Assigning a zero clearly shows the teacher, the student, and the caregiver that something went wrong, that the student didn't fulfill her responsibility, that she owes something. Many of us may assign zeros for missing work not in order to accurately report a student's knowledge, but to send a message to a student that she didn't submit an assignment and spur her to change her behavior. Does assigning zeros specifically, or failing grades in general, motivate students? We'll focus more on the relationship between grades and motivation in chapter 12, but for now, a one-sentence summary: There's no research that finds that failing grades motivate students, and plenty of research that has found the opposite—that a student who receives 0s and Fs becomes less motivated, not more motivated. Guskey (2009) found that "no studies support the use of low grades as punishment. Instead of prompting greater effort, low grades more often cause students to withdraw from learning."

Because our Driving Principle for the pillar of Accuracy is that our grades must accurately represent a student's performance, does the zero make our grades accurate?

One explanation of entering a zero in the grade book is that a student has answered none of the questions correctly on the assignment. Because she did not submit the assignment, this is true. However, it is also logically true that the student who has not submitted an assignment has also not answered any questions *incorrectly*.

Shifting our perspective, does the zero represent that the student has absolutely no knowledge of the content addressed by the assignment? Of course not. If the student has been present at all in the class, she knows *something* about the content. If a grade is to reflect what a student knows, an award of zero certainly does not describe a student's knowledge accurately.

To explain further, consider this math problem: Suppose we want to know the average weight of ten fish in a pond. After we catch and weigh eight of them (we aren't able to catch the remaining two), these are their weights:

> **Fish 1:** 3 pounds   **Fish 6:** 2 pounds
>
> **Fish 2:** 3 pounds   **Fish 7:** 2 pounds
>
> **Fish 3:** 3 pounds   **Fish 8:** 2 pounds
>
> **Fish 4:** 3 pounds   **Fish 9:** Not caught
>
> **Fish 5:** 2 pounds   **Fish 10:** Not caught
>
> *Based on our data, what is the average weight of the ten fish in the pond?*
>
> A. 2.25 pounds
>
> B. 2 pounds
>
> C. I am unable to give an average because I haven't caught and weighed all the fish.

In our traditional grading calculations, the correct answer is B, 2 pounds: we divide the total weight of the fish we've measured (28 pounds) and divide by the total number of fish (10). 20 / 10 = 2. "Wait," you say. "We shouldn't divide by 10 because we don't know the weight of the final fish; the weight of the unweighed fish certainly isn't zero pounds." Unfortunately, that's exactly what we're doing when we assign missing work a score of zero; we don't know what a student's performance would be on that assignment, but because we don't have the assignment (we haven't caught that fish), we record it as a performance of zero knowledge. Not having evidence of what a student knows isn't the same as having evidence that she knows nothing!

The crux of the issue is that when a student does not submit an assignment or assessment, we don't know *what* grade to award. If a grade is supposed to accurately reflect what a student knows, assigning a zero when we haven't received any data creates inaccuracy; we can't assume a missing fish has zero weight. We have no evidence to accurately know whether the student understands the content, so how do we record the weight of the fish we haven't caught?

First, we could decide to not enter any information for that assignment; because we haven't received the assignment, we have no information to report about the student's performance. We could also enter some nonnumerical information to represent that the assignment is missing, an "M" or highlight it in red if our software allows it. In both of these cases, we would want the missing assignment to be excluded from the overall grade calculation, because to include it as a zero would misrepresent the student's performance and render the entire grade inaccurate—remember our fish. This simple strategy may be unsatisfying; few teachers believe that a grade is accurate if assignments are excluded because the student didn't complete them; we may feel it gives students a free pass. This leaves us with two options.

The first option is to award no grade when there is missing information; in our fish example it's answer C: We can't derive an accurate answer unless and until we weigh every fish. Similarly, if I don't have enough information from the student to accurately describe her academic performance (e.g., the student did not hand in a summative assessment or project), then the grade simply cannot be reported. We could enter a grade of "Incomplete," which puts the student and all decisions based on that course grade in limbo—an awkward but defensible position for the teacher: with a commitment to grade accurately, the teacher cannot assign a grade when the student hasn't provided enough evidence of her level of mastery. Surely the student knows more than zero, but the teacher needs to know how much more. Once the student submits the information, the teacher can provide an accurate description of the student's performance.

Some teachers, when there are missing assignments, take a more active stance: Rather than assign an inaccurate zero, they require the student to complete the work. Reeves (2008) writes,

> *Defenders of the zero claim that students need to have consequences for flouting the teacher's authority and failing to turn in work on time. They're right, but the appropriate consequence is not a zero; it's completing the work. (p. 86)*

After all, in the world outside school, when someone doesn't complete a task she is responsible for, her consequence is that she has to complete the task. If my daughter doesn't take out the garbage, the consequence is that she has to take out the garbage!

If a student is missing an important assignment or assessment, we assign an accurate grade not if, but *when* that student completes it. Keep in mind that this approach of holding students accountable for work isn't easy. When teacher and author Myron Dueck stopped allowing students to get a zero for skipping a major assessment and instead mandated they complete it, he hadn't anticipated the reaction of Ellen, one of his students. She called the idea "stupid," and then proceeded to tell her father as well as other teachers about the policy who, she reported, all called it stupid. Ultimately, she made an odd request: "Can I please just have a zero?" Dueck (2014) continues,

> *Since my confrontation with Ellen, I have lost count of the number of times students have asked for zeros in place of actually completing their work. Students have offered to clean the classroom, buy me lunch, and wash my car if I would reconsider, just this once, bending my "no zeros" policy. Now, when I hear teachers preach about the need to use zeros to enforce student responsibility and accountability, behind my desire to smirk is the story of Ellen. (p. 30)*

Many students, especially those who have experienced years of academic struggle, may actually prefer receiving a zero for a missing assignment than to do the work; it's less damaging to their self-esteem to fail because they didn't try than to fail when they did. And, if we teachers are honest with ourselves, it may be easier to assign a zero when a student misses an assignment than to pressure and support the student to complete it. It can be time-consuming and exhausting for the teacher to call parents and caregivers or require students to stay after school until assignments are completed. Yet if we're committed to making our grades accurate, we can't give a grade until we have sufficient evidence of a student's actual level of achievement.

A second option is to assign a number other than zero when an assignment is missing. To understand why and how let's first examine our 0–100 scale more deeply.

The 0-100-Percentage Scale: Early Use and Enduring Flaws

Traditional grading uses a 100-point scale. When we give an assignment or test, we assign a number of points possible, students earn up to that many possible points, and that ratio of earned points divided by points possible is converted into a percentage. A student takes a test and earns 47 points out of 60, for example. It makes no difference which 47 points the student earned—whether those points represented excellence in a few topics or mediocrity across multiple topics—the student's score is 47 divided by 60, or 78 percent. Teachers use this method of scoring for nearly all types of performance, whether it's for a small assignment worth only 5 points or a major assignment worth 500 points. We describe a student's performance as a percentage, and a percentage by definition is on a 100-point scale.

The 0–100 scale gives us the ability to distinguish 101 levels of student performance. But do we need 101 levels, and can we really distinguish between a student who scored a 78 percent and one who scored a 77 percent? Not really. What the

101 levels do help us do is to compare and sort students. That was actually why schools began using the percentage scale in the first place.

The 100-point scale appears to be first used in the 1860s and 1870s at a few universities in order to distinguish among the students. Harvard, for example, divided the 100-point scale into six divisions (students scoring 90–100 were classified as "Division One," those scoring between 75–89 were "Division Two," etc.), which evolved into the summa cum laude, magna cum laude, and cum laude categories. Other colleges followed suit (Smallwood, 1935).

The larger societal trends of the early twentieth century, discussed in chapter 2—the increasing emphasis on sorting and classification, the importance of efficiency, the attention to scientific precision—all made the 0–100 percentage scale a perfect fit for K–12 schools, but flaws quickly became evident.

Researchers in the early 1900s found that when teachers used the 0–100 scale to score student work, there was enormously wide variance from teacher to teacher. Starch and Elliott (1913) found that when 147 high school English teachers were asked to evaluate a piece of student writing on the 0–100 scale, the same paper earned thirty different scores, ranging from 64 percent to 98 percent. Starch and Elliott's study was immediately attacked on predictable grounds: Judging good writing is highly subjective. The two researchers then replicated the study using geometry papers graded by 128 high school math teachers and found even *more* variance; teachers' scores for the same student work ranged from 28 percent to 95 percent. They found that a primary cause of this variance in both studies was that teachers were basing their grades on many different considerations—a similar reason for the variance we have in our schools today and discussed in more detail previously in chapter 4, and which this book's practices help to solve. However, there was another reason for such wide variance: the 0–100 scale itself.

Starch (1913) wondered whether teachers who evaluated student work might be particularly prone to error. He tried a similar exercise with carpenters, who he asked to estimate the length of rods, and found that their variance was similar to the teachers'. The biggest cause of the variance wasn't variation of professional judgments; the problem was the number of distinctions in the scale they were using. An easy way to minimize variance, Starch found, was to adjust the scale:

> [M]easurements made by means of a mental scale are subject to the same amount of inaccuracy in one field as in another. It simply means that the mind can not discriminate any more accurately. If we are attempting to evaluate a paper by a scale of 100, 99, 98, 97, 96, etc., we are attempting the impossible. The mind simply cannot discriminate between a paper of grade 85 and another of grade 86. If the second is appreciably better then it more likely should have a grade of 90. The situation is analogous to asking a person to estimate the width of a room in inches when you should ask him to estimate it in yards. Estimates in terms of large units, of course, do not have greater absolute accuracy, but they are more apt to be uniform. (p. 634)

Starch found that a "fine" scale, with 100 different descriptors of performance, is much more prone to error than a "coarse" scale with fewer designations. He recommended the use of a four, or at most, 9-point scale—A+, A-, B+, B-, C+, C-, D+, D-, and F, with no "medium" grades such as A, B, C, D—and later found that a 5-point scale led to increased consistency (Starch, 1915). His and other studies contributed to the movement in the early twentieth century away from a 100-point scale and to an ABCDF scale. Few K–12 schools continued to use the percentage scale for the next several decades.

Then, with the emergence of grading software in the 1990s, the 0–100 experienced a resurgence in popularity, apparently not based on pedagogical justification, but because of technological capability and adopting a false belief that more gradations make our grades more accurate, when in fact it makes them less so (Starch, 1913). Starch's experiment was retested a few years ago with similar results: Seventy-three high school English teachers were *trained* to use a specific approach to evaluating student writing, but when they gave a score on the 0–100 scale the scores ranged from 50 to 96 for the same essay (Brimi, 2011).

The 0-100 Scale's Orientation Toward Failure

But even aside from its susceptibility to statistical error, there are much larger and more glaring mathematical weaknesses in our 100-point scale. The first mathematical problem is that the scale is disproportionately weighted toward failure and therefore sends the message that failure is more likely than success.

How? Let's look at the grading scale used in nearly every school:

TRADITIONAL GRADING SCALE	
90–100	A
80–89	B
70–79	C
60–69	D
0–59	F

This traditional scale divides 101 points into five different chunks. One chunk (A) includes 11 points, three chunks (B, C, D) each include 10 points, and one—the F—covers a range of 60 points. In order to move from a D to a C, a C to a B, or a B to an A, a student must increase their percentage by no more than 10 points, but for a student with an F, it may require an increase of up to 60 points to earn her way into the D range, the next level up. In other words, our 100-percentage point scale is "non-linear," with disproportionate divisions.

Our scale allocates sixty of its 100 numbers (0–59) to the failure scale while only forty numbers (61–100) are allocated to passing.[1] What does this say to our students about learning and achievement? That we value failure over success—why else would we want to describe failure in sixty different ways but proficiency (B or above) in only twenty ways?

	NUMBER OF GRADATIONS	SCORES THAT REPRESENT FAILING (F)	PERCENTAGE OF SCALE REPRESENTING FAILING SCORES (F)	SCORES THAT REPRESENT MEETING STANDARDS (B OR ABOVE)	PERCENTAGE OF SCALE REPRESENTING SCORES OF MEETING STANDARDS (B OR ABOVE)
0–100 Point Scale	100	0–59	60%	80–100	21%

To put it simply, failing scores occupy three times the area of our 100-point scale as the range dedicated to describing success. And to reveal not just the punitive orientation of the scale but its absurdity, let's look at what happens if we were to make each letter range of scores proportional and extended the 10-point bands for A, B, C, and D (10 points per letter):

TRADITIONAL GRADING SCALE (COMPLETE)	
90–100	A
80–89	B
70–79	C
60–69	D
50–59	F
40–49	G
30–39	H
20–29	I
10–19	J
0–9	K

Seems nonsensical to describe so many levels of failure, right? Why would we ever feel a need to award a J, and what would be the pedagogical justification for

---

[1] We'll assume that a D is a passing grade, although in many schools, a C is the lowest passing grade. This renders the 0–100-point scale even more disproportionately oriented toward failure: 70 numbers represent failure, and only 30 numbers represent passing.

distinguishing a high failure of an F or G from a low failure of a J when they are all failures? Our scale communicates that we anticipate so many kinds of failure that we *need* to distinguish among all its different varieties—a message that certainly runs counter to what we want to say about learning and our expectations for students.

Allocating so much of our scale—nearly two-thirds of it—to failure seems wrong on its face, but its real harm occurs when the 100-point percentage scale is applied to assignments across a term: It becomes nearly impossible for a student to overcome low grades.

> *This non-linearity of [the 100-point] scale not only increases the probability of an assigned grade being an F but makes the grading process susceptible to having a few failing grades dominate a much larger number of passing grades. (Carifio & Carey, 2013, p. 22)*

Nowhere is this more obvious than looking at how the zero affects a grade. Earlier in this chapter, we examined the inaccuracy caused by the zero when it signifies a missing assignment, but now let's see its impact within a series of scores. For example, let's look at a hypothetical student's grades on three assignments:

	LETTER GRADE EQUIVALENT
Assignment 1	B
Assignment 2	B
Assignment 3	F

Assuming each assignment were equally weighted, if we were to determine the right final grade for this student, we might average her scores and award her a C-, perhaps a D+. One grade we obviously would not award is an F.

But now let's look at what happens when we substitute percentage equivalents from the 0–100 scale for the letter grades. Let's assume the student earned two B scores of 85 percent (the B range is usually 80%–90%), and was assigned a zero as the F because the assignment was never submitted:

	PERCENTAGE SCORE	LETTER GRADE EQUIVALENT
Assignment #1	85%	B
Assignment #2	85%	B
Assignment #3	0% [missing]	F
Average	85 + 85 + 0 = 170	?
	170/3 assignments = 57% (F)	

The student's average is a 57 percent, an F (that it is a high F is unlikely to be of much consolation). Certainly, the student could have avoided this consequence if she had submitted the assignment, but that's not really the point. Her one missing assignment dropped her two 85 percent scores nearly 30 percentage points. But maybe the damage of the zero is severe because our example only has three grades. What happens if our hypothetical student earned two more B grades, for a total of four 85 percent scores, but still had one missing assignment:

	PERCENTAGE SCORE	LETTER GRADE EQUIVALENT
Assignment #1	85%	B
Assignment #2	85%	B
Assignment #3	0% [missing]	F
Assignment #4	85%	B
Assignment #5	85%	B
Average	85 + 85 + 0 + 85 + 85 = 340 340 / 5 assignments = 68% (D)	?

Despite doubling the number of assignments earning 85 percent (solid Bs), the student now only has a D. If we had a student who had earned four Bs and one F, we might debate whether the student's average should be a B-, C+, C, or C, but it is unlikely we would suggest our student should receive a D. The single zero continues to have a devastating effect. Imagine how difficult it would be for a student to salvage her average if she receives two or three zeros in a grading term. As one high school student legitimately complained, "It's so hard to bring your grade up, but so easy to bring it down." Douglas Reeves (2004), in his well-known article, "The Case Against the Zero," addresses the devastating mathematical effect of a zero on a 100-point scale. Teachers may feel as if a zero is an appropriate punishment for not turning in an assignment, but Reeves, with a sardonic sense of humor, suggests it is equivalent to banishing students to Siberian labor camps for a parking violation; the mathematical consequence is so disproportionate that it doesn't fit the "crime" of a missing assignment. We never would average four Bs and award a D, just like we wouldn't average two Bs and award an F. Doing so would be grossly inaccurate and a mathematically unsound method of grading. And yet, when we assign a zero and average the percentages on a 100-point scale, that's exactly what we do. We're not giving the student an F, but assigning what teachers have called an "atomic F," or a "Super F." It punishes the student and makes redemption mathematically impossible. It's giving a student a K on the A–F scale.

It is not some radical insight that the 0-100 grading scale is flawed because of its disproportionate orientation toward failure. The adult world's professional exams—which we use to determine competency and licensure in occupational specialties—explicitly reject the 0–100 percentage scale, substituting it with alternate scales and translated scores. These high stakes assessments never even mention a percentage. For example, California's teacher candidates earn between the scaled scores of 20 to 80, with 41 representing a passing scaled score on each section. Aspiring lawyers must pass the Uniform Bar Exam, which has a 400-point scale, and although states can each set their own pass rate on the exam, most states require a passing score of between 260 and 280. Even elementary schools, at least through the primary grades, rarely, if ever, use a percentage scale; they use descriptive language to describe students' levels of performance (e.g., "Meets Expectations," "Approaching," "Developing").

A humbling but reluctantly honest reason many of us continue to use the zero on a 100-point scale may be because the zero satisfies a psychological need. While Reeves sardonically recognizes teachers' need to "punish the little miscreants who fail to complete our assignments" (2004), this need among us to feel satisfaction, to "hold students accountable" for not following our directions, is real and powerful. Guskey (2004) suggests that teachers, particularly at the secondary grades, assign a zero because they recognize that their power over students is relatively limited, and want students to really "feel" the consequences for not performing.

But if we can recognize that the 100-point scale is mathematically inappropriate and unsound, particularly when we assign a zero, we have two more accurate alternatives: Establish a grading floor, often called a "minimum grade," or change the scale itself.

Minimum Grading

We can correct the 100-point scale's disproportionality toward failure by instituting a "minimum grade"—that is, setting a percentage such as 50 percent that no student can score below:

MINIMUM GRADE GRADING SCALE	
90–100	A
80–89	B
70–79	C
60–69	D
50–59	F

In this way, we've made the gradations of the letter scale more proportionate—10 points separate each of the letter grades—which means that a 50 percent is the floor. Our grades now require from the student the same degree of improvement from an

F to a D as we would require to move from a B to an A. We really don't need sixty different descriptions of an F for mathematical reasons or want them for pedagogical reasons. Minimum grading assigns a value to failure that is more mathematically accurate and reasonable than the 100-point scale.

But wait: How can a student get 50 percent for not turning in anything? Will our grades be inflated so that students receive passing grades when they should fail? What gives us confidence that our grades will be mathematically sound? Will the student who deserves to fail but who receives 50 percent minimum Fs still fail (although this is a question that we should feel slightly uncomfortable asking)?

Fortunately, we have peer-reviewed research that shows what happens when a minimum grade of 50 percent is applied not just to a class of students, but throughout an entire school. In 2012, researchers from the University of Massachusetts (Carifio & Carey, 2013) reviewed seven years of grades from a large comprehensive urban high school. The school, which calculated semester grades based on an average of the grades of the two quarters, instituted a schoolwide policy that in all semester courses, any grade that was below 50 percent in the first quarter would be raised to 50 percent, meaning that it became more possible to pass the course at the semester. The school's purpose behind the policy was to target a specific student population: The students who have an early failure in a semester course and who, even though they receive passing or even high grades in the second quarter, are consigned to fail because of a low, unsalvageable first quarter grade. The researchers asked what many teachers feared: Would the minimum grading policy result in "social promotion" and grade inflation in which students would be promoted undeservedly?

The researchers looked at seven years of data under the school's policy: 343,000 grades assigned to nearly 11,000 students. They found that the policy did not lead to widespread social promotion or grade inflation. They write, "Any claims that minimum grading was leading to large numbers of students passing courses they would otherwise be failing were clearly not true" (p. 26). In only 0.3 percent of the grade sets did a student receive a 50 percent grade in the first quarter of a semester course and ultimately pass the course at the semester, presumably with no more than a semester average of 75 percent or C, and more likely a D average.[2]

---

[2]Assuming that the first quarter and second quarter of the semester were equally weighted, if a student had a 50 percent minimum grade for the first quarter, the highest score in the second quarter—100 percent—would result in a 75 percent or C average for the semester. It is, however, fairly unlikely that a student who had below a 50 percent average the first quarter would score a 100 percent, or even as high as a 90 percent average, for the second quarter (which would yield a 70 percent average, the minimum for a C). Therefore, it is reasonable to assume that the student who passed had a second quarter percentage that earned them a D for the semester average.

As the researchers found (Carifio & Carey, 2013), minimum grading addresses a very narrow set of circumstances:

> *Students fail for many reasons, but minimum grading is a specific grading practice targeted at a very specific cause of student failure: poor performances early in the learning process that put the student in so deep of a hole that recovering is not a reasonable possibility. As such, minimum grading targets a small but well-defined subgroup of students. Further, students who consistently post failing grades are not likely to benefit from minimum grading. Nor will students who post consistently good grades. Only students whose failing performances are intermittent, and who are now failed when their course grade is unfairly skewed by one or two failing performances will benefit from receiving a minimum grade. (p. 20)*

Seven years of minimum grading didn't lead to widespread passing rates, it didn't give a free pass to the student who had a pattern of failing grades, and it didn't inflate grades. The 50 percent minimum grade was found to prevent the disproportionate and unsound mathematical impact of sub-50 scores, especially the 0, on the 100-point scale. Minimum grading "minimiz[es] the impacts of intermittent catastrophic performance failures that certain groups of students experience, and even have tendencies to experience" (Carifio & Carey, 2015, p. 131).

Which of our students have tendencies to experience "intermittent catastrophic performance failures"? It is students whose lives are more likely to have disruptive events (such as children of undocumented immigrants) or who have a weaker safety net when those events occur (such as children of low-income families). Imagine the student who has to miss school to take care of an ill (and possibly uninsured) sibling or older relative, the student who increases her after-school work hours to earn money while a parent is out of work, or the student who witnessed extreme violence or tragedy, or the student whose family becomes homeless. Minimum grades allow these students to pass, and don't we want that?[3]

Carifio and Carey (2013) also found that the 50 percent minimum policy isn't just about improving the accuracy of grades. The researchers acknowledged that teachers often fear that minimum grading will dilute their authority and undermine the functioning of the classroom:

> *The concept of minimum grading is particularly challenging and even threatening to such educators, as it appears to be (at first glance) a major diminution of teacher authority, power of management and a major lessening or weakening of what is thought to be the major power and causal variable by such people for influencing and shaping student behavior. (p. 27)*

---

[3]Interestingly, the researchers found that the 925 students who benefited from the policy across the seven years were from all different ethnic backgrounds and special needs categories. And 90 percent of them were boys.

However, the researchers found the opposite to be true: The minimum grading policy contributes to a classroom and school culture that better supports learning.

> *Minimum grading actually empowers teachers and schools rather than disempowers them, as it lessens, dampens out and neutralizes most of the negatives aspects of grades and grading in school learning and in the behavioral processes while creating a climate of caring, hope and support, particularly for those students whose growth and development will most probably always be an intermittent and somewhat chaotic process and path. Minimum grading is a first step and key component in creating a culture of compassion and caring in a learning organization, classroom or school. (p. 24)*

Across seven years, thousands of students, and hundreds of thousands of assigned grades, minimum grading created more compassionate, caring classrooms, and gave teachers *more* power to support student success, not less.

And for those interested in the financial "bottom line" of a minimum grading policy, Carifio and Carey (2015) calculated its financial impact. They suggested that over the seven years of the policy, the additional 1159 passed classes due to the minimum grading policy translated into over $2 million that the district did not need to allocate to seats for remedial, repeat, or summer school courses. The authors conclude, "Minimum grading is a policy that accomplishes so much at such small costs, while achieving such large savings in both financial and human capital terms, that one must really wonder why it is not the norm currently but rather both the classroom and institutional exception . . ." (p. 26).

Maybe this minimum grading is making some sense to you, and a question emerges: *Maybe it's right for the student to get nothing lower than a 50 percent if she tries and shows very weak performance, but what about the student who doesn't even attempt the work?* Why should both of these students get the same grade? The question seems to be saying, "I want to give different kinds of Fs, and the 50 percent minimum doesn't let me distinguish between different types of failure." And so, we illuminate more absurdity of our traditional grading: We can't distinguish among Fs. The student who gets a 38 percent gets the same F as a student who gets a 4 percent. There's no F- or F+, a nonsensical and possibly cruel idea. We've been led to believe that we're distinguishing between different types of failure because we have a 0–100 scale, but we're actually not. Instead, we're allowing students to dig different size holes, most of which they can never get out of, regardless of whether they have sub-50 percent performance or no performance.

For the teacher who understands the benefit of the 50 percent minimum but wants to distinguish the student who tries and fails from the student who does nothing, one option is to set a different minimum: say, 50 percent for the student who has a missing assignment, and a 52 percent or 55 percent for the student who tries but has too many errors. This allows us to distinguish between the different performances (or from the one with a performance and the one who has no performance), and although it gives both students hope of passing the class, it puts the one who has demonstrated attempts in a slightly better position.

Despite the evidence and reasonableness, we might still be afraid that the 50 percent would decrease student motivation. Though we'll address the intersection of grading practices and motivation more comprehensively in chapter 11, it's worth a sneak peek: If students get something for nothing, then what incentive is there for them to do anything other than nothing? The study of seven years and 343,000 grades found that minimum grading *increased* motivation for those students who were not consigned to failure because of a catastrophic first quarter (Carifio & Carey, 2015).

To those of us who have spent their careers with the zero, this can be a difficult pill to swallow:

"I had real trouble initially with a no zero policy. If a student didn't do anything, they deserve a zero! But a 50% is still an F. An F is an F, and it will show as an F. I thought about the students I had last year who would work very hard to improve their grade, even do extra credit, but their grade wouldn't change because previous assignments were a zero. I had students who asked, 'Why do anything to improve my grade if my grade is still going to be an F no matter what?' I just had to let go of the zero." (Mike, Middle School Math Teacher for seven years)

Perhaps it might make us feel better to know that not only a district in Massachusetts, but schools in many other districts and schools across the United States have minimum grading. In fact, the entire country of New Zealand uses a 50 percent minimum in their schools. Intellectually and logically it makes sense, but emotionally, psychologically, and perhaps even pedagogically, it may still feel wrong: We might feel that minimum grading risks our authority, that we're losing something.

These feelings are normal. Despite conceding that the minimum grade is the right policy, we may still find minimum grades too uncomfortable to implement. With reluctant admission, we can feel like we need our zero to send an ambiguous message to students: handing in nothing gets you nothing. Plus, as challenging as it is for us to understand the 50 percent minimum, it might be even more difficult to explain to students and caregivers. The minimum grade might satisfy half of the Driving Principle of our Accuracy pillar—it makes our grades more mathematically accurate—but it seems unlikely to make our grades easy to understand.

Fortunately, we have another solution to overcome the mathematically inaccuracies of the 100-point scale. We'll keep the zero, but we'll replace the 0–100 scale itself.

The 0-4 Grading Scale

As mentioned above, the world is replete with other ways of describing measures of content mastery or readiness. We've cited some examples already. There is no percentage score on either the SAT nor ACT, or bar exam, or medical boards.

Same with the driver's license test or teacher credential exams. Nearly every test that measures competency outside of secondary schools uses something other than a 100-point scale.

If alternatives are all around us, it shouldn't be a surprise that there's a solution right in front of us: the Grade Point Average (or GPA) scale. Every school that assigns grades converts them into a GPA for high-stakes purposes, such as honor roll, college applications, scholarships, and insurance premiums. Could we use the same scale in our classrooms?

GPA SCALE	
4	A
3	B
2	C
1	D
0	F

Compared to the 0–100 scale, it seems almost too simple. A single digit number is correlated with a letter grade, and there are five gradations (thirteen if you add pluses and minuses)—similar to what Starch recommended to solve the flaws he identified, and Brimi confirmed, in 1913. Let's compare the 4-point scale to the 100-point scale:

	NUMBER OF GRADATIONS	SCORES THAT REPRESENT FAILING (F)	PERCENTAGE OF SCALE REPRESENTING FAILING SCORES (F)	SCORES THAT REPRESENT MEETING STANDARDS (B OR ABOVE)	PERCENTAGE OF SCALE REPRESENTING SCORES OF MEETING STANDARDS (B OR ABOVE)
0–100 Point Scale	100	0–59	60%	80–100	21%
0–4 Point Scale	4	0	20%	3–4	40%

As we saw earlier, the 0–100-point scale allocates three times as many gradations to failure as to meeting standards (60% vs. 21%), and compared to the 0–4 scale, dedicates triple the proportion to failure and has half as many gradations representing meeting standards. Would we prefer to use a grading scale in which nearly two-thirds is dedicated to failure and one-fifth to success, or a scale in which one-fifth is dedicated to failure and two-fifths is dedicated to success? Stepping back for a moment, how could we ever justify using a 100-point scale that is so oriented toward failure when we have an alternative that is so much more aligned with how we want our students to understand their likelihood of success? Why would we use the 0–100 point percentage scale to distinguish between the student who received a 74 percent and a 75 percent when we constantly, at least in high school, translate the grade to a 0–4 for GPA calculation anyway, rendering that minute distinction irrelevant and forgotten?

And if we love having the zero, the 0–4 scale lets us use it without fear that it will consign our students to unredeemable failure. The punishment for a missing assignment now more proportionately fits the crime. Let's use our earlier example of the three grades and replace the percentage scores with the 0–4 score equivalent. How does the use of the 0–4 scale affect the student's overall average?

	PERCENTAGE SCORE	0–4 SCORE
Assignment 1	85%	3 (B)
Assignment 2	85%	3 (B)
Assignment 3	0%	0 (F)
		Average = 6 total / 3 assignments = 2

The average of the three scores is 2, a C on the GPA scale—what we initially thought the student deserved a few pages ago. Compared with the 0–4 scale, which is more accurate and so much easier to understand, it seems untenable and unnecessary to use the 0–100 scale. Clearly, the continued use of the 0–100 scale can only be defended on the shaky grounds that it is traditional.

If you are surprised and feel some anger or frustration by the inaccuracies and punitive tendency of our ubiquitous 0–100 scale, strap your seatbelt on, because in chapter 8 we'll learn about two more common grading practices that are just as inaccurate, but because of conceptual, not mathematical, weaknesses.

Summary of Concepts

1. It is the extremely rare student who knows absolutely nothing about a concept that was taught, so assigning a zero almost never accurately represents a student's achievement. The zero also disproportionately punishes students when used within a 0–100 point scale.

2. The 0–100 percentage scale emphasizes failure over success and offers so many fine gradations that are not only unnecessary but that make it susceptible to

error and variance. The 0–4 scale is more oriented toward success, is simpler to understand and use, and is less prone to error and variance. Minimum grading can correct the problems of the 0–100 percentage scale.

Questions to Consider

1. For Teachers: If you've assigned a zero, was it intended primarily to affect students mathematically or psychologically? Knowing that it is mathematically unsound as well as inaccurate, does that change your opinion of it? Would it change your opinion if you discovered that there is no evidence that receiving a zero motivates students, but in fact it often demotivates them? (See chapter 11.)

2. Because the zero is never an accurate description of a student's knowledge, some teachers use a 1–5 scale instead of a 0–4 scale. Would this scale make the grade more accurate? More equitable? More motivational?

CHAPTER 8

Practices that Are Mathematically Accurate (Continued)

- **Weighting More Recent Achievement**
- **Grades Based on an Individual's Achievement, Not the Group's**

In this chapter, we will answer the following questions:

1. How does averaging scores render grades inaccurate and also less equitable? What are more accurate and equitable options?

2. Why is it more accurate, and therefore equitable, to base grades on what individual students learn from group work, not the group work itself?

In this next set of more equitable grading practices, we'll continue to follow the Driving Principle for our Accuracy pillar:

Driving Principle: Our grading must use calculations that are mathematically sound, easy to understand, and correctly describe a student's level of academic performance.

In contrast to the practices in the previous chapter, rather than identify practices that make grades more accurate because of mathematically sound computations and scales, we'll apply a less computational lens and approach it as a more straightforward pedagogical challenge: How can we most accurately describe a student's level of performance?

The Problems With Averaging

When I work with teachers, I ask them to determine a final grade for a hypothetical student with the following unit grades:

91%, 92%, 40%, 94%, 94%

Almost without fail, every teacher will pull out their phone and average the scores. When I ask teachers why they chose to average the score, they often look at me with confusion: Why *wouldn't* the score be averaged? There's a deeply embedded belief that averaging a set of scores is the most accurate and fair way to grade—a belief that is bolstered and reinforced by its use in all grading software. Why would we reject this tried and true method of calculating scores?

Perhaps we should ask a sixth grader why we shouldn't always average. Middle school students learn (and some of us even teach) a really important mathematical concept: Given a group of numbers, there are multiple ways to derive one number that represents that group. (In mathematical terminology, it's the process by which to determine the "central tendency" of a set of numbers.) Three computations we teach our twelve- and thirteen-year-olds are the mean, median, and mode. The mean is the average, derived by totaling the numbers in the set and dividing by how many numbers you have (or how many members are in the set), the mode is the number that occurs most frequently in the set, and the median is the "middle" number when we organize the numbers in the set from smallest to largest.

Let's apply these different approaches to our set of five scores and see which most accurately describes our student's overall performance most accurately.

Average (mean): We add the numbers (91 + 92 + 40 + 94 + 94) = 411

Divide 411 by the number in the set (5) = **82.2%**

Mode: We find the number that occurs most frequently in the set (91, 92, 40, 94, 94).

The most common number is **94%.**

Median: We order scores from smallest to largest (40, 91, 92, 94, 94)

The middle number is **92%.**

The average, or mean, score for this student is 82%, the mode is a 94%, and the median score is a 92%. Which one best describes our student, who consistently performed at a high level but seems to have had one horrible-no-good-very-bad day?

Her mean score of 82% translates into a B–, but considering that she never actually performed at the B level, this seems a strange way to summarize her performance. Here we see the primary disadvantage of using the mean: It is susceptible to "outliers"—a number far outside the other numbers in the set—that skew the result. Her score of 40 percent is so far away from the other scores that it gives us an average that doesn't accurately describe her overall performance. When a set of data has outliers, many mathematicians and scientists avoid averaging to avoid this inaccuracy.

On the other hand, the median and mode are calculations that resist outliers. Our student's median and mode scores of a 92 percent (A–) or 94 percent (A), are more accurate descriptions of her "tendency" of performance. One might be worried that the median or mode essentially ignores the 40 percent score, but it's not actually ignored; it holds as much weight in the calculation as every other number in the set.[1] And really don't almost all students have outliers in their performance—a bad day or two? Don't we all? At the very least, the assumption that the average is the superior method of deriving a grade should now be in serious doubt. The median and mode not only are reasonable alternatives to averaging, but when there are outliers in a student's performance, they are more mathematically accurate than the average.

Yet there is a broader problem with all of these methods: They apply a mathematical calculation to a set of student scores without regard to when those scores happened. When we want to describe a student's overall performance over time, should it matter *when* she earned each score?

Here is a concrete example: Ellis, an incoming ninth grader in your class, has never been taught how to write a persuasive essay; he went to a middle school that, for whatever reason, didn't teach it. You give an assessment in September, and Ellis's performance reveals his inexperience—there's no thesis or clear organization of ideas, few details, if any, support his ideas, he's got sentences that seem out of sequence, and there's no concluding idea. The essay gets the grade it deserves: a D–. But it's only September, and you, as his teacher, provide instruction and guided

---

[1]This argument that we're "ignoring" the low score seems less credible when we recognize that the high scores are being "ignored" as well. The median "ignores" the high score of 94 percent as well as the low score of 40 percent. With the mode, we ignore the 91 percent and 92 percent. This is not disqualifying the numbers; it's considering them appropriately within rules of the calculation.

practice with feedback, and at the mid-term assessment in November, Ellis's essay is at the C level. Your instruction continues with more practice and feedback, and when it's time for the last essay of the semester in January, Ellis has made steady improvement and his essay is quite strong: an A. You're so proud of his progress (and your effectiveness as his teacher)!

Ellis's three assessment scores are D– (beginning of semester), C (mid-point), and A (end of semester). To simplify this hypothetical, let's assume this is a persuasive essay course where the only skill that is measured is a student's proficiency at writing a persuasive essay, and these are the only grades he received. What should be his semester grade?

Applying a calculation of the mean, median, and mode all give us a C+ or C, but do any of these really capture and communicate Ellis's writing skills? If we include the D– and the C scores in our mathematical calculation, we're essentially lowering his grade based on his inferior skills early in the learning process, *before you taught those skills to him* and before he had a chance to learn them. After he learned how to write a persuasive essay, he demonstrated excellence. Why would we lower his grade because he didn't initially know how to do the skill that you ultimately taught him? You can't ask anything more from him: By the end of the term, he excelled at what you wanted him to learn.

Before I propose what Ellis's grade should be, let's enroll some other students in Ellis's ninth-grade English class:

- **Tonya:** She went to Ellis's middle school, and also has no previous experience with how to write a persuasive essay. She also got a D– on the first assessment. She struggled much more than Ellis through the first half of the term because of some challenges at home, and she earned a D on November's mid-term assessment. However, things in her home stabilized, and something suddenly "clicked" in her head around winter break. On January's final assessment, she earned an A.

- **Jason:** He attended a different middle school where teachers taught him to write a persuasive essay, so he was much more familiar with its organization, tone, and other elements when he walked into your class. On his first essay assessment, he earned a B. He spent the semester honing his skills, and gradually improved so that he earned an A on the final essay.

- **Maria:** She attended the same middle school as Jason, and even attended a summer writing program in the summer before ninth grade. Her September assessment was very strong and she earned an A. Her writing remained strong throughout the term, and she finished with an A on the final essay.

Here's a visual representation of our four ninth graders:

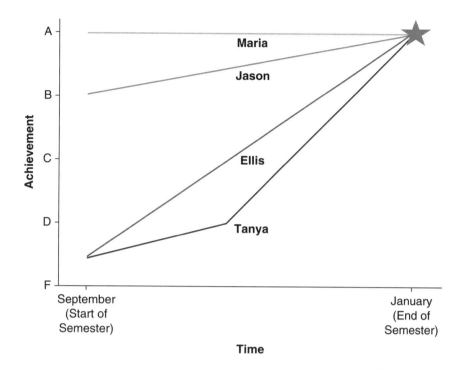

Each of our ninth graders started at different places, for different reasons, and progressed at different rates, but by the end of the semester all have written a persuasive essay at the "A" level. If we include earlier scores in some computation—whether mean, median, mode, or something else—each of these students would have a different final grade even though they all mastered the skill. Jason's, Ellis's, and Tonya's final grades would be lower than an A, thus inaccurately describing their level of mastery on the skill. We need to have a more accurate option to describe the student performance whenever that performance has improved over time (which, presumably, is true for nearly every student).

Weighting More Recent Performance

Instead of reflexively averaging performance over time, or even using the mean or mode, we should consider assigning a grade that is the most accurate description of their skill level—in this case, how well they did at the end of their learning, their most recent performance.

Think about it. In most cases when we measure and describe someone's skill, we describe her most recent performance at that skill. A person who passes the bar exam on her third try doesn't have her scores averaged. A marathon runner's time in a race isn't calculated by averaging all of the times in her training sessions. When we want to find a plumber, we don't ask to see her evaluations as an apprentice. When our supervisor conducts classroom observations as part of our evaluation, we're judged primarily on the quality of our most recent observation, not on the entire set of those observations. Even one's golf handicap is based only on the ten most recent scores, not averaged across the player's entire career.

When we consider scores from earlier in a student's learning process, our grade reflects not a student's achievement but the student's learning trajectory: For example, what skills did the student start with? Did she learn skills quickly or slowly? We know that learning occurs with many different rates and pathways depending on the student, her circumstances, the content, and the teacher. It shouldn't actually matter to our grading whether the student's progress was constant and steady or full of fits, lulls, or epiphanies. What ultimately matters is that the student learns the material and demonstrates competence. When we recognize and allow for this diversity of learning routes, we realize that a grade, if it is to describe a student's level of understanding, won't be accurate if it is an average (or a median or mode calculation, for that matter) of the student's performance over time. Instead, a grade is accurate when it reflects a student's current level of performance, not the history of her performance. Regardless of the rate at which a student learned, a grade should reflect whether she ultimately learned the material.

And it's not just a matter of accuracy; it's a critical element of equity. If we apply the traditional grading practice of averaging scores over time to our hypothetical set of students, Maria and Jason would have the highest grades because they started the semester quite close to the target: They were lucky enough to attend a middle school that taught persuasive essay writing. Maria would earn the highest grade thanks to the summer writing program (which could have been due to her parents identifying and paying for it). Tonya would earn a lower grade because troubles at home slowed her down, but she finally succeeded. In other words, grades that average scores over time reflect the advantages or disadvantages of students' circumstances. As we'll discuss more in the next chapter, we don't want our grades to represent students' prior learning experiences or educational support before our class, and we don't want to reward or penalize students for home environments that slow or accelerate their rate of academic progress. We don't want to lower Ellis's or Tonya's grades because of circumstances outside their control. What matters is whether each student learns the material and shows competence. If we grade students equitably and accurately, each of the students in the hypothetical all earned an A. They all started at a different place and have different learning paths, but they all demonstrated mastery. As Mohammed, a middle school humanities teacher for four years, explains,

"Two different students . . . one didn't need any help, and the other one took a long time to get there, but in the end, they both learned what they were supposed to learn. They should receive the same grade. It doesn't matter how they got there. Students who get 100% all the time, they're still getting 100%. But the ones who took a long time but in the end were able to show the same performance a little later in the term, they are also now getting 100% instead of being punished because it took them longer to get there."

This isn't a radical approach at all. Elementary teachers almost universally assign grades this way. A student's report card reflects what the student currently can do, not where she's been. It would be ludicrous to describe whether a kindergartener knows all fifty-two letters—twenty-six upper case and twenty-six lower case—based on averaging how many he knew three months ago and how many he knows now. All that matters is her most recent performance. Although this idea is treated as common sense by elementary teachers, it initially can create a lot of confusion and discomfort for secondary teachers. Averaging performance over time is so deeply embedded in how we think about school and so hardwired into our grading software that it becomes extremely difficult for us to imagine *not* averaging scores over time.

Temporarily setting aside the difficulty of overcoming the technical hurdles, let's address some philosophical and practical concerns that teachers often voice:

- *Will giving more As decrease the value and meaning of each A? In other words, won't Maria be upset if she receives the same grade as Ellis?*

Both concerns originate from the concept of the curve—that there is a natural and necessary distribution of performance within any population, and As only have value if there are Fs. In chapter 2, we saw that this concept had its heyday in the Industrial Revolution. Though the bell curve has some utility when applied to some characteristics of a population—height, for example—we know that the curve has no validity when it measures performance against an external standard. For example, when you demonstrate proficiency in driving, you get a driver's license. The DMV doesn't limit the number of people who can score proficient on the driver's license exam, and we don't believe that the driver's license itself has less meaning if a lot of people pass the test. Bowling alleys recognize high scores—perhaps above 290—regardless of how many people achieve that score. Whether the alley's list has five people, twenty, or 100, the value of that achievement doesn't change.

Meeting an external standard, like writing a persuasive essay or passing the driver's license test, or even exceeding it, is not like taking a limited resource, like gold or oil, which fluctuates in value depending on how much there is. Proficiency at driving is an external standard, and as soon as you meet that standard, you are awarded a symbol of that proficiency. The driver's license exam doesn't change its difficulty or its passing score depending on how many people pass it, and the cutoff high score in the bowling alley doesn't change if a deluge of bowlers start scoring 300. The bull's-eye on a target doesn't get smaller as more people hit it.

Close (2009), in *Fair Grades*, writes,

> *Grades (A, B, C, D, F) are not scarce resources. They may be constructed as such, but they are not inherently so. If we design our courses and our grading systems as if certain grades were a scarce good, we have already adopted an ethically questionable model of grading. (p. 365)*

When Ellis, our student who started further behind than Maria, earns an A, Maria's A doesn't become less valuable. They both met and exceeded the standard, and the As denote that achievement. Whatever we define as "meeting the standard" doesn't change; they both demonstrated that they can hit the bull's-eye, and isn't that what we actually *want* to happen? Equity means not only that we don't fear that too many students will meet an academic standard, but that we actually believe and *want* as many students as possible to meet the standard!

When we say the opposite—that there's a point at which there are too many As—we pit students against each other, infusing characteristics of performance goal orientation (see chapter 5) and inequitably reward those students with resources and stronger education backgrounds. We warp what learning means when we say that if Ellis gets an A, he's somehow devaluing Maria's A or taking something away that is rightfully hers. A century ago, before standards, our primary job as educators may have been to compare students to each other and sort them, but with external standards we no longer need to make students compete for their grades. It should feel liberating to know that we don't have to choose between Ellis and Maria to decide who gets an A; if they both showed excellence, each A is equally valuable and an accurate description of each student's performance.

- ***What if a student's performance decreases over time, so that her most recent level of performance is actually lower than an earlier measure?***

We would expect that all students would improve their performance over time, but that doesn't always happen. We know that the trajectory of learning isn't a simple linear progression. Sometimes we learn something but that knowledge evaporates soon after the test, or our understanding is only superficial and we can't apply it in deep ways. Plus, students' lives are unpredictable, sometimes chaotic, and even though they can show proficiency at one moment, if home or environmental distractions become too powerful, they can show a weaker performance. Is awarding students the grade based on their most recent performance a hard-and-fast rule, or should we allow for exceptions?

Our solution rests in our pillar: An equitable grade needs to be *accurate*. It should be clear by now that there is no sacred mathematical formula that guarantees accuracy and fairness, and, in fact, the universal application of one formula to all students in all circumstances can ensure unsound mathematics and inaccuracy. We have to apply our professional judgment to decide which performance (or performances) is the most accurate representation of a student's knowledge and skills. If a student had a poor result on an assessment after showing proficiency earlier, then we should ask: Is that most recent low score an accurate performance? We might investigate whether circumstances in the student's life so negatively impacted her most recent performance that we should discount the performance and use an earlier performance because it is more accurate. Did our assessment reveal, allow, and facilitate the student's true demonstration of their level of mastery, or did our assessment somehow affect the student's performance, yielding incorrect information about the student's knowledge? Do we care only that the student showed proficiency in the content or skills at some point in the term? If so, we should use the student's highest performance. In other cases, we may want the content to be deeply understood and known throughout the term, in which case we would assign the grade to reflect only the most recent performance: the "What Have You Shown To Me Lately?" grade (with apologies to Janet Jackson). All of these questions help us ensure that the grade is accurate.

- **If early scores don't matter and only the final performance matters, won't students simply slack off and not take early assessments seriously? If a students' performance over time isn't included in their grades, what will motivate them to learn throughout? Won't this actually teach them the wrong lesson and hurt them in the long run?**

While we might see the merit in not penalizing Ellis for his weaker background and agree that grades based on a student's most recent performance is more accurate, we might worry about students who are not Ellis but think they can be like him. We might fear that students, seeing that their last performance is what matters, would perform less than their potential early in the term, believing that they don't have to work until later when the test scores really count. What if Maria doesn't study for tests in the first part of a term because the early scores don't really factor into her grade? We don't want students to get the message that early performance doesn't matter and that they can learn something in a hurry and only at the end when it counts. On the contrary, we want them to value hard work and long-term persistence and to understand that learning takes time. Won't considering the most recent performance mislead students about how learning requires sustained effort over time?

When we describe student achievement according to a student's most recent performance, we don't show that early performance is irrelevant. Instead, we teach students that early mistakes don't consign you to mediocrity or failure, that learning takes time and dedication, and that everyone can grow and succeed. We give an assessment, and then if they don't do well, we let them know that they can learn from their mistakes and on the next assessment, they'll get another chance. We can talk all we want about a growth mindset, but in traditional grading that averages every performance, we actually undermine the idea of growth—lower performances muffle ultimate achievement, weighing down the impact of improvement. Grading based on a student's most recent performance shows them a growth mindset in action and aligns with the important values of continuous improvement and persistence, rather than undermining those values.

Behind this concern is an assumption that students, given an opportunity, will "game the system," and that if a test, or any task, isn't graded, the student won't study and prepare for it. What makes us so suspicious of our students? Why do we think that given a chance to study and show us successful achievement, students will resist that opportunity? Teachers who consider only the most recent performance have found that students rarely if ever choose to opt out of learning or to do badly on a test because they know that their later performance will replace earlier scores. Students perform badly on tests for much more rational reasons, like lack of confidence, environmental challenges, anxiety, other schoolwork, and weak skills. As Denise, an eleventh grader explains,

"It's fair to grade us on our latest test because in [subject], we go through the topics pretty fast. A lot of times we don't really get the chance to understand everything. The first test we take we're trying to do as best we can. Then [the teacher] will go over information again so we can really understand. I just feel like sometimes you don't get all the information you need to pass the test on the first go-round."

Finally, assigning grades based on a student's more recent performance hints at the important benefits of retakes and redos in equitable grading, which we will address in chapter 11.

Examining the Group Grade

Professional work environments are becoming increasingly collaborative, with teams of people working together across cities, states, and countries. Students are therefore expected to learn how to "collaborate," to work with other students to generate complex ideas, solve problems, and create projects and presentations. We want students working together to identify and utilize their unique talents, compensate for and support others' weaknesses, and to know how to manage, organize, compromise, and coordinate so that the group functions effectively. We also know that students can learn from each other, sometimes more effectively than from the teacher. For all these reasons, teachers assign group projects, group presentations, even "group quizzes" to facilitate collaboration and shared learning.

Some teachers take the seemingly logical next step: They recognize, reward, and, at times, punish students based on the quality of work they produce with their peers. With a "group grade," the group's performance or product earns a grade that is shared by every member of the group. We believe that a group grade fosters mutual accountability and responsibility motivates the higher-performing students to support and encourage the less engaged students. Maybe the weaker students will work harder and learn more, not wanting to disappoint their peers in the group.

Yet we often don't get these results. Despite thoughtful project design and worthy goals, we inevitably get an earful from students—usually higher-performing students—who complain about the other group members—usually the lower-performing students. "The lazy students aren't doing their part, and I'm going to suffer," the hard-working students complain. Students allege unfairness, and although we sympathize, we believe that a group grade can motivate students to learn the life skills of managing, supporting peers, and negotiating conflict. Unfortunately, we may be underestimating the complexity of interpersonal dynamics among our students and fail to realize that they are reluctant to put pressure on each other. The stronger students don't challenge the weaker students; instead, because they care so deeply about getting high grades, they do more than their share of the group's task and resent lower-performing students, and the teacher, because of it. To weaker students, a group grade is both a threat of exposing their lack of content knowledge and skills to their peers as well as a windfall: When stronger students do more of the team's work, weaker students can avoid showing their weaknesses and still receive the same grade as the stronger students. The weaker student is almost guaranteed to receive a grade higher than what she usually receives, and perhaps higher than what she deserves.

Besides frustrating the hard worker, the group grade violates the Accuracy pillar's Driving Principle: **Our grading must use calculations that are mathematically sound, easy to understand, and correctly describe a student's level of academic performance.**

First, even though each student receives a grade based on the quality of the group's final product, that grade doesn't necessarily reflect each student's contribution to that product or, more importantly, each student's content knowledge that the project was designed to teach and measure. For example, if the group is assigned to research and report on a concept, and the quality of the final report is a B, it is nearly impossible for the teacher to distinguish, much less to evaluate, each student's individual role in earning that B. More significantly, even if the report's tasks are divided and assigned to individual group members (as some teachers do) and the teacher is able to somehow document each student's contribution to the final report, the teacher has no way to accurately evaluate each student's knowledge of the complete content that the group report was designed to teach. In other words, a student may be getting a grade based on the quality of the group's report, but we have no confidence that the level of knowledge demonstrated by the report (on which the grade was based) represents each individual member's level of knowledge.[2] Rather than support teamwork and mutual accountability, a group grade undermines those goals. If a teacher knows (and how could she not know) that some students in a group will contribute more than others, why would she award every group member the same grade? After all, how would we feel if our entire grade level or department team received the same evaluation?

At its essence, a group grade confuses means with ends. The purpose of group work is not to create some product in which all members participate, but for each student to learn specific skills or content *through* the group's work together. A group report is intended to teach important content to the entire group, and the only way to accurately assess the success of that group's work together is to individually assess each group member's understanding of the content the group work was designed to teach. If the group works together like a well-oiled machine and completes a high-quality project, but not all members of the group learned the content that project was intended to teach, what good was the collaboration and project completion? We can't argue that at least the group learned how to work well as a group, because the best measure of whether students worked well as a group is whether they learned the intended content. Whether the project is a successful learning experience depends on individual accountability after the project, not during it; we can only get valid evidence of a student's content knowledge and, therefore, assign an accurate grade when we assess each student after the project is complete. Grading students based on work they do collectively is invalid and therefore inequitable.

In sum, assigning a single grade to all students in a group compromises each student's individual accountability to understand the project's content and yields grades that are invalid and inaccurate.[3]

---

[2] Group work has other pedagogical weaknesses that make assigning a group grade inaccurate. For example, if a project consists of four content elements, it may be that each student is responsible for one part. If the group's grade is meant to reflect performance across all four areas, we essentially exempt each student from learning and demonstrating proficiency in the other three content elements for which she wasn't responsible. Additionally, some teachers try to create artificial mutual accountability schemes where the group of students allocates points to each other based on each member's relative contribution. The problem with this is that we can't confirm the accuracy of how the group awards points to its own members.

[3] Some teachers assign a grade based on how the group works together, such as how well each student collaborates or shows respect to other members of the group. As we'll see later in the chapter, evaluating behavior makes the grade even more susceptible to bias and inaccuracy and relies on outdated understandings of motivation. Additionally, using grades as a behavior management strategy—to incentivize the student to work productively in a group—relies on the assumption that extrinsic motivation improves learning. We'll address this assumption and use of grades within our discussion of "soft skills" in chapter 13.

Encouraging Productive Group Work Without a Group Grade

Does that mean students shouldn't be assigned group work? Of course not. Students need to learn how to work collaboratively and to experience how effective teamwork can yield more innovation, creativity, and better results. But rather than fragment that understanding by awarding a grade based on what the group produces—a grade that is guaranteed to inaccurately reflect what each individual student has learned—we should reestablish the relationship between the quality of the group's collaboration and the impact on each member's learning. After all, as Melia, a high school art teacher for eleven years, recognizes,

"Group work is a behavior. The standard isn't working cooperatively or working happily in a group. That's one of the practices we're developing but it's not the standard, so it shouldn't be included in the grade. Plus, I realized that if one person does the work and everybody else in the group doesn't, by assigning a group grade I was giving people who hadn't done the work credit for that one person's work, encouraging those who hadn't contributed to continue do the one thing that I don't want anyone to do in group work: not contribute."

So how do we get students to participate in productive group work while assessing only the knowledge each student gained from that group work? This question implicates the larger questions of how to motivate students to engage in effective learning behaviors without grading those behaviors—strategies we address in chapter 13—but for now, here are some strategies to explicitly build the cause–effect relationship between group work and its learning outcomes:

1. Before the project, explain that the purpose of the group work is for all students to learn the content, and each student will have to individually demonstrate that learning on an assessment after completing the group work.

2. Brainstorm with students about their experiences with group work—not only about what makes groups productive or unproductive, but what each student will need from her group in order to learn the material. How do effective groups check in with each member on her understanding? How can groups ensure that each student learns all of the content even though the tasks required to complete the work might be distributed among the group's members? Provide, or co-construct with students, group work norms or a rubric that reflects expectations See **www.gradingforequity.org** for sample group work rubrics.

3. Be patient. Any shift away from traditional grading and assessment practices takes time for students to see the bigger picture, to understand that group work is not an end that earns points or a grade, but a means for learning the content that

will be assessed separately from the group work. Give them clear and frequent feedback related to the rubrics and norms and keep reminding them of the authentic purpose of group work with its link to individual learning.

4. After the group work, assess each student individually to determine whether each learned the content or skills the group work was designed to teach. This provides valid information for grades and valuable feedback to the teacher and student on the true effectiveness of the group work.

Assigning a group grade is not accurate or equitable, and it misleads students about what group work is for. Instead, we should help students realize that the real goal of group work in schools is not to make a high-quality product based on academic content, but to improve each student's chance for learning that content through the production of a high-quality product. As Mohammed, the middle school humanities teacher, realized,

"21st century skills—cooperative learning, project-based learning, and engaging with other people—is really a big focus in secondary education, so I sort of automatically started grading that and not focusing on what those skills produce. It was unclear to me the difference between formative and summative assessment, and I was emphasizing what students did during group work more than what students actually learned through group work. I had to relearn that and think about it differently."

We'll address this important idea in equitable grading—that the means of learning should be tightly connected to its ends—in much more detail in chapter 13's discussion of "soft skills."

Our Accuracy Pillar: A Final Thought

We've learned that in order for our grades to be accurate we have to use mathematical principles and calculations, but you may have begun to realize that the mathematics of grading isn't just about the mathematics of grading. Examining the zero, averaging, group work, and the 0–100-point scale raises questions of curriculum design and content priorities as well as larger issues of pedagogy, values, and beliefs about learning. Equity depends on accuracy, and we've seen a few ways in which the choices we make—mathematical or pedagogical—can promote or limit equity. In the next chapters, we'll introduce our second pillar of equitable grades— that they must be bias-resistant. The implications for teaching and learning may be even more profound.

Summary of Concepts

1. Averaging a student's performance over time results in inaccurate descriptions of what a student ultimately learned and inequitably lowers grades for students who took a longer time to learn and demonstrate proficiency. Instead, a student's most recent performance can more accurately and equitably describe her achievement.

2. Assigning a single grade to all members of a group can create resentment and undesired dynamics within the group, and often yields inaccurate inequitable descriptions of student performance.

3. Assigning a common grade to all students for their group work confuses means (to collaborate to capitalize on the diverse learning needs and strengths of peers) with ends (to increase learning). It rewards them for working together to create a product regardless of whether each student learned from that group's work.

4. Awarding grades based on student learning subsequent to the group work refocuses students on its purpose and provides us with opportunities for formative feedback.

Questions to Consider

1. For Teachers: Many of us give students a grade "bump" when they have shown improvement or growth over a term. By allowing (and encouraging) students to demonstrate growth over time through improved performance, and recording that most recent performance, do we still need to include a separate bump for growth, or does the improved score itself recognize and reward growth?

2. For Teachers: How easy should it be for a student to be able to calculate her own grade? How could we use a student's own grade as an opportunity to teach mathematical principles of median, mean, mode, scale, and percentages, and thereby empower students to be more critical consumers of statistics?

3. Think of an example in the professional workplace in which group work (or more likely, called "collaboration") is expected. What is the rationale, and how is the effectiveness of that collaboration determined?

CHAPTER 9

Practices That Value Knowledge, Not Environment or Behavior

- **Grades Based on the Required Content of the Course, Not Extra Credit**
- **Grades Based on Student Work, Not the Timing of the Work**
- **Alternative (Nongrade) Consequences for Cheating**
- **Excluding "Participation" and "Effort"**

In this chapter, we will answer the following questions:

1. How do traditional grading practices invite biases and nonacademic information into student grades, and how can we make our grades more bias-resistant?

2. What is inequitable about including extra credit in the grade? What's the alternative?

3. How do our implicit biases operate when we incorporate students' nonacademic behaviors into their grades? What are the consequences?

4. Despite our good intentions, why are the inclusion of participation and effort in a grade so problematic? What are alternatives?

Pillar 2: Bias-Resistant

> **Driving Principle: Grades should be based on valid evidence of a student's content knowledge, and not based on evidence that is likely to be corrupted by a teacher's implicit bias or that reflects a student's environment.**

> *Since institutions continue to support, not dismantle, the status quo, we continue to see racially inequitable outcomes even when there are good intentions behind policies or ostensibly neutral profit motives behind actions, even when there are no racist actors. (Powell, Heller, & Bundalli, 2011)*

In chapter 2, we learned how the factory model of schools was designed primarily to sort students into their appropriate station in society, and how the system of letter grades efficiently facilitated that sorting. That reporting system, informed by two other premises of the Industrial Revolution—that across a student population there was a statistical distribution of academic potential (the curve) and that students are most effectively motivated through extrinsic means—endures today to perpetuate ideas and outcomes which not only contradict what we know now about students and learning, but which are patently unjust. The disparate outcomes of our schools have been persistent and wide ranging, and grading has been a key mechanism of our schools to perpetuate disparate outcomes and makes it too easy for it to predict a student's achievement based on their race, native language, special education needs, and family income.

In the previous chapter, we focused on how mathematics of grading—ensuring that our grading computations render grades that accurately reflect a student's academic performance—promote equity. We saw how the use of averages, particularly when a student's performance has "outliers," is a mathematically inaccurate method to calculate a grade, but it is also biased against students with a weaker education background—who are more likely to have low grades initially—and those who take longer to learn a concept. Similarly, the 0–100 scale is oriented toward failure and therefore yields inaccurate scores, but it also disproportionately harms students who have intermittent, catastrophic failures—something historically underserved groups are more likely to experience. When grading practices are truly accurate, they remove some biases in traditional grading. We'll see in this chapter how the reverse is true: When we reduce our biases in grading, our grades become more accurate.

In chapter 4's primer on implicit biases, we saw how unconscious biases based on a student's race, gender, income, language, or special needs can result in disparate consequences, such as more frequent and harsher disciplinary actions. Teachers' implicit biases also affect how we interpret our students' behaviors, so when we used our interpretations of behaviors to evaluate and grade them, we must ensure that our implicit biases don't reflect and result in the same disparities that we see too often in disciplinary consequences.

For example, with equitable grades we wouldn't include a score on a report to be completed over spring break and submitted electronically because that policy rests on a biased assumption that all students have access to academic support during the vacation if they need help with the report and that all students have access to a computer. The policy would penalize students who didn't have access to support or a computer, and grades for that report would inequitably reflect a student's surroundings or family income and education.

We need a grading system that prevents our implicit biases from "infecting" our grades. In other words, our grades need to be **bias-resistant**. If we want to interrupt and dismantle the education structures that have allowed and perpetuated the achievement and opportunity gaps, we have to find ways to reduce the influence of biases that operate without us even realizing it.

Many teachers already take steps to prevent implicit biases from altering their judgment: Students write their names on the back of essays or type all responses so that the teacher's previous experience or feelings about the students don't influence her evaluation. Teachers sincerely want the grade to reflect concrete objective evidence so that it is the student's work, not the teacher's subjective judgment of the student or anything else that warrants the particular grade. While these are valuable strategies, our grading has systematically perpetuated the achievement and opportunity gaps because our practices, though believed to benefit students and seemingly neutral on their face, actually promote and authorize our biases to operate. These practices include the following:

- Providing extra credit points

- Penalizing for lateness (tardiness or submitting work past the deadline)

- Punishing cheating in the grade

- Evaluating student behaviors

- Including homework in the grade

In the next two chapters, we'll see how these practices allow our biases to cloud and warp the accuracy of grades, and therefore can disproportionately harm historically underserved students. We must identify alternative practices that protect our grades from the explicit biases embedded in, and the implicit biases invited by, traditional grading practices.

Bias-resistant grading practices help us to focus on a student's knowledge and not her circumstances or behavior (or how we perceive and interpret her behavior).

We want our grades to be accurate reflections of a student's level of content mastery and not to be lowered because of how we judge nonacademic aspects of the student. Importantly, we also don't want to *raise* students' grades because of their circumstances or identity. Teachers are compassionate and empathetic and may reward the student facing challenges of poverty, language, race, or other circumstances. They raise the grade of this kind of a student to encourage her to continue to work hard and to recognize the merit of overcoming her struggles. They assign the student a grade that is higher than her level of content mastery, essentially exchanging effort or growth for achievement, and (mis-) characterize it as equity: "The student had more to overcome, and with fewer supports, so her grade should be bumped up." While this may seem fair, even just, it is neither of these. Instead, it is inequitable and deprives the student of important elements of equity: honesty and dignity.

When a student doesn't demonstrate mastery of content but we assign a grade that reflects that, we are lying to the student, falsely communicating that she has demonstrated mastery when she hasn't. Students need to know where they stand in relation to the standard, because if we don't tell them now, someone or some institution is going to tell them later. They'll mistakenly believe they are academically prepared for the next year's course, or college, or some other challenge, and they'll have a rude and tragic realization of their underpreparation. We dignify our students when we tell them the truth.

Does this mean that we check our empathy and compassion at the schoolhouse door? Are we supposed to be unfeeling umpires simply calling balls and strikes? Of course not. Equitable grading practices give students hope, support, and opportunities for redemption. But they are, above all, accurate reflections of what a student knows, resistant to our biases that lower *or* raise grades because of student's circumstances or identity.

Let's see how.

Examining Extra Credit

What's not to like about extra credit? It solves so many problems.

- The classroom needs supplies—crayons, paper, notebooks, and tissue boxes, for example. Extra credit encourages students to bring in those supplies and support their classroom environment and saves the teacher from spending her own money for supplies.

- There's a movie, exhibit, or performance that is related to classroom content. Extra credit persuades students to attend the outside event and make connections between the classroom content and the world outside.

- It's the end of the term and some students are very close to the next higher letter grade (e.g., a student has a 79.4 percent—very close to the 80 percent qualifying for a B). Extra credit motivates students to earn a few extra points to secure the better grade.

- There's an upcoming exam for which students need to study. Extra credit incentivizes students to complete the optional review activity so they're better prepared.

Teachers also award extra credit for handing in assignments ahead of time, for bringing food to a potluck, and for attempting challenging extension activities related to the content. When I taught high school, I wrote extra credit questions about popular culture on my American history exams. I reasoned that the extra credit would add variety and some fun to the exam, would strengthen my relationships with students, and would give struggling students an opportunity to feel smart. Extra credit is by definition not required, which grants the teacher nearly unfettered creativity to offer any task, at any time, for any value, and about any content. Extra credit offerings can motivate students, salvage low grades, allow students to extend learning, and because all extra credit is optional, it doesn't seem to punish students who choose not to do it.

But is extra credit really equitable and bias-resistant? Does it conform to our Driving Principle that a grade should reflect a student's knowledge and not the environment that is outside her control?

No. Here are four reasons why:

First, as we mentioned in chapter 3, our inherited grading systems treat grades, and all the points that comprise them, as a commodity. Extra credit is one of the most obvious examples of this. When teachers offer extra credit, we reinforce for students that our class isn't really about learning or mastery of standards, but about acquiring enough points, however possible. The grade is no longer a valid reflection of what a student knows, only the points she accumulates. No wonder that when we get near the end of a term, students plead for extra credit assignments that will allow them to earn points they didn't or couldn't earn earlier. We can't complain that students are point-grubbers when we give them extra points to grub.

Second, even when extra credit is related to the course content—like seeing a movie based on a book, or doing an extra project to show deeper or applied understanding of the content—students are taught that points are fungible, that weak learning in one content standard can be compensated for by more work in another standard. "I don't need to learn about the dispute between the Federalists and the Anti-Federalists if I take advantage of all the extra credit in the Constitution unit." Extra credit tells students that learning is a "Choose-Your-Own-Adventure" game where you select how to get the points you need to get the grade you want. Or that learning is an arcade, where if you earn enough tickets (points) across all the games you can exchange them for the prize (grade) you want.

Third, extra credit undermines a teacher's own curriculum and instruction. When we offer extra credit, the points a student earns acts to backfill or compensate for points that she didn't earn earlier in the term. An extra credit assignment supplants the earlier assignments that students were responsible for—the learning activities designed to teach them the content of the course—with assignments that may or may not have anything to do with course content. The points a student earns for bringing in tissue boxes for the classroom or cans for the food drive replaces the points lost when the student couldn't correctly use the quadratic formula. With extra credit, teachers send the message that those assignments or content understandings really weren't so important. Extra credit renders a grade inaccurate because it reflects information unrelated to a student's knowledge of the content. If a student has demonstrated a C+ level of course content mastery, why should extra credit points lift the student to receive an inaccurate and misleading B-? Plus, creating extra credit assignments means that the teacher creates assignments in addition to those she's already created in the required curriculum. Why create additional tasks and obligate ourselves to grade additional assignments if our initial assignments were designed to teach the content?

Fourth, extra credit violates the second aspect of our Driving Principle—it's inequitable because it reflects a student's environment over which she has no control. Extra credit, although it's optional and open to all students, doesn't allow all students to take equal advantage because it requires extra resources beyond the course requirements. Extra credit is *extra*, beyond the requirements of the course, and often requires money (materials, tickets to a movie), time, or adult support beyond what the school provides. As a result, students of lower-income families or who have fewer resources are less likely to be able to complete extra credit offerings, and when the extra credit extends course content beyond what's addressed in class, academically struggling students, especially if they had difficulty with the required curriculum, aren't likely to do the more challenging extra credit work with that standard. Research confirms that lower-achieving students simply do not complete extra-credit assignments as often as do higher-achieving students (e.g., Padilla-Walker, 2006; Padilla-Walker, Zamboanga, Thompson, & Schmersal, 2005; Hardy, 2002), which should compel us to "reconsider the usefulness of extra credit" (Hardy, p. 233). Without us realizing it, extra credit not only devalues a teacher's curriculum but actually increases the achievement gap—offering opportunities that only those students who have resources, supports, or stronger education backgrounds can take advantage of.

If the Work Is Important, Require It; If It's Not, Don't Include It in the Grade

To make grades more equitable—more accurate and bias-resistant—we must stop offering extra credit opportunities. If the work teachers assign is important, students shouldn't be able to avoid the work or replace those points with alternate tasks, particularly when those alternate tasks aren't related to the content. Instead, students should have to do, or redo, assignments that they did not complete or do well (see chapter 11 for more on redos), or if the content of an extra credit assignment is valuable for student learning, it should be included in the required curriculum. Doing so invests our assignments with more meaning and importance (students can't opt out of an assignment knowing there's an extra credit "cushion"), makes the playing field more level for all students, and saves teachers from generating (and correcting) additional assignments. Eliminating extra credit makes our grades more bias-resistant and accurate, and if we now have to buy our classroom's tissue boxes ourselves instead of "buying" it with a few bonus points, it's a small price to pay.

Grading the Work, not the Timing of the Work

In traditional grading, students are penalized in their grade when an assignment is submitted late: Rather than refuse the work because it is late, teachers allow students to turn it in but for less credit. It's a common policy even though it can be a record-keeping nightmare. For each day late, students lose a few points or a letter grade, a policy that requires teachers to carefully record for each student the number of days each assignment was submitted late, sometimes distinguishing the excused days—those days missed with legitimate reasons and with sufficient documentation—from the unexcused days—those which aren't approved by the school or which were not accompanied by sufficient documentation. After all, the reasoning goes, if a student couldn't meet the deadline there should be some punishments, and if she had extra time to complete the assignment, she shouldn't be able to earn the same grade as a student who turned it in on time (and who therefore had less time). We believe we're teaching students responsibility, the meaning of deadlines, and being fair.

However, reducing grades for late work both creates inaccuracy and violates our bias-resistant Driving Principle.

First, the practice creates inaccurate final grades. For example, a student who has demonstrated A quality work but who submitted the work past the due date has her grade lowered to a B, which is an inaccurate description of her level of performance on that assignment. We are collapsing two distinct aspects of her achievement—her academic performance and the timing of that academic performance—resulting in a grade that isn't accurate.

Additionally, late work penalties can disproportionately hurt the most vulnerable students. Students turn in assignments late for all sorts of reasons. They have few resources, weak prior knowledge, overwhelming schedules, a lack of engagement, stress, and simple forgetfulness. They may not have been able to entirely control all the circumstances that caused the assignment to be late, and our implicit biases influence the assumptions we make about whether they had. They may learn at a slower rate and need more time to complete assignments to actually learn from them. When grades are lowered for work submitted late, many students, rather than submit work past the deadline for less credit, will choose to stop working on the assignment after the deadline has passed and will stop learning. Other students may resort to copying in order to meet the deadline, in which case they'll meet the deadline but won't have learned.

What's the Alternative to Lowering Grades for Late Work?

When teachers accept late work without a grade-based penalty, grades are more accurate reflections of student academic performance; learning becomes more important than deadlines. When we don't penalize for late work, we send the message that learning has a more flexible timeline and pace, and it's better to produce high-quality work submitted after the deadline than to cut learning short. After all, as educators, we would always prefer that students continue learning rather than truncate it. Kim, a high school English teacher for seventeen years, explains,

> *"I realized that it was more important for students to do the work that I assigned than it was to make them conform to my timeline. If the work was important, it was important whether they did it by the due date or they did it a week later."*

When teachers stop reducing grades on assignments submitted late, one of their biggest surprises is that they not only get more completed work—students who need more time use that time—but also that the quality of work *increases*. When students are allowed to have more time to complete assignments, they can work around unpredictable events or overpacked schedules, have less incentive to copy, and can take more pride in doing their best work. As Jaden, a middle school student, shares, "I don't copy if I have an extra day to do [assignments] because it gives me more time to try to understand what I'm doing instead of rushing. If you have more time, then it's just pointless to copy because you can actually do it yourself."

Of course, at some point the learning has to stop, and no teacher wants to suffer a deluge of outdated and irrelevant work in the last days of a grading term, but there are middle grounds. Some teachers allow assignments to be submitted without penalty until the date of that unit's summative assessment, because the purpose of those assignments is to teach students the content; once the assessment is over, the prior daily assignments have no value. Other teachers choose to accept late assignments until a week before the end of the grading term so they have enough time to review it and enter grades.

Meeting deadlines is important, but it's a "soft skills" behavior that is separate from academic content mastery. We'll address how we teach these critically important skills to students without including them in the grade in chapter 13. For the time being, it's enough to confirm that because meeting deadlines is not academic content, a student's ability to meet a deadline should not be included in her grade.

Alternative (Non-Grade) Consequences for Cheating

Cheating is another student behavior, and one that elicits some of the strongest reactions from teachers. Many view cheating, which includes copying another student's work or using technology or other mechanisms to access or copy information, not as simply a lapse in a student's judgment, but as a personal affront to the teacher's dedication, a slap in the face to the subject area, and an offense to the learning process. We know that cheating on an exam in college can result in harsh punishment—failure of the course, suspension, or even expulsion—while cheating in other aspects of adult life—embezzlements and other crimes of shortcuts—can even lead to fines or even jail time. Even though the student likely was driven to cheat for reasons that had nothing to do with her personal feelings toward the teacher, educators feel hurt and undermined and want to teach these students a harsh lesson: Cheating is the cardinal sin of learning. It is akin to an act of treason—violating the trust between the student and the teacher, and casts doubt on the validity of a student's current and even her *prior* performance. Some educators even believe that cheating isn't just a bad action; it can be a step down the road of moral degradation. One teacher I spoke with believed that cheating on a test could, if unpunished, lead to marital infidelity!

Teachers' most frequent punishment for cheating is to give the student who cheated (and any accomplices) a zero for the test or assignment. It's the toughest punishment we teachers have at our disposal. We assign the zero because we want students to understand how severe a transgression cheating is, and we hope the zero teaches that lesson.

The first problem with this consequence is that we're including student behaviors in a grade that is supposed to only represent a student's academic performance. Cheating is not a reflection of that performance; if a student gets a grade penalty for cheating, she now has a "hodgepodge" grade, a grade that combines the behavior of cheating with the rest of her academic performance. Secondly, assigning a zero when a student cheated makes the grade inaccurate. As we discussed in chapter 7, that zero is a false representation of the student's content knowledge. Even if the student did cheat, it is likely untrue that she knew nothing (zero knowledge) about the content; it's that *we don't know what the student knows because she cheated*. Assigning a zero rejects any evidence (and even the *possibility* of evidence) of what a student has learned. Viewed from this perspective, the zero is an odd punishment for cheating: "You cheated on a test, so as your consequence, your grade isn't going to reflect what you know!" If we're honest, deflating a grade isn't the logical consequence for cheating.

Students cheat for lots of reasons (some of which we'll see in the chapter's examination of homework and copying), but at its core, a student cheats because she doesn't believe that she can be successful on the assignment or test without cheating; she doesn't know (or have sufficient confidence that she knows) the answers and believes she is unable to earn the score she wants unless she cheats. Students may cheat because they realized too late that the homework they ignored would have helped them, or they couldn't learn the content fast enough, or there was some circumstance or event that prevented them from sufficiently preparing (e.g., a school play, sports event, or a family commitment or emergency), or maybe they just didn't want to study. At the very least, when we suspect cheating, we might treat it as a symptom of a student's academic or personal struggle, and that alone might warrant a different kind of consequence than irredeemable punishment.

The real irony of assigning a zero for cheating is that it lets the student off too easy: She never is held accountable for the content in the assignment or assessment. She doesn't have to reveal what she actually knows and what her gaps are and avoids learning the content. Penalizing students with a zero for cheating is inequitable because, along with including a behavior to render the grade mathematically inaccurate, it denies students the opportunity to show what they know and discounts whatever they may have learned, and it essentially exempts cheating students from learning.

Of course, we can't have students cheating, and there needs to be a meaningful punishment, but do teachers have other options other than rendering the grade artificially low and inaccurate, and exempting the cheating student from the work? Let's find the right punishment by coming at this problem from a new perspective: criminal law and its understanding of crime and punishment.

Criminal law identifies five potential aims of punishment:

Deterrence: The threat of punishment deters people from doing the offense. (When someone gets put in jail for doing an offense, others don't do the offense because they don't want to be put in jail.)

Incapacitation: The punishment prevents that person from doing more bad acts. (When someone commits an offense, we put her in jail so she can't do more harm.)

Rehabilitation: The person must learn to correct that bad behavior and contribute positively to society. (When someone commits an offense, we require her to gain the capacity to not want, or need, to commit the crime in the future.)

Restitution: The person who did the action must do something to make the victim "whole" again. (When someone steals from or harms someone, she must repay or compensate the person for the damage or loss.)

Retribution: The person who did the crime harmed society, so society harms that person. (When someone commits an offense, we punish her so that she feels the pain commensurate with the damage she caused.)

In schools, most of the consequences for student misbehaviors, such as detentions, serve *retributive* and *deterrence* purposes; we harm the student because the student harmed others, and we want the threat of detentions to prevent other students from misbehaving similarly. For more extreme misconduct, we use suspensions or expulsions to incapacitate the student, excluding them temporarily or permanently from our school community. Our assignment of the zero, aside from its mathematical inaccuracy and its function as a "Get Out of Learning" card, is primarily a punishment of retribution; the cheating student has harmed the learning environment, and the learning environment (represented by the teacher) must exact some harm: a grade that weighs down the student's grade disproportionately. The zero also functions as a deterrent, a warning to other students that their grades too could be imperiled if they are caught cheating. But is retribution and deterrence the approach we should be taking in our punishments for academic "crimes"?

Recently, punishments designed to serve these purposes have been called into question. Though zero-tolerance and "no-excuses" behavior policies were all the rage for decades, research has consistently found that a punishment premised primarily on retribution and deterrence is not an effective strategy for improving behaviors and has a disproportionately negative impact on students of color (see, e.g., Skiba, Michael, Nardo, & Peterson, 2002). Instead, many schools are beginning to apply rehabilitative consequences for student misbehavior, such as restorative justice practices in which students reflect on their mistakes, recognize how those behaviors affected others (perhaps including some restitution), and learn productive behaviors for the future. Except for the most egregiously dangerous and harmful behaviors, consequences that are rehabilitative rather than retributive better align with a learning environment in which mistakes are expected. People can be redeemed, and fissures can be healed.

Are there *rehabilitative* consequences we could apply to our students' cheating?

If we want (and even encourage) students to learn from mistakes and to master course content, then we have to reconsider the zero as a punishment for cheating. Cheating should primarily have a rehabilitative consequence, not a retributive one, with deterrence as a secondary effect. The consequence for cheating that aligns most closely with these purposes is not to assign a zero, but instead to require the student to complete the test or assignment and reveal her true level of content knowledge. In other words, the student who cheats should be required to rehabilitate herself by doing the assessment or assignment. Rather than allow the student to evade showing what she knows and earn a zero grade that doesn't reflect her knowledge, she should be required to do the work without cheating. Perhaps she must complete that assessment, or future assessments, with closer monitoring until she has restored our trust—in other words, *restitution*. We might consider withdrawing some privilege or responsibility of the student's or require her to research consequences for cheating in "the real world" that would awaken her to the seriousness of the behavior—a consequence that is both rehabilitative and a deterrent. We could also require additional restitution—that she apologize to the teacher and possibly her peers—and make amends by undertaking an additional responsibility in the classroom.

While we may have felt that the zero was the most appropriate and available consequence, we now see we have many more creative and effective options for cheating—options that have a rehabilitative purpose and preserve the integrity of the grade as a valid reflection of academic performance. The consequence for cheating shouldn't be to allow a student to opt out of learning or to make the grade inaccurate. Cheating, at its base, is not an act of learning but a behavior—something that is contrary to everything learning is about, but a behavior nonetheless. For that reason, while the student should definitely receive a consequence—and one that deters her from ever cheating again—the punishment shouldn't be reflected in her grade.

Excluding "Participation" and "Effort" From the Grade

"She grades you for everything. You can get an F for walking in that class with a hood on, or hat on, or something like that. She pushes her authority around. She wants everything done right, and if you didn't do it right then she'll just take off points, even if it's little mistakes." (Katelyn, middle school student)

Biases find a home in traditional grading practices when teachers evaluate student behaviors. The two most explicit examples of this is when teachers consider a student's "Participation" or her "Effort" in the grade. By expanding our analysis from chapter 4 and better understanding the subjectivity deeply embedded in these concepts, we'll realize why we can't include these categories in a grade. Our Driving Principle for bias-resistant grades means that we must limit the impact of our biases by limiting elements of a grade that are judgments of our students' behaviors. If we incorporate student behavior into a grade, we are at risk allowing, and even helping, the education system to continue to hurt students not in the dominant cultures and to further entrench the achievement and opportunity gaps.

PARTICIPATION. For most teachers, the Participation category functions as a catch-all for rewarding the behaviors the teacher wants. As we saw in chapter 4, each teacher likely has a different definition of what behaviors comprise Participation. Some Participation behaviors are about being ready to learn—bringing a notebook, coming to the class on time, asking questions—and others are about supporting the learning of the entire class—being respectful, staying on-task, and being committed to the classroom activities. Like other grading practices we've examined in this chapter, teachers include nonacademic information, like missing deadlines, in the grade because of noble intentions. For example, teachers award daily points for bringing materials to class because they know that students can't be successful in class if they aren't prepared. Perhaps we're giving them points for asking good questions or contributing to the class discussion.

Awarding a grade for behaviors that support learning has been a strategy that schools have used for decades to make students act in ways that conform to a stereotypical type of student. For example, we don't just give credit for asking questions in class, but we reward them for only talking when they are called on. In 1992, Stiggins and Conklin observed teachers and reviewed students' essays on what they thought affected their grades. As described by Kelly (2008),

> The students reported the importance of classroom behaviors like being attentive, completing assignments, and trying hard, all of which are likely to be associated with a growth in achievement. But they also reported that it was important to be "nice, kind, [and] polite" and to "establish a good relationship with teachers" (Stiggins & Conklin 1992: Table 4.2). These data and the high school profile data on teachers' assessment practices led Stiggins and Conklin to conclude that there is "a stereotypical personality type that teachers respond to favorably"— students "who appear attentive and aggressive during class and who therefore receive higher grades than others, not because they have learned more material but because they have learned to act like they are learning more." (p. 35)

Regardless of the criteria, the category focuses more on a student's conduct than what she has learned, and is a subjective and therefore bias-infected judgment of a student's behavior.

"I realize that I do give kids grades based on how much they conform to my expectations of what a great student is. I started to ask myself, 'How much do I help students because they are good at asking for help, versus those students who aren't used to asking for help or used to getting it?' I can't tell you how much of their grade was based on their ability versus how much was based on following the rules of how to set up an assignment or when it's turned in." (Melia, high school art teacher for eleven years)

It therefore shouldn't be a surprise that students who don't fit into that archetype are reluctant to engage in the associated behaviors that schools reward (rejected by students of color as "acting white"). Students who haven't been successful in school, and who have experienced school as an antagonistic place where they have been tracked, disproportionately suspended, and then told they are failing, are less likely to engage and invest in that very institution than the students who have had a pattern of success. They aren't succeeding in what Robert Fried (2005) calls "The Game of School," in part because they are judged against a set of criteria that don't reflect who they are.

Like the points we award or subtract for homework and meeting deadlines, we end up severing the relationship between the habit we want students to learn and its purpose. We award points for a behavior irrelevant of how it contributes to an outcome. If students have their notebooks, they receive 5 points regardless of how they use the notebooks. Rather than show them the causal connection between preparation and success, we separate the cause and effect and treat them independently.

Rewarding certain behaviors is meant to support student learning but it forces students to fit within a set of behaviors anchored to the teacher's subjective, implicitly biased idea of what a successful student is—behaviors that more often than not are the behaviors that their teacher has and values, embedded within that teacher's specific culture, upbringing, and learning styles. In truth, we often superimpose the behaviors we engaged in that made us successful. In doing so, we often ignore the diversity of learning styles, contexts, cultures, and needs among our students. Even if we want the entire class to utilize notebooks to take notes during the class period, some students may not learn best by taking notes. Although a teacher may believe that a student must contribute to a discussion to learn, and awards points for that contribution (or subtracts points when a student does not contribute), some students learn by absorbing the discussion silently or by reading on their own. If some behaviors that we find valuable for learning don't help certain students in their learning, why would we punish students for not showing those behaviors, and why reward those students for exhibiting behaviors that don't help them?

Finally, it's worth mentioning that participation points reward students for doing what teachers ask and acting in ways teachers prefer (following directions, adhering to classroom rules) not only because teachers believe that if students act in those ways they'll learn, but also because these student behaviors will make the teacher's job easier and hopefully more successful. Participation points are the carrot that extrinsically motivates students to behave, and by using that grading practice, we may be confusing skill development with our own desire for obedience and control.

Viewed against our Driving Principle, including points for Participation behaviors has no place in a student's grade. It doesn't include valid evidence of a student's content knowledge, and it is based on criteria that is entirely subjective and inevitably corrupted by our implicit bias.

EFFORT. Unlike Participation, rewarding or penalizing on the basis of effort is rarely a separate category in a grade. For many teachers, the consideration of effort in a grade is a safety valve (or "grade hack" listed in chapter 4) when the grading software doesn't yield appropriate final grades. If the grading software computes a student's overall percentage to be on the cusp of a higher grade (e.g., an 89.9%, a B, but only 0.1 percent from a 90%, an A-), the teacher can consider the student's effort. If the student worked hard, the teacher feels justified in manually adjusting the grade despite the grading program's calculation. Faced with grading programs that may not yield the proper grades in the teacher's professional opinion, what's wrong with boosting grades in order to recognize a student's hard work? Perseverance and resilience (sometimes called "grit") are so important to success in school and life; shouldn't students be rewarded when they show effort?

Yes and no. Hard work and persistence are important skills for life not for their own sake, but only when hard work gets us closer to a goal. It's another example of where traditional grading detaches the means from the ends. Let's say a student gets a review sheet and spends two hours just looking at it but not applying effective study skills, and therefore doesn't score well on the test. Would we want to reward that student for effort that wasn't effective, that didn't get her closer to her goal? Of course not—that would be misleading students into believing that all that matters is how much time they spend. Hard work without effective strategies that lead to success isn't what we want to encourage. The reward for greater effort is the higher score on the assessment, and thereby, a higher grade. As Close (2009) vividly analogizes,

> *Contaminating the grade with information beyond the academic content of the course makes the transcript unreliable, even useless, in determining levels of knowledge and competence. Imagine a USDA meat grader who grades the farmer's beef carcasses in part on the great effort that the farmer expended in getting the beef to market or because of how much progress the farmer had made in raising beef cattle after a long career as a philosophy professor. (p. 369)*

Plus, trying to evaluate a student's effort is a minefield, opening the door for our bias and subjectivity. Like our subjective definition of Participation, we usually impose our idea of what effort looks like—maybe it's asking questions, participating (see previous section), or staying after school for extra help. But consider the student whose single parent works a night shift and who wakes up before sunrise so she can cook breakfast for her younger siblings, get them dressed, walk them to school, and get to your class only a few minutes late. How much effort is she putting in if she doesn't always have homework completed and dozes off occasionally? Or what about the African American student who has been suspended for her "defiance" (a catch-all that we know disproportionately punishes black and brown kids) or missed a month of school due to her grandmother's illness or has failed as many classes as she has passed, and generally doesn't trust teachers or believe school is really there to help her succeed? How much effort is it if she comes to class every day, listens, and partially attempts assignments every day even though she has no confidence that she will pass the course?

Plus, our evaluation of effort is based on starkly incomplete information. We base effort on incomplete information: only on what we see in the classroom. Students' time with us is a fraction of the time and effort they might be spending on learning our subject—and we can't possibly know what effort students are investing when they're not in the classroom. As Tyler, a high school student, reports,

"My teacher only allows retakes if he knows that you're trying hard. But how do you show him that you're trying hard? What if you can't come to tutoring because you have sports? What if you can't come during lunch because you have clubs? Even if you're studying at home and by yourself, he doesn't know that. You could just be asking questions about things you already know how to do just so he thinks that you are trying."

Effort credit is rife with bias, clearly violates our Driving Principle, and should not be included in the grade. The most accurate and non-biased reflection of effort is increased academic performance.

To adhere to our Bias-Resistant pillar's Driving Principle—that grades should only be based on valid evidence of a student's content knowledge, not on a student's environment or based on evidence that is likely corrupted by a teacher's implicit bias—we should exclude the following from a student's grade: extra credit, the timing of when students submit assignments, and behaviors that traditionally are included in categories like Participation and Effort. By excluding these elements of our traditional grading, we're detoxifying our grades of the information that contributes to inequitable grading and instead protecting the grade against biases and ensuring that it only represents what a student knows.

In the next chapter, we'll continue with making our grading practices bias-resistant and take on one of the most challenging issues: whether to include homework in the grade.

Summary of Concepts

1. Bias-resistant grading prevents our implicit biases—which are impossible to ignore or erase—from misrepresenting students' academic performance. Even when we increase students' grades out of compassion or empathy, doing so misleads them and deprives them and their families of the dignity they have always deserved: knowing the truth about where they are in their learning, where they have to go, and that we're here to support them.

2. Eliminating extra credit helps us to immunize our grades from inequities, no longer rewarding or penalizing students based on their environment or resources, and adding credibility and value to the required curriculum and assignments. If the work is important, it should be required.

3. As much as we want students not to miss deadlines, and certainly never want them to cheat, when we incorporate these (mis-)behaviors into a grade, we

warp the accuracy of the grade to describe student academic performance. We also miss the underlying causes of the behavior—such as inadequate preparation and insufficient supports. Instead of entering a low grade that effectively ends the learning, we should allow late work to be submitted when it is done and punish cheating by requiring the student to complete the assignment or assessment, perhaps with non-grade consequences.

4. It is inequitable to include student behaviors in a grade. Weighted categories such as Participation and Effort reward and punish students based on subjective criteria and are flush with opportunities for implicit biases. Instead, when these categories are not included in a grade, students can be taught how participation and effort are means for learning, not ends in themselves.

Questions to Consider

1. In the professional world, what are some different consequences when something misses a deadline? Do those consequences exempt the person from ultimately performing the task?

2. Some consider cheating on an assessment not an act of disobedience, but as a signal that though she is struggling, she is still engaged and cares about her success. Why is cheating arguably a reflection of greater engagement than if the student simply skipped the assessment?

CHAPTER 10

Practices That Value Knowledge, Not Environment or Behavior (Continued)

- **Grades Based Entirely on Summative Assessments, Not Formative Assessments Such as Homework**

In this chapter, we will answer the following questions:

1. What makes the inclusion of homework in a student's grade so problematic and inequitable?

2. What is the most equitable way to weight summative assessment performance in a student's grade, and how might this expand our concept of the purpose and design of assessments?

The discussion of homework and grading implicates many complex issues. We'll organize our discussion into the following topics:

- The two approaches teachers traditionally use to include homework in the grade

- The impact of grading homework on students, explained through their own voices

- How to reframe homework's purpose and value by not including it in the grade, and its benefits

The analysis of homework and grading will lead directly into one of the more exciting and, for some, unnerving practices of equitable grading: including only summative assessment performance in a grade. We'll see that rather than restricting us and our students, considering only summative assessment performance expands our options and leverages our professional expertise.

Homework

Teachers traditionally assign a grade for homework using one of two approaches:

1. The correctness of responses on the homework, or

2. Evidence that the student completed, or even just attempted, the homework

Let's hold each of these approaches up against our Bias-Resistant pillar's Driving Principle:

> **Grades should be based on valid evidence of a student's content knowledge, and not based on evidence that is likely to be corrupted by a teacher's implicit bias or reflect a student's environment.**

Grading homework for its correctness violates this Driving Principle because grades become inaccurate representations of student knowledge. Consider the first time we introduce a topic, concept, or skill. We expect that on the homework for that new content, students would make mistakes (if they didn't make mistakes, they have already learned the content and shouldn't need to take our course). We enter that less-than-perfect score into the grade book,[1] and although it doesn't count for Much in the grand scheme of the entire term's assignments,

---

[1]Some teachers assign a grade for the correctness of homework, but to soften their judgment, they write comments on the homework for the students to read and learn from. In this way, homework provides a communication line between them and the student, for the teacher to individually tailor feedback and to validate the student's time and effort on the homework. The problem is that research shows that when a teacher writes comments on student work, once a grade is written on it, the student not only doesn't benefit from the feedback, they don't even read it (Butler & Nisan, 1986). As soon as students see a grade on their work, they perceive themselves as being evaluated at the end of learning, not as receiving formative feedback during their learning. The comments seem irrelevant to them if they already feel judged.

those points count and are included in the end-of-term grade calculation. We review these less-than-perfect student assignments and address students' mistakes so they correct their misunderstandings and misconceptions. Later, having learned from their mistakes, students demonstrate on the summative assessment that they have mastered the concept. However, that summative assessment score gets combined with their prior lower homework scores, thus rendering an overall grade for that content that is lower than their test scores. Even though students made mistakes when learning the concept—exactly what we *wanted* them to do—grades that should reflect content mastery are lowered, rendering an incorrect description of their levels of competence—the same unsound mathematics and inaccuracies we saw in chapter 7's examination of averaging.

Let's recognize that the most important pedagogical reason for homework is that it is practice. As addressed in chapter 3, even though mistakes are crucial for learning, when we penalize students for errors during the learning process we inadvertently send a message that mistakes are bad. Homework is the space for students to make mistakes, and if mistakes are necessary for learning, then to grade homework based on whether the answers are correct sends contradictory messages. When we award homework points based on how correct students' answers are, we simultaneously tell them that mistakes during practice are to be avoided and that mistakes during practice are to be desired. We can't deduct points for incorrect answers on homework—which penalizes students for mistakes—and at the same time tell students that homework is just practice and that mistakes are a necessary part of learning! When we do, it's no wonder that we confuse students about what learning is and make it much easier for them to measure success simply by point totals.

The other critically important pedagogical purpose of homework is that, in addition to reinforcing skills the teacher taught that day, homework is a **formative assessment**: a way for the teacher to check what skills students learned from the day's lesson and what they haven't yet learned. Teachers use and even depend on student responses on homework to modify instruction and address students' errors and misconceptions before students take the **summative assessment**—the test or final task used to evaluate student's content mastery. Despite the many debates about homework, all teachers agree that at its core, homework helps students to practice what they learned in class and it gives the teacher valuable insight into her students' understanding.

Grading homework for correct answers also can have a disparate impact on vulnerable students, making a weaker student reluctant to attempt an assignment she believes she may not do correctly. She may find it easier and safer simply to not take that risk, choosing instead not to hand in the homework at all (or skip the class period entirely). If we truly empathize with the struggling student, that's an understandably rational decision. Often, the result of grading homework based on its correct answers is that only the students who have academic confidence, a stronger academic background, or supports will submit homework and secure that they have correct answers.[2] The weaker students—those who most need our help—won't attempt the practice, will learn less, and therefore will be less prepared for the summative assessment. And when fewer students submit homework, teachers get less information about student misconceptions, and that information becomes skewed upward because they're not getting homework assignments from the most struggling students. Teachers become less likely to know, much less to address, student mistakes or misunderstandings.

Many teachers, recognizing this essential purpose of homework, award points not for the correctness of students' responses, but for students' attempts at completing the homework irrespective of whether answers are correct. "I want students to know that mistakes are okay," the teacher decides, "so I will reward them for trying the homework practice even if the answers are wrong. I want them to feel confident and comfortable making mistakes, and if I can motivate them by giving points if they just attempt homework, they'll be learning from the homework and I'll be more likely to see their misunderstandings and address them." With this approach, students only lose points if they leave homework questions blank, if parts of the homework aren't attempted.

In comparison to grading homework for correct answers, this seems much more bias-resistant and pedagogically preferable. Unfortunately, this policy puts teachers on a different path toward the same dead end. Including homework in the grade with this approach continues to result in grades that are based on inaccurate and invalid information and inequitably privileges certain students.

Let's assume that the plan works perfectly: All students—those with weak backgrounds and those with strong backgrounds—attempt all parts of the homework, with some correct answers and some incorrect answers. With no points awarded or subtracted for correct answers, each student gets a perfect homework score in the grade book's Homework category for attempting the entire assignment. This policy continues throughout the unit, with some students consistently getting homework answers wrong but still receiving full credit for submitting an attempt. On the unit's summative assessment, some students show mastery of the material and others don't. However, when the scores are totaled in the grading software, students with 100 percent homework completion have higher grades beyond the grades they scored on the assessment. (Review the omnibus grading and category weight calculations in chapter 4.) Some students who did not show proficiency on the exam have cumulative grades that reflect proficiency. The result is grades that are inaccurately inflated reflections of students' levels of content mastery.

---

[2]This assumes that the homework a student submits is actually that student's work and not copied from or assisted by someone else—an assumption that is often not true, as we'll see in a few pages.

We see that giving points for homework whether based on correct answers or just for completion violates the first part of the Bias-Resistant pillar's Driving Principle: Grades aren't based on valid evidence of a student's content knowledge, and therefore misrepresent that knowledge. Students who demonstrate mastery of the content based on summative assessment scores but who haven't turned in homework earn final grades that are deflated and suggest that they know less content than they actually do. For other students, it's the reverse: They dutifully submit homework, and even though they didn't master the content based on the summative assessment, the homework points inflate their grades and suggest they do.

So far, this analysis has been entirely theoretical. How do students experience having homework included in their grade?

The Impact of Including Homework in the Grade: Student Voices and Copying

Does grading homework, whether based on correct answers or just for completion, encourage more students to do the homework, helping them to practice and learn? Well, yes, but with a huge caveat: More students may turn in homework, but it actually can result in fewer students doing the homework they're turning in. As Danny, a middle school humanities teacher, found, "I used to give a grade of credit, no-credit for homework assignments, but I noticed that kids are doing the homework, but only to please me, not to learn from it."

Awarding points for homework provides a grade "cushion" to many students—adding points that compensate for low summative scores. Students depend on the homework points and will do whatever they can to earn those points, such as getting others (caregivers, older siblings, friends) to help them complete it, and when students feel they need to, they copy others' homework. For many students, that is a system that works perfectly and doesn't require them to learn:

> "We have the biggest homework copier in my grade and he has a high cumulative GPA too. He doesn't have to worry about actually trying to figure out and do the work. He barely passes the test but if you get all As on the homework assignments you get a high grade and really don't need even to know anything." (Kiandra, high school student)

Teachers know that homework copying is a major problem in schools. In 2010, the Josephson Institute of Ethics surveyed 43,000 students from both public and private high schools, finding that more than 80 percent of students admitted to having copied another student's homework. I have interviewed over 150 middle and high school students, and every student has told me that they have copied homework at some point. Though we might first believe that this widespread copying reflects our students' moral failings, I've found that when teachers include homework in the grade—whether it's based on the accuracy of a student's answers or just for turning in something—those points actually incentivize students to do whatever they can to complete the homework. Students copy primarily because they want the homework points.

"I feel the reason for copying is not that, 'Oh, I want to cheat', but it's just that it's in my grade. And if I don't do the work then it affects me big time. That's why some of us copy, not because we want to be lazy, but because our grade depends on it." (Isaiah, high school student)

Let's give students the benefit of the doubt and presume that if students could complete the homework themselves, they would. If students are making a rational decision to copy homework to earn the points, what is it about homework that tips the scale toward copying and away from doing the work themselves, and how might including homework in the grade particularly pressure our more vulnerable students to copy? There are clear trends in student voices from my interviews:

First, if students knew how to do the homework, or had access to sufficient supports, they'd do it.

"Most of the time I copy because I just don't get it, or I can't find the information I need. That's happened a couple times where I actually can't find the information I need for my homework. And I'm freaking out and so I'm just like, 'Can you send me the homework?'" (John, high school student)

"Let's say I go in and ask to the teacher [a question], and the teacher gives me an explanation of how to do it, and I don't get that explanation. If I don't get his point of view, I'll just copy and get the points—it's the easiest way." (Ysidra, high school student)

"I think one of the reasons I copy is sometimes in class [the teacher] goes too fast. If it's too fast then it's really hard to get it." (Naomi, middle school student)

When students have homework with content that they don't understand and with no supports outside of school to help them learn it, they copy rather than lose points. This situation doesn't affect all students equally. Let's consider an example: After a mini-lecture introducing the Great Depression, the teacher's homework is a worksheet on the Great Depression with questions. If I have a reasonably strong educational background it shouldn't be too difficult for me to do the homework, but even if it is, if I have caregivers who have college degrees and are available to help me, then I still should be able to complete it. On the other hand, if I have a weaker educational background or special education needs, that same homework may be difficult for me to complete. I might need more support outside school, but if I don't have an adult who can read and understand the article as well as the questions or who doesn't have time and energy to help me, I'm stuck. My teacher provides help before or after school, but that too is dependent on my resources—transportation and time. As long as the homework is going to count for a grade, it's completely understandable that I would copy in order to complete it. Maybe I'm hoping that I'll learn from the copying, or that we'll go over the homework and continue having discussions so that I'll learn what I need to know. Including homework in a grade may have a disparate impact on historically underserved student populations: My ability to complete homework depends on my environment and circumstances; when I have fewer supports, I'm left with fewer options to complete homework other than to copy.

Homework also requires sufficient time outside of class, and many students find themselves overloaded:

"The reason I copy is because I don't have enough time in my schedule to do all my homework from all my classes. I always get assigned so much. I dance from eight to ten, and I also do cross country which is from three to four. I'm always trying to do everything I'm supposed to do in that small time period but it's so much. And I need help understanding some of my work, so if I don't finish it on time, the teacher, he wants it now. He won't give me extra time." (Vanessa, high school student)

"Sometimes we get long packets and your other classes are giving projects at the same time. Your English teacher will give you a huge project and then your elective teacher will too, and then on top of that, my math packet. The teachers are stacking it on too much. I'd rather just copy—at least I'm doing something, even if I just copied. But that's probably not the best thing to do." (Nicholas, middle school student)

"I'm trying to balance not just a grade in one class, but six. That's one of the things I think most teachers forget—we aren't in just their class. Many of us are taking more than six classes that each have their own requirements and homework. And so when a teacher assigns a very heavy assignment with a very short timeline it's really, I feel, almost inconsiderate to the student to have to shift that around five other classes that have other requirements as well." (Tiffany, high school student)

Our high schools have six to eight periods a day, and it's likely that each teacher assigns some homework each day. Students might have one or multiple extracurricular activities that occupy hours every day. And while some students' activities are limited to classes and after-school activities they choose, some students' responsibilities are neither school related or chosen:

> *"Most of the time when I copy it's because I didn't have enough time, because sometimes I have to go home and I have to work in the house. My father is not there for me at all. He's really not there at all. So I have to do things a lot on my own, and at times I don't even have time to do my homework because I'm trying to help support my family and everything. And then the teachers come to me and then they start telling me, 'Oh, why didn't you do your homework? You know you're just lazy,' even though I keep explaining to them I have to do everything at home."* (Marco, high school student)

Other students might have jobs, earning income that their families depend on. And while students of all backgrounds and circumstances may have packed schedules, students who need more time to complete homework because of their academic weaknesses or special learning needs, are disproportionately affected. When time is scarce and a student has to choose between sleep or completing homework, copying is the more efficient and healthy strategy to get homework points.

A third response to including homework in the grade is that homework can lose its value and meaning for learning. Even though a primary purpose of homework is to help students learn material to be successful on the summative assessment, when homework is a means for points it can be more difficult for students to see how homework is connected to their learning. When students can't see how the homework fulfills this purpose, they see homework simply as a hoop to jump through, irrelevant to prepare them for future success.

> *"If the homework is something that I'll have to know for a test, then I'll take the time to learn it. If it's something I already learned but it's still time consuming, then I feel like it's pointless to sit there and really try to take all that time if I already know it."* (Rashawn, middle school student)
>
> *"I copy homework that I feel is busy work and won't benefit me in terms of learning, but I know that I still need to do it because it's going to count towards my grades."* (Rose, high school student)

It's what we know about learning in general—students want to know that content is relevant and important to their students' lives and their futures. And even if the content isn't the most engaging, students at least want to know that the homework has a meaningful purpose—that it isn't just busy work but is an investment of their time that will be rewarded. And particularly when students are from communities that have had negative experiences with schools and other institutions of power, they have less reason to trust the connection between the teacher's assigned homework and future success. The value of homework isn't self-evident because it is assigned by someone in authority.

Another reason students copy homework is that when homework is included in the grade, they can feel increased stress that overwhelms their capacity to complete the homework.

"[A reason students copy is that] [y]ou had a family issue and you're scared that your teacher won't understand. I know that's how it is for me a lot. The teacher won't understand. She'd say, 'Oh that's too bad. You guys should have gotten it done.'" (Lakota, high school student)

"Last year I tried my best in chemistry. I'd say to other students, 'Hey, can you help me explain? Tell me how to do this. Explain it to me, please.' Sometimes they just don't want to explain. They're just like, 'Here take it.' And I'd say, 'No, I want to learn,' but they don't want to tell me, they don't want to explain it to me. It's like they have no time. They're stressed out too. They say, 'Here you go. It's right there.'" (Delaney, high school student)

Brain research confirms that when we are stressed, our cognitive capacity decreases; we simply aren't able to think and process information as when we are relaxed and feel safe. We've known for decades that students' ability to learn and their achievement decreases when they experience stress (e.g., Goldstein, Boxer, & Rudolph, 2015; Kaplan, D., Liu, & Kaplan, H., 2005; Papay & Spielberger, 1986; Stewart, Lam, Betson, Wong, C., & Wong, A., 1999), and the effects of stress have a stronger negative effect on performance for students with learning disabilities (Fisher, Allen, & Kose, 1996). Although nearly every teenager experiences stress—arguments with caregivers and dating relationships, for example—some students experience more stressful events than others depending on their unique circumstances, such as pressure by their parents to succeed, stress from the death of a loved one, or the anxiety caused by parents' divorce. We also know that some groups of students as a group experience more stress than others, further inhibiting executive functioning and higher-order thinking, and weakening their tolerance for academic struggle. For example, the undocumented immigrant family's children live in daily fear that they or their caregivers will be detained or forced to leave the country. Black and brown students live with the stress that any involvement with the police could end in death. The child growing up in poverty feels stress from not having clean clothes, living in poor and often violent communities, or in extreme situations, of experiencing the dangers of homelessness (Gillock & Reyes, 1999).

Finally, some students, as adolescents, don't complete homework because of mistakes:

"I've copied homework because I left my book in my locker and I didn't have time to get it before I went home and my class was literally the next period. I had a bad

(Continued)

(Continued)

grade—it was a wavering A where it was literally just 90-point something. When you're that close to getting a B you don't want to do anything wrong. If we didn't have the homework, [the teacher] would just give us a zero." (Annika, middle school student)

"There are those times when I get home at 9:00 or 10:00 at night and I have to do all my homework for the next day. And there might be just a tiny thing that I just forget. And I'm like, 'Oh my gosh, just let me see yours and then I'll just go back and study it.' But a lot of people copy and then never look back, never look at the homework again." (Joel, high school student)

All teenagers struggle with executive functioning (see, e.g., Blakemore & Choudhury, 2006). It's not easy for teenagers, in the midst of rapid physical, mental, psychological, and social changes to always be organized and remember to do, and how to do, every assignment for every class each day. When every homework assignment is included in the grade, perfectly predictable mistakes are treated as unacceptable and can compel students to correct these mistakes by copying. Plus, considering the challenges disproportionately experienced by historically underserved groups, it's reasonable that some students would need to deprioritize homework. Take a student who is homeless, or feels unsafe walking to school, or isn't sure where her next meal is coming from. Is it so surprising that she might forget to do her algebra assignment?

These quotes should also show us that extrinsic motivation isn't the solution to students not doing their homework or copying it. For students in these situations, we could make each homework assignment 10, 1000, or a million points and they still wouldn't complete it. Not doing homework has nothing to do with not having enough external incentives.

Students aren't copying because they're malicious or intentionally disrespectful; they may not even want to copy. They're doing it because they know that they'll be penalized for not doing it, and copying therefore seems to be a reasonable and expedient choice. If they can't do the homework, they figure, at least they can earn the points. Although it matters whether they learned the material when it comes to the test, whether they learned doing the homework is incidental; the priority is that they complete it.

If we knew about students' circumstances—their pressures, schedules, difficulties—we might forgive them for copying, and at times we might even agree with them. The challenge for us is that we don't know about students' circumstances and shouldn't expect them to tell us. Our implicit bias can make us see students' copying as a sign of laziness or disrespect, and with this biased assumption we punish their laziness by recording a zero when we catch them copying homework.

Considering all these reasons why students copy, and how we inadvertently encourage it by awarding points for homework, we see how including homework scores in a grade violates both parts of our Bias-Resistant pillar's Driving Principle: A student's grades do not validly reflect a student's content knowledge when she receives points that reflect someone else's knowledge (the person or website she copied from), and homework scores often reflect a student's environment over which she has limited control. Students are less likely to complete homework themselves if they have fewer resources, caregivers who have less formal education or who have limited English fluency, and if they have more environmental stress. Students have no control over these elements of their lives, and yet the successful completion of homework often depends on these elements. We've heard from several students; our last voice is from Danny, a middle school humanities teacher for six years, who remembers vividly the challenges he faced with completing homework as a student:

"When I was a high school student, homework affected me drastically. I was a long-term EL [English learner]. When I was a senior in high school, I was probably reading at a third-grade or fourth-grade level. I struggled. I had these really, really harsh English teachers who would grade me on homework, but it's like, how can I complete this homework when I just don't comprehend it? And I didn't have any adult to motivate me to do it or anybody to help me to ensure that I was doing the homework correctly because my parents were immigrants and they knew less English than I did. I would refuse to do the homework because I didn't know how, so I ended up failing a lot of my English classes in high school, didn't graduate, and had to go to adult school to finish my studies. And it's only because I wouldn't do my classwork, I wouldn't do my homework. Whose fault was it, mine, the teachers? I don't know, but it was just a horrible experience. Transitioning to not grading homework and not grading classwork was easy for me because the last thing that I want my students to experience is to fail a class for not being able to complete homework and classwork. I feel like it's not really their fault."

Without us realizing it, including homework in a grade acts often to perpetuate inequalities and the achievement gap.

The source of this problem? Like too many aspects of school, homework is framed as a measure of a student's compliance with the teacher. The teacher assigned homework; did you do it? We know that teenagers aren't eager to do what adults tell them, and so we—teachers as well as caregivers—are in a constant struggle to get students to do their homework. We dig as deeply as we can into our extrinsic motivation bag of tricks and offer points within a weighted "Homework" category. The incentive for doing homework becomes reduced to a behavioristic reward system: Do the homework the teacher assigns and you get points. If we are honest with ourselves, we know that particularly for our underperforming students, the problem with them not doing homework is not that we're not offering enough points.

For students whose lives are chaotic or who need more supports than are available to them, their not doing homework is not a problem of motivation even though we try to solve it as if it were. Mangione (2008), in "Is Homework Working?", writes, "We may think that grading homework sends a message that it isn't optional, but the fact is, the students who are most at risk will almost always opt out" (p. 615).

Students have been taught to do homework not for their own learning, but because teachers told them to do it and they awarded points to students who follow directions. As early as elementary school, students get homework points, even if it is simply completing a reading log. Throughout middle school and high school, homework is treated as an end in itself, a separate category in the grade book software, separate and independent of the primary effect of doing homework—improved performance on a summative assessment. Rarely do teachers make clear to students the relationship between homework and results.

Could students understand that homework isn't for the teacher but is for them? Could our grading practices intrinsically motivate our students to do the homework, to make them understand that if they practice—the primary purpose of homework—they will have success on summative assessments? If they understood that by doing homework they could improve their performance, would they actually choose to do or at least attempt the homework for no other reason because it helped them learn? Could we eradicate copying at the same time? How do we not disproportionally harm our vulnerable students—those who need more time to do homework or those who don't have fewer supports and resources outside the school—and who most need the practice that homework is designed to provide? This seems like a really tall order. Is it possible to have an equitable grading policy when it comes to homework?

Reframing Homework

In order to align with our Bias-Resistant pillar's Driving Principle, in which the grade validly represents what the student knows and does not reflect the student's circumstances, we must not provide or subtract points for homework. In other words, homework should not be included in the grade.

As described back in chapter 5, we know from a century of research after Skinner that though extrinsic punishments and rewards may be effective when it comes to incentivizing menial, repetitive tasks like stuffing envelopes, extrinsic motivation fails when tasks require creativity and complex thinking. Because most of us consider homework to be more intellectually demanding than stuffing envelopes and to require complex and creative thinking (at least we intend it to be), extrinsic motivation strategies are likely to fail. To motivate someone to successfully perform intellectually demanding tasks, intrinsic motivation is much more powerful and effective.

The good news is that we're not starting from square one; our students actually already understand the concept of practicing not for immediate rewards but for performance in the future. Students spend hours shooting free throws, rehearsing a dance performance or religious rituals, doing multiple rewrites of rap lyrics, or kicking goals in the backyard, all readying themselves for an improved performance in the game or concert. Those free throws in practice don't count toward their points in a game. The musical scales they practice aren't heard during the performance. The lyrics and the choreography they rehearse aren't witnessed, but students understand that if they practice, they improve their performance. We practice because we are investing in our future success. We need to help students understand how academic practice is no different.

Even with all the theoretical rationale and logical justifications, it sounds scary. "If I stop giving points for homework, no one will do it!" you worry. In other words, if there's no carrot or stick, the mule might just sit there. It's a reasonable concern, but if students entered school motivated to learn intrinsically (remember my first-grade son from chapter 3?) and we taught them to be motivated by extrinsic rewards, we can unteach them. Many middle and high school teachers have helped their students make the transition to do homework for themselves, not for the teacher, and no longer include homework scores in grades. Although this transition takes time, teachers have found that when they make the leap to not include homework in the grade—and because the twentieth century notion of extrinsic motivation is so entrenched even as it has been debunked, it can be an anxious leap—there are incredible benefits that transform learning in the classroom. Once teachers explicitly reconnect the purpose of homework—to practice and prepare for the assessment—to more successful results on the assessment, intrinsic motivation reawakens in students. You'll be shocked that you had for so long accepted and propagated a system that relied so heavily (and so quixotically) on extrinsic motivation. Jillian, a middle school math teacher for thirteen years, shares her experience:

"I've significantly lowered the percentage of what homework is worth. Before homework was worth 25% and now homework is worth 5%, but I've actually seen them do more homework this year than in the last few years. Students were just doing homework for the points and their grade, rather than doing it because it helps them. They see homework problems on the exams and they think, 'Ok, maybe I should do more of the homework not just so I can get homework points.' Now they start to realize its purpose."

Let's look at all the benefits that happen when teachers stop including homework in a grade.

Benefit 1: Students no longer have any incentive to copy. Once you stop awarding points for homework, students have no reason to rely on another person's homework or to take shortcuts. There's no extrinsic reward for the homework itself. The benefit to the student shows up on the summative assessment, and only if she does it herself. Students may continue to seek help from their classmates, but they complete homework because they see its effect on their own learning.

Benefit 2: Teachers can reallocate their time. When teachers award points for homework, they spend time every day in class and outside of class checking those homework assignments and entering scores into the grade book software. When homework isn't included in students' grades, less time is spent in class documenting who completed the homework and chastising those who didn't, and more time is allocated to teaching and learning, to attend to individual students' needs and to reteach concepts that students haven't yet mastered despite the practice opportunity. "I'm not as worried about making sure that every student gets in every piece of work," explains Sarah, a special education teacher for six years. "I can really be more focused on, 'Do you get the gist? Do you remember what we read about yesterday?' rather than focusing on 'Did you do enough worksheets?'" Outside of class, the impact can be just as large. Instead of the teacher spending hours inputting hundreds of homework grades into the grade book, she can spend more time designing curriculum and developing more engaging instruction, and even invest more time in self-care.

Benefit 3: Students learn to take responsibility for their own learning. We often justify giving points for homework on the grounds that it teaches students responsibility. But awarding points for homework is teaching compliance (I do something because someone told me to do it), not responsibility (I do something because of its relationship to my success). It also isn't true preparation for college or the professional world. Yes, sometimes we have to do things because someone in charge tells us to, but to teach this lesson in every course every day in every grade positions our schools and classrooms in the same role as those of the early twentieth century: to essentially acculturate and assimilate students to be effective manual laborers in factories, not to be college-degreed professionals. In the professional world, work done at home is not a specific and separate part of the job description, independently rewarded. Work done at home is whatever the professional deems must be completed in order to perform her best in her job—a judgment left entirely up to the professional. In college, this is generally true as well; there is no such thing as daily homework that is included in a grade.

When homework isn't included in a grade, students have to learn to (a) internalize the purpose of homework (Do I see the causal relationship between doing homework and learning?), (b) understand the tangible benefits of homework (Do I understand that by learning through homework I will be more successful on the assessment?), and (c) be able to self-assess their own level of understanding (How much practice do I need to master the content or skill?). True responsibility (what we'll call "self-regulation" in chapter 13) is to understand whether you need more practice to do well on the assessment, and if so then to do the homework, and if you don't need that practice, then to not do the homework, and then to observe the consequences. This is how we teach students responsibility—and ownership—over one's learning.

Benefit 4: We no longer "double-punish" students. In traditional practices of including homework in a grade, when a student doesn't do homework, she loses points, and when she doesn't do well on the semester assessment (which would presumably happen if she doesn't do the homework practice) she is punished twice—she loses points for not doing the homework and later loses points for incorrect answers on the assessment. This is unnecessary double punishment. When homework isn't included in the grade, students learn the purpose and value of homework. They see that by not doing the homework they are less prepared for the subsequent assessment. Two failing grades don't teach this lesson any more persuasively, and they are harder for students to recover from mathematically.

Benefit 5: We allow for different learning styles. It makes no sense in our traditional practices when a student scores high on an exam but has her grade lowered because she didn't do the homework that we thought she needed to do to score well. For that student, our belief was incorrect; the homework was *unnecessary* for her learning, and she shouldn't bear the punishment for our mistake! Whether they pay close attention in class, take their own kind of notes, or have a very good memory, we shouldn't expect or require students to learn only through homework. When homework is not included in a grade, students who do not need to complete every homework assignment in order to learn are able to succeed. We (and our students, with our help) discover what they need to do to learn.

Benefit 6: We don't penalize students for environmental factors or circumstances that prevent them from completing homework. When we don't include homework in the grade, we recognize that many students don't complete homework because of factors outside their control—limited transportation options, ill or needy family members, home responsibilities, fewer resources (technology or other support)—and we don't penalize them for those factors. Of course, they are still responsible for learning the material and successfully performing on the summative assessment, but we no longer add the unnecessary stress of homework points to lives already filled with pressure.

Benefit 7: Our feedback to students is heard and valued. We might believe that a grade based on correct answers on homework gives the student important feedback: Did I answer questions correctly? However, research has found that once we put a score or a grade on an assignment, the student is less likely to review comments or learn from that grade (Butler & Nisan, 1986). Students are concerned only with the points they are awarded, not learning. Plus, the grade on the homework functions as evaluation, not as feedback—we're being a judge, not a coach. When we don't award points or include homework in the grade, we place a greater value (and a greater likelihood that our students place value) on the feedback we give, whether that comes in the form of comments on the homework or from reviewing the home-work content in class. Not grading homework can allow and even incentivize us to give more authentic feedback rather than assume that assigning points is sufficient feedback to affect performance, which it generally isn't.

So what does this look like in practice to reestablish the severed link between home-work and assessments and dissolve the idea that doing homework has value only because the teacher assigned it? Teachers stop entering homework data in the grade book program. Others keep a record of which students completed homework assignments in a separate document. Some enter homework information in the grade book but set the homework category in the grade book to a very low weight in the overall grade, perhaps even 0 percent—in this way, it has no mathematical effect on the final grade calculation. If a student doesn't do well on an assessment, the record of her homework completion can help the student reflect and internalize the connection between the two, and it can help the teacher tell the story about why a student got the grade she did. Students can struggle with this restructuring of the grade and reframing of homework—we have taught them too well that home-work is for the teacher, and you only do it to get the points. But over time, students realize the relationship between homework and assessment, that homework is for them to practice, to make mistakes, to learn.

As I wrote at the beginning of this section, homework is an incredibly complex aspect of schools, and one that we can't possibly address in its entirety here. What we can do is focus on not including it in a grade, thereby ensuring that regardless of what the homework is, it doesn't warp the accuracy of students' grades or infect grades with inequity.

The previous chapter and this one have endorsed the exclusion of many elements of student behavior that are traditionally incorporated into the grade: extra credit, late work, cheating, and homework. With so much removed from the grade, what's left?

Grades Based Entirely on Summative Assessment Performance

If we truly believe in and want to adhere to the Bias-Resistant pillar's Driving Principle, then the only thing that gives us valid information about student's knowl-edge and minimizes our implicit biases is students' performance on assessments. If we include scores based on a student's behavior—lateness, participation, or effort—then we're including information that invites biases and subjectivity. If we include scores on formative assessments—anything that gives the student practice and the teacher feedback, such as homework and in-class assignments, we're including infor-mation while the student is in the midst of learning, including (and presumably) their mistakes. The most accurate information about what a student has learned is her demonstration of that knowledge when the learning process is complete:

her summative assessment performance. Equitable grading that is accurate and bias-resistant includes *nothing other than a student's summative assessment results.*

As we know, summative assessments have one primary purpose: to accurately measure what students know at the end of the learning process. That's why summative assessment scores usually have the largest category weight in traditional grading—usually between 40 percent and 70 percent—so the final grade is heavily influenced by summative assessment performance. But now we're suggesting that summative assessment results should count for 100 percent of a student's grade!? This may come as a bit of a shock, as too extreme, harsh, unfair, and radical. Two questions leap at us if summative assessment scores are the only source for students' grades: (1) How would this affect how teachers approach assessments? and (2) How do we prevent this emphasis on summative assessments from creating even more stress for students and inequitably punishing students who don't test well?

First, How does this affect how teachers approach assessments?

When we include only summative assessment results, a student's grades depend on the equality, range, and creativity of our assessment design. We become open, and obligated, to consider how we can expand assessment strategies so that students have a full opportunity to demonstrate what they know. We need to allow and invite students to portray their knowledge visually, linguistically, and even verbally, all in service to ensure that we accurately access a student's content understanding. Bernardo, a high school history teacher for five years, explains his approach:

"I changed my approach to assessment. I decided to give students different options for assessments. One of the things some of my students struggle with is writing. If the reason why they're not performing well is because they can't write a paragraph to inform me what they've learned, I'm giving them multiple options. A lot of students like PowerPoint so they can do a presentation. A lot of them like drawing, so they could illustrate and explain it to me. They're still showing me that they've learned the material but they don't have to be frustrated with not being able to produce. Giving students the opportunity to choose whatever assessment method they felt most comfortable with gave me much better results."

Including only summative assessment performance in the grade doesn't just free (and push) us to expand our repertoire of assessment design strategies, it also allows (and requires) us to apply our professional judgment to every assessment result, ensuring that every score we incorporate into a student's grade is an accurate reflection of her learning.

How can we be sure that our assessment results are accurate? By triangulating the results with other assessments we've given. If a student demonstrated a lower performance on a standard when we summatively assessed it via multiple choice questions than when we earlier formatively assessed it through classroom discussion, then we might try to summatively reassess the student in an alternate way. If the results of that assessment aren't the same as our first, multiple-choice assessment, we'll have to decide which assessment result is a more valid reflection of her knowledge, and why. If we find one of the assessments to be less valid, then we don't have to include those results in the student's grade. If a student demonstrates knowledge on a valid assessment, why would we include results from an assessment that reflected her knowledge inaccurately?

Of course, a student needs to be able to convey her knowledge through multiple means including a multiple-choice test, an essay, or an online assessment. The world in front of them will ask them to demonstrate knowledge in those forms and may not give them choices—but whether they know how to respond with particular test formats can and should be assessed separately from determining whether they know the content of the class. Our first priority should be to validly assess, and correctly describe, a student's level of content mastery.

What about our second concern—that when summative assessments are worth 100 percent of the grade, even with multiple types of assessment possible, students will still feel pressure and anxiety, jeopardizing the atmosphere of support and safety we want for our classroom and inequitably causing some students to perform badly? That's why equitable grading marries the emphasis of summative assessments with offering retake opportunities. As we'll discuss more in chapter 11's discussion of retakes and redos, a summative assessment makes students much less anxious if they know if they make mistakes on a summative assessment, they can have another chance to demonstrate understanding.

We see the synergy between equitable grading and our new paradigm of assessment. When the grade is comprised entirely of summative assessment scores, it becomes incumbent upon us as educators to ensure that our assessments are clearly measuring those standards and not the "noise" of confusing or biased tasks or unnecessarily challenging response formats. When students' results on these assessments are the sole source of their grades we face a healthy pressure to get assessments "right" and the opportunity to take whatever assessment strategies are appropriate to correctly ascertain a student's level of mastery. Our students spend enough cognitive load making sense of the complexity of our current world; let's use assessments as a bridge for us to access their understanding, not as a hurdle for them to convince us of that understanding. Plus, equitable grading ensures that we tightly connect our assessment and the content we taught—did we give students a chance to practice the content or skill on the homework, and if not, is it fair to ask them to demonstrate the knowledge of that content or skill on the summative assessment?

When summative assessments are worth 100 percent, teachers can be left with an empty feeling: "What do I do with all the data that I have always collected—the homework completion, the daily preparation, the quizzes, the classwork, the homework?" Does that mean that the other information—the quizzes, the class-work, the homework, coming on time, asking questions—is no longer important? Of course not! Those activities are designed specifically for students to learn, to equip them with the skills and information they need to perform successfully on your assessments. They are all means to an end, and students need to see the relationship between those means and the ends. Continue to enter it in the grade book, but in a category worth 0%. Even though homework completion, preparation, or attendance aren't included in the grade because those factors are heavily influenced by students' circumstances, that information is likely related to students' academic performance. Preserving that data can help students understand that relationship.

That information can be especially valuable when we need to tell the story of that student's achievement to a caregiver or an administrator: "Jaime received a D on his summative assessment, which means that he has not yet mastered the material. The reason for this is likely because he rarely completed his homework and came late every day." Now our grade is clear: The D was only based on what Jaime knows, but we have other data to explain why he had a weaker level of content standard mastery. It also helps Jaime make a much clearer cause–effect relationship between homework, promptness, and achievement than if we lumped it all together. He didn't get a D because he came late or because he didn't do homework or because he's incapable. He got a D because he didn't demonstrate sufficient knowledge of the content, and he can learn the content by coming on time, doing the homework, and contributing to discussions. It's a much better life lesson to learn to do things that teachers say because it will help you learn than to do things teachers say because otherwise you'll lose points. Theresa, a humanities middle school teacher for nineteen years, talks about how the accountability for not doing homework is embedded into the structured relationship between homework and tests:

"I told my students, 'As long as you're ready for the spelling test on Friday, you're good.' Did not including homework in the grade make kids just stop doing homework? No. The kids who were already doing the homework, the kids who were already studying at home, they continued doing that. It didn't change anything for the kids who weren't doing their homework either, other than to give them credit for showing what they know. If you can do well with very little studying, then you can get by with very little studying. But if you are doing poorly on the test, well, maybe we need to start studying more! There's accountability, but it's just not a daily accountability."

Increasing the category weight of a summative assessment to 100 percent is a wide river to cross for many of us, and while the preceding explanations may be persuasive to the logical side of our brains, perhaps you still remain skeptical. How will we show students that something like homework is valuable if there's no grade attached to it? It might even feel undermining: You've done so much careful and creative planning to develop engaging homework so that students do it, and now it doesn't even count? Why would students do first drafts of an essay, you think, let alone second and third drafts, if there's no grade assigned or credit awarded for them? They know from other aspects of their lives the relationship between investing in practice and realizing a successful performance. They just have never been taught that there's the same kind of relationship in school. They can actually succeed if they practice, and they won't be penalized for the mistakes they make. It's giving them more responsibility, not less, and it's giving them more supports, not less. They have to own their performance—they're not going to fail or pass because of any number of missed assignments or acting in ways the teacher doesn't like or because they were absent. They're going to succeed or fail only based on what is in their brain—what they've learned and what they show us. Nothing else. It's a classroom that rewards students based on what they know, not how they behave or what they do. Mohammed, a middle school social studies teacher for four years, found this approach had a transformative effect on struggling students:

"Some students don't have the support at home, and for all different reasons if they can't get through middle school, they're probably not going to get through high school. And if in middle school some kids don't believe that they can learn, then once they get to high school they're not going to make it. For whatever reason, those students don't do the daily homework and at the end of the quarter, they're normally screwed mathematically. But when these kids that have been failing have an intelligent conversation about things that we learned, I can say, 'Wait. You just learned exactly what we've been asking you to learn this whole time and guess what? Now you're passing this class.' And it is that simple. All of a sudden they realize that they can pass this class. And not only that, they can actually learn the information. It's so exciting to them because they normally fail. Seeing that achievement in their eyes, seeing them believe in themselves and realize that they can actually do it is great."

We're afraid that we'll be creating a pedagogical high wire for ourselves, that students will be crushed by the pressure, and that even though we'll still assign homework, students (and their caregivers) will rebel if we stop including it or behavior in the grade. These are real fears, but what's amazing is that the opposite happens, over time.

As Mohammed found, some of the most rewarding results are that students think differently about themselves, the class, and their relationship to the teacher. No longer is their role to follow every direction of the teacher—a potentially and all-too-often antagonistic relationship—but instead to work in partnership, to do the work the teacher assigns because it benefits them. If they want to succeed, they do so by learning the material—there is no longer any substitute path to success (completing credit, turning assignments in on time, or copying), and there are no longer the same subjective judgments about their participation or effort that will slow them down or boost them. Students earn a grade based on what they themselves have learned, nothing more, nothing less. It is more honest, more accurate, and more equitable than what we have traditionally done.

Grades to Teach Students, Not to Control Them

"Homework and classwork—those are very fundamental skills that we use as teachers, and our greatest currency is grades, so for me to not give grades for non-summative assignments, you're taking away my currency." (John, high school science teacher of eighteen years)

"A lot of the push back I get from colleagues is that they use grades to control behaviors. I understand that, but once you see that, you can't unsee it, so it's a matter of getting them to have that 'aha' moment where they say, 'Oh, I'm grading all this homework because I want to control how much they do or whether they do it. And once that goes away, they start to make strides.'" (Vicki, middle school teacher of twenty-seven years)

Unquestionably, when we assign 100 percent weight to summative assessments, we take away some of the teacher's traditional tools for behavior management. No longer can we incentivize students to do what we say (or as Vicki, a middle school teacher, said, to "control" student behaviors) under the threat that they'll lose or gain points. We are sending the message that their circumstances or how they're perceived is not what's recognized, but only what they know, and if the way we assess what they know doesn't accurately tap into their knowledge, then it's up to us to adjust how we find that out.

This chapter doesn't ask us to compromise our expectations for students: We want students to work collaboratively, to do their homework, to submit assignments on time, and not to cheat or copy. We just have to stop relying on our grading as a classroom management strategy, believing that grades is the only language that students can hear. The Bias-Resistant practices in this chapter and chapter 9 reestablish the relationship between behaviors and academic performance, prevent us from judging behaviors with our unavoidably biased perspectives, and support greater accuracy in our grades. Rather than constraining and limiting teachers, equitable grading actually frees and empowers. No longer do we have to spend the endless minutes and hours of checking off every homework assignment, giving a daily participation grade, or acting as handwriting detectives to determine if students are copying homework. We can focus on the craft of teaching and the assessment of learning. In our classrooms, what counts is what a student knows.

We're actually raising our standards. Under traditional grading, when students don't do homework, hand in an assignment late, or cheat, we give them a lower grade and then exempt them from learning. Under more equitable grading, we don't let students off the hook; giving students full credit for late work shows that we expect them to complete the assignment and requiring the student who cheats to redo the task shows that she doesn't get to opt out of learning.

The practices in this chapter have been about redefining the learning process for students. We're teaching that learning can happen all the time, even when it doesn't show up on a homework assignment or when a student doesn't subjectively appear to be participating. We're reestablishing the relationship between practice and performance—that the work we do in class is to prepare us for success later, that being a student means doing class assignments and learning activities not to accumulate points but because hard work now prepares you to succeed later. Kim, a high school English teacher for seventeen years, describes how her grading policies and natural consequences helped students reestablish this relationship:

"When I first stopped including homework in the grade, students at first would test it and they would not do it, thinking they could do it later. What would happen is that they'd find that they weren't prepared for the assessment at the end of the unit, and then they would realize that the homework was important for their learning. It wasn't about getting a grade or accumulating points. They saw a reason—there was an intrinsic motivation to do their homework as a result of letting them not do it."

We're teaching more honestly and equitably, and therefore giving more dignity to our students and their families by making the grade only about what a student knows. And as Kim explains, re-connecting the means of learning with its ends shifts students' motivation from external incentives (the points teachers award) to the internal drive in all of us to show academic mastery. The next three chapters introduce equitable grading practices that build students' intrinsic motivation not just as a beneficial side effect of more accurate and bias-resistant practices, but explicitly, by empowering students with hope, transparency, and agency.

Summary of Concepts

1. It is inequitable to include student performance on homework in a grade. It is unreliable (we don't know who did the homework or what assistance she accessed or received), and it reflects a student's environment and circumstances, much of which is out of her control (caregivers' education, financial access, family relationships and responsibilities). Also, if we include in a grade rewards or penalties for mistakes or incompleteness, we warp the accuracy of a grade, encourage earning points by any means necessary, and contradict our message that mistakes are necessary for learning.

2. A grade should reflect only a students' level of mastery in a subject, which means that all formative work (homework, classwork) and behavior (punctuality,

participation, effort) should be excluded, leaving only a student's performance on summative assessments. This compels us to think more broadly about summative assessment design and the evidence of student knowledge to ensure that students have the means to demonstrate their knowledge. It also gives us the opportunity to reassert the purpose of homework: for students to practice and prepare for summative performance, and not for students to comply with the teacher for points.

Questions to Consider

1. Look back at Tangela and Isabel in chapter 4. If summative assessments were the only element in the grade, what grade would each receive? What are the implications? What message do we send each of them? How might it change how they and their caregivers think about each student's progress? How might it change how each would respond moving forward?

2. Ask some middle school or high school students about why they copy homework, or what gets in the way of students completing homework. What is more important to you—that students do as much homework (and presumably, learning) as they can themselves, or that they copy it so that they get the points? What would need to change to explicitly communicate this priority?

3. For Teachers: Look at the grade book for one of your classes. Compare students' test or summative assessment scores with their homework scores. For which students are their summative assessments higher than their homework scores? If a student learned the material, how much does it matter if the student turned in homework? For which students is it reversed (homework scores are higher than summative assessment scores)? If a student turned in homework but did poorly on assessments, what does it suggest about whether homework served its purpose (or who might have done that student's homework)?

4. For Teachers: Try this simple, risk-free experiment: Print out a copy of the grade book for one class of students. (Do this in the evening or when you're confident that students will not be accessing their grades.) Change the percentage weights, lowering the weight for homework and participation categories, and raising it for summative assessments. Print out the altered version, and then return the weights to their earlier percentages. Compare the final grades. Under which weighting system do final grades describe students' levels of content mastery more accurately? Which system's final grades describe students' content knowledge less accurately? For which students (or what kinds of students)? Does this change your opinion about how much to weigh summative assessments?

CHAPTER 11

Practices That Support Hope and a Growth Mindset

- **Minimum Grading and 0–4 Scale (A Revisit)**
- **Renaming Grades**
- **Retakes and Redos**

In this chapter, we will answer the following questions:

1. How can we apply contemporary understanding of motivation to how we grade?

2. Why are retakes and redos so important to the learning process, and how can our grading practices accommodate them?

3. How can we implement a retake and redo process that overcomes logistical challenges and our own reticence?

4. How does altering technical elements of our grading (category weights, percentage scale, the naming of grades) affect student motivation?

Pillar #3: Motivation

> *Driving Principle*: **The way we grade should motivate students to achieve academic success, support a growth mindset, and give students opportunities for redemption.**

Doctors a decade ago were advised by national health organizations to pay much more attention to the pain that patients were experiencing and to alleviate that pain. The understanding, based on research at the time, was that OxyContin and other related opiate drugs were not addictive. Consequently, the use of pain medications ballooned, and doctors were finding that they needed to prescribe increasingly greater amounts of pain medication to help patients "manage" their pain. Researchers learned only later that the pain medication was not only addictive but actually *decreased* patients' tolerance for pain; the level of pain patients could withstand after taking the medication was far less than the level of pain they had been able to tolerate before taking the medication. In other words, doctors were using a practice—prescribing pain medication—that they thought was helpful, but that was inadvertently causing patients to have less pain tolerance as well as more addiction, therefore requiring doctors to continue, and increase, the use of the practice.

A practice (prescribing OxyContin) based on a faulty understanding (people's pain could be alleviated without causing addiction) inadvertently resulted in behaviors (patients developed less tolerance for pain and therefore felt greater pain) that not only reinforced the faulty understanding but that justified continued use of that practice even though it actually was harmful. As we'll see, many of our traditional grading practices related to student motivation are similar: they are self-justifying even though they are based on incorrect assumptions and harmful.

Building on our two pillars of equitable grading practices—that they are accurate and bias-resistant—in the next three chapters we'll focus on our third pillar: that equitable grading practices are also motivational, particularly for historically underserved students.

Our Understanding of Motivation

Motivating students is one of the most important elements of a teacher's work. Compulsory education laws get students in the seats, but we need students to engage intellectually with what happens there. The "horses" are led to water, but we need them to drink. We use many different strategies to motivate them to work in our class (and presumably, to learn). Some of our strategies are about carrots and sticks (punishments and rewards), some are interpersonal (persuasion, shame, encouragement), and some are pedagogical and instructional (offering more choices, using hands-on activities, choosing relevant curriculum). We know that grades can be a powerful motivator for many students. For some students, all they need to hear is that an assignment will be worth points or will affect their grade, and they respond. For others, those incentives, and even the possibility of a failing grade, can seem to fall on deaf ears. What do we know about motivation, and how can a better understanding lead to more effective and equitable grading practices? Could it be that we, like the doctors prescribing OxyContin, justifying a false belief about motivation by reinforcing it ourselves, inadvertently making it harder for our students to break the habit of extrinsic motivation and become intrinsically motivated?

To begin, let's review what we've learned in the last century about what motivates students to learn. What is motivation? How does it work, and what are those implications for our classrooms generally and for our grading in particular?

Urdan and Schoenfelder (2006) describe motivation as "a complex part of human psychology and behavior that influences how individuals choose to invest their time, how much energy they exert in any given task, how they think and feel about the task, and how long they persist at the task" (p. 332). It's more than "engagement," which is about a student's involvement and attention to the task at hand. Motivation is about a student's willingness and attitude with which they approach a task.

As mentioned in chapter 2, one of the most well-known and influential researchers of motivation is B. F. Skinner. Drawing on the work of early behaviorist psychologists such as Pavlov and Watson, Skinner in the 1930s and 1940s "radical behaviorism" suggests that motivation is primarily affected by external reinforcement, also called "operant conditioning." For example, if a student is rewarded for coming punctually to class, she'll be more motivated to repeat that behavior in the future. Conversely, if that behavior is not reinforced—she is not rewarded for coming on time or punished for coming late to class—she will be less motivated to be on time in the future. Much of Skinner's work is premised on the idea that humans (like all animals) are motivated by external reinforcements. In the learning context, these external reinforcements can be concrete (stickers and stamps), less concrete (praise or phone calls home), or more symbolic (honor roll). Behaviorism conceives of a cause and effect relationship between a human action and the reward or punishment: I do something and there is some external response that informs my future actions.

By the 1970s, research showed that this framework oversimplified motivation, and in some cases was downright wrong. I don't just do something because something outside of me encouraged or discouraged me from doing it. I also can be intrinsically motivated—engaging in a behavior or activity because it interests me or I enjoy it. One of the most cited articles in motivation literature was a study conducted by Lepper, Greene, and Nisbett (1973), in which they observed preschool classrooms to identify children who liked to draw, and then individually invited each of those children to draw the researchers a picture. However, the researchers changed one element depending on a random assignment of each of the students into three groups:

- "Expected reward" group: The researchers created a "Good Player" certificate and told the children that if they drew a picture they would receive the award.

- "Unexpected reward" group: The researchers did not mention the award at the outset, but at the end of the session, the researchers handed a "Good Player" certificate to the children who had decided to draw.

- "No reward" group: The researchers invited the children to draw, didn't mention the award at the outset, and didn't give them one at the end of the session even if the children drew something.

Two weeks later, the researchers observed the students in their preschool classrooms during a drawing activity and compared their interest in drawing to what it had been earlier. The students in the "unexpected reward" and "no reward" groups drew just as much and with the same quality, but the children in the "expected reward" group showed a significant decrease in interest in drawing and the quality of their drawing was significantly below the quality of the other groups. The promise and contingency of a reward in the future—not simply receiving a reward (which the second group received)—reduced students' intrinsic interest.

At the time, this finding was very controversial. After all, this threatened what had seemed an established fact: offering rewards is an effective motivator. The researchers replicated the results in several other studies with children, and then other researchers made similar findings with adults. In 1999, Deci, Ryan, and Koestner reviewed 128 studies on motivation over nearly three decades and confirmed the results:

> "[T]angible rewards tend to have a substantially negative effect on intrinsic motivation. . . . When institutions—families, schools, businesses, and athletic teams, for example—focus on the short-term and opt for controlling people's behavior, they may be having a substantially negative long-term effect." (p. 659)

That conclusion is now established fact among psychologists and education researchers: Contingent extrinsic rewards—do this and you'll get that—undermine intrinsic motivation.

Of course, even if this is true (and it is, replicated and reinforced in study after study), maybe we are willing to sacrifice some of our students' intrinsic motivation in order for them to complete tasks, or to behave properly, or to do their best work. What is the impact of extrinsic, contingent rewards on these elements of learning?

Research has found that extrinsic motivation can encourage people to adhere to specific, simple-to-control behaviors (such as providing stickers to children who stay seated) and can increase productivity for rote, formulaic tasks (such as stuffing envelopes). When the task requires creativity and expansive complex thinking (one of the key distinctions between the deep thinking required of our contemporary curriculum standards and the less complex cognitive loads of the standards during the No Child Left Behind era), extrinsic motivation *lowers* performance (Amabile, 1996; Kaufman & Sternberg, 2006). Extrinsic, contingent rewards narrows people's focus on the short-term and immediate goal instead of allowing their brains the freedom and flexibility to be creative, original, and to imagine alternative possibilities. In several experiments in which people were asked to solve complex problems or complete creative tasks, those who were offered money for their work were less successful in solving the problems or in producing high-quality work than those to whom no extrinsic reward was offered. Those who were motivated entirely intrinsically were more creative and successful in completing complex tasks.

Extrinsic motivation has also been found to also increase unethical behavior. Extrinsic motivation doesn't just narrow our focus so that we are less creative; contingent rewards encourage us to see only a short-term goal, a target that we pursue as directly as possible, even via shortcuts. Note countless examples of businesses that sacrifice integrity in order for a financial reward: Wells Fargo's opening new accounts for customers without their permissions comes to mind, and we're all familiar with how financial rewards for increases in our students' standardized test scores can lead teachers, administrators, and even superintendents to cheat.

In sum, extrinsic rewards may reap short-term results but can smother intrinsic motivation and its benefits and cause undesirable side effects. Daniel Pink (2011), in *Drive: The Surprising Truth About What Motivates Us*, captures the implications of the decades of research on motivation:

> In environments where extrinsic rewards are most salient, many people work only to the point that triggers the reward—and no further. So, if students get a prize for reading three books, many won't pick up a fourth, let alone embark on a lifetime of reading—just as executives who hit their quarterly numbers often won't boost earnings a penny more, let alone contemplate the long-term health of their company. Likewise, several studies show that paying people to exercise, stop smoking, or take their medicines produces terrific results at first—but the healthy behavior disappears once the incentives are removed. However, when contingent rewards aren't involved, or when incentives are used with the proper deftness, performance improves and understanding deepens. Greatness and nearsightedness are incompatible. Meaningful achievement depends on lifting one's sights and pushing toward the horizon. (p. 57)

Grades are clearly an extrinsic, contingent reward—if you perform well in the course you'll get a higher grade. Grades also function as an extrinsic, contingent punishment—perform well in the course or you will get a failing grade. Even though we may believe that learning is an internally motivated endeavor, our observations and experiences have led many of us to believe that most of our students need extrinsic motivation to learn and that grades effectively motivate students to perform better. We've seen how students on the cusp of failure rally to avoid repeating a course, and how students will commit to extra studying and seek more support so they can earn a high grade on an important exam. Is there research specifically on the effects of grades as a motivation tool?

Grades and Their Impact on Student Motivation

Research suggests that the students who are motivated by grades as a reward see them as a positive recognition of their success (Guskey & Bailey, 2001; Marzano, 2000). In other words, some students will work hard to get the grade they want and to avoid the grades they don't want (Haladyna, 1999). However, Docan (2006), in his summary of the research, suggests that we may be sacrificing long-term rewards for short-term results, even when students earn high grades:

> A wide variety of research demonstrates that extrinsic reinforcers, such as grades, work to decrease intrinsic motivation and interfere with the process and quality of learning. Unfortunately, grades may distract from the learning process and focus attention on the final result—that of getting a grade. Additional research demonstrates that learners who are motivated extrinsically are less likely to experience positive emotions such as enjoyment and are more likely to use a negative emotional tone, such as displaying frustration in the classroom. Even "good" grades can create unmotivated students. Cleary discovered that students who were rewarded with good grades became apprehensive writers. Moreover, Benware and Deci discovered that learners motivated extrinsically are often passive information processors. This passive approach ultimately may discount what a student learns, while simultaneously favor the importance of getting good grades. (p. 23)

We've witnessed this among some of our most "successful" students. They care deeply about the grade, but only about the grade. They (and sometimes their parents and caregivers) carefully monitor their grade, nowadays so easy to do on our grade book software's student portal, vigilantly ensuring that they complete the necessary tasks and accumulate the required points so that they achieve the A. We bemoan that many students sound as if they are more interested in the grade than in learning. Ezra, a high school student, put it succinctly: "Either you're trying to learn, or you're just trying to get the good grade." He continued,

"A lot of students are doing exactly what they need to do just for the grade and not really learning anything. They're not really absorbing the information but they're just doing what they need to do to get that good grade, throwing out whether 'I need to learn it,' or 'I should learn it.' A lot of students will cheat or just kind of just learn the basics just so they can barely pass the test, just to get the good grade, instead of learning it and kind of taking it in and saying, 'This is how you do it, this is how you can expand upon it.' That part is shut off, is cut off, in a lot of situations."

For successful students, the extrinsic motivation of grades yields attitudes and behaviors that we don't want in our students, but we can console ourselves that at least they're getting the grades they want, successfully navigating the schools and reaping postsecondary rewards.

The flip side to high grades as an extrinsic reward is using low grades as an extrinsic punishment. Many of us assign Fs believing (or perhaps merely hoping) that those Fs will motivate struggling students to work harder, to improve their behaviors and approach to learning. These students often have weaker education backgrounds, who come to our classes often already behind academically and with a history of struggle in school. And when they get an F (for a low performance, a missing assignment, or wrong behavior) and their next performance has not sufficiently improved, we give them another F, presumably to reiterate their subpar performance and to motivate them to improve. Each time we must think that the most recent F will be the one that finally spurs the student to turn around her performance.

As we might suspect, no research supports the idea that assigning low grades as punishment encourages students to try harder or do better (Dueck, 2014; Guskey, 2000; Guskey & Bailey, 2001; Marzano, 2000). In fact, Guskey (2008) writes, "Instead of prompting greater effort, low grades often cause students to withdraw from learning. To protect their self-images, many students regard the low grade as irrelevant or meaningless. Others may blame themselves for the low grade but feel helpless to improve" (p. 14).

We've seen this happen in our classrooms: A student who has received several Fs balls up and throws away each subsequent failed test paper or "loses" a progress report. She doodles throughout the class, or becomes a greater discipline challenge, or may simply stop coming to class. We know one reason why. As we learned in chapter 7, once a student gets a series of Fs in traditional grading, it can become mathematically impossible for them to pass the class, much less to excel. But beyond the mathematical consequence, each failing grade has a much more powerful impact on motivation—it erodes it. Students lose the confidence that success is possible for them. Geneva Gay (1995), one of the pioneers of culturally responsive pedagogy, describes how with each failure, students have less confidence in their ability to succeed, and each failure "confirms what they already know about the task—they can't do it."

Though students' external behaviors may suggest disinterest and dismissal of their low grade (which can infuriate us even more), it often is actually a coping mechanism to protect themselves from profound fear and self-doubt. In the face of low grades, students can resort to "self-protection," seeking to preserve a sense of self-worth and resist the deep implications of academic failure:

> *Despite attempts at self-presentation and the importance of appearing "able" in the eyes of others, self-protecting students seem unable to escape their own fears that they lack the ability to avert failure should they invest the effort necessary to succeed.*

The fact that helplessness, self-handicapping, truancy and disengagement were all associated with a heightened fear of failure suggests that while these behaviors may appear to be the product of not caring enough, they may in fact be consequences of caring too much about the prospect of failure and what it means. . . . It is largely assumed that parents and educators can control student effort by rewarding achievement and punishing the indifferent. However, this basic policy of intensification may only make matters worse, if it increases fear of failure among students who do not believe they are capable of succeeding. (De Castella, Byrne, & Covington, 2013, p. 38)

These are the students who are absent on the day of the exam, who come too late to participate in activity, who "forget" their homework at school, who shrug off when they get answers correct, or who accept failure through passive resistance, such as putting a head down during a test. They protect their low self-esteem and manage their fear of failure by not engaging or risking that failure, and in so doing undermine any likelihood of success. When grades are a pervasive part of a classroom culture, students with less confidence in their academic knowledge often dare not even try for fear that they will not receive the extrinsic rewards of a passing or high grade and that their inferior performance will be revealed (Urdan & Shoenfelder, 2006).

Fear of failure also can drive students to search for other sources of self-worth. They may reject school altogether, make excuses for their failure, or focus on other ways to find, and define, their success—through extracurricular activities, sports, or socially. "In this way, 'failure accepting' students may in effect be downplaying and 're-defining' their failures in a way that is less threatening to self-esteem" (De Castella et al., 2013, p. 39). It makes sense: If I have experienced repeated failing grades, it's pretty clear that the classroom is not the place where I can succeed, so I look for other places where I can excel, where I can "fit." Students with a history of low grades but who are required to continue attending school until graduation or they "age out" can feel they have no choice but to resign themselves to endure, painfully, the academic elements of school.

Knowing all this—that the research clearly shows that grades as extrinsic, contingent rewards and punishments limit learning and have huge deleterious effects on lower-performing students—why do we continue to use grades as contingent rewards and punishments?

I offer some hypotheses:

1. Teacher education has not caught up with psychology's current understanding of motivation theory. We were never taught anything different than what was used on us, so not only do we not have any other strategies to motivate them than extrinsic techniques, we don't even know that we should be considering anything other than those techniques.

2. Extrinsic motivation techniques continue to be used in school because although our curriculum and rhetoric espouse deeper and more creative thinking, our

schools actually want to propagate the Industrial Revolution's interest in preparing the majority of our students to perform less complex tasks. We *want* students to respond to extrinsic, short-term rewards and aren't interested in all students being successful or optimizing their creativity and deeper thinking.

3. Teachers need to exert power where they have it. Guskey (2009) writes, *"Secondary teachers may perceive that they have little direct influence over the privileges students most value or the punishments they most fear. . . . But teachers do control grades, and grades can indirectly influence those privileges and punishments. . . . The threat of a zero and the resulting low grade, therefore, allows teachers to impose their will on students who otherwise may be indifferent to the teachers' demands."* (p. 12)

Whatever the explanation, we have to change the way we think about the relationship between student motivation and our grading. Although we may ascribe a student's lack of motivation to immutable personality characteristics or weak parenting, we may be witnessing how students who have experienced repeated failure across years and subjects cope within an extrinsic contingent reward and punishment structure. Rather than describing a student as "unmotivated," it may be more accurate to say we have a grading system in which they are "motivated to fail" (De Castella et al., 2013). After all, those students who are the farthest behind and must work the hardest to succeed have the least incentive to do so when the schools have used the grading system to describe them as failures. The experience of repeated failure leads many students to cope with that failure in ways that nearly guarantee future failures—a self-reinforcing cycle—unless we change how they experience grading. And our successful students' experiences with consistently high grades leads many to be motivated by points and to have little compunction to cheat and copy, and to experience harmful consequences to their mental and physical health—the complete opposite of what we want learning to be—unless we also change how *they* experience grading.

A few authors, such as Alfie Kohn (1995), have rejected grades in their entirety. In *Punished by Rewards*, he exhorts schools to eliminate all extrinsic motivation tools, including grades, and in "The Case Against Grades" (2011), he writes, "We have to be willing to challenge the conventional wisdom, which in this case means asking not how to improve grades but how to jettison them once and for all" (p. 33). Some schools and colleges are persuaded by his case and the research, and have the political capital, financial freedom, and the willing family and postsecondary communities to switch to grades that are narrative or simply Pass/Fail.

But for the rest of us, A–F course grades are here to stay. We have to figure out how to reduce the impact of grades as a contingent, extrinsic reward and refocus students on learning. For our struggling students with repeated failure in school (and whose families for generations have experienced a history of academic failure), it becomes our moral imperative to stop using grades as punishment and instead to reframe and reemploy them to give more students a sense of self-efficacy, endless capacity, and hope. As Stiggins (2005) writes,

Procedures that permitted (perhaps even encouraged) some students to give up in hopelessness and to stop trying must now be replaced by others that promote hope and continuous effort. In short, the entire emotional environment surrounding the prospect of being evaluated must change, especially for perennial low achievers. (p. 65)

The next three chapters describe grading practices that are not only accurate and bias-resistant but motivate all students to succeed—not just the ones who have performed successfully in the past—based on our contemporary understanding of motivation and learning. In this chapter, we'll explore practices that support hope and a growth mindset by allowing and promoting revision, redemption, and relearning. In chapter 12 we'll then address practices that "lift the veil" on how to succeed by making the path to success transparent, clear, and attainable. Finally, in chapter 13 we'll describe how equitable grading and assessment practices can build students' "soft skills" even when the evaluation of these skills are not included in the grade.

Let's divide our Motivational Pillar's Driving Principle—**The way we grade should motivate students to achieve academic success, support a growth mindset, and give students opportunities for redemption**—into its components.

At first glance, there seems to be something hypocritical here. After challenging the way that traditional grading emphasizes extrinsic motivation, we now want grades, and external reinforcement, to be motivating? Yes and no. Equitable grades motivate, but they motivate in ways that are quite different than the traditional motivation of receiving 5 points for each homework assignment. As we discussed in chapter 10, when we reward students with 5 points for completing the homework assignment or bringing their notebook to class, we're rewarding the means to academic success, but when we reward students with a high grade, we're rewarding the ends. Equitable grading transforms our external motivation from short term and immediate to a motivation that is longer term. We're providing space for students to internalize the motivation to do the necessary steps in order to ultimately have academic success.

We also want our grading to support a growth mindset so students understand grades as a temporary description of a student's level of mastery in a subject, not something that is a static definition of who a student is. We want to counter the "I'm a D student in math" fixed mindset. Building on our earlier discussions of ensuring mathematical accuracy, we want students to see that errors and incorrect understandings aren't etched in stone and do not consign them to low grades. Instead, in equitable grading, mistakes and low scores can be corrected and grades can be updated as students gain competence. High grades are always within reach of every student, even if she makes mistakes along the way.

We'll begin by examining the research on mistakes in learning and transition to the equitable grading and assessment practices that dislodge students from fixed mindsets and that ensure that success is always attainable. We'll see how equitable grading needs to be accurate, bias-resistant, and motivational—qualities that work together to nourish one of the most important keys for learning: hope.

The Role of Mistakes in Learning

Whenever I talk with teachers about the learning process, they all emphasize the importance of mistakes. Not only are mistakes acceptable and likely, they say, but mistakes are *necessary* for learning. Without mistakes, they assert, learning can't happen. Teachers want to create "safe" classrooms, where students take risks and feel comfortable making mistakes.

And yet, as we saw in chapter 7, under our traditional grading practices, mistakes often consign a student to failure. A student is terribly weak in a subject, for whatever reason, and earns a 20% in the first quarter of a semester-long course. Under traditional grading, in which the final semester grade is calculated as an average of the first quarter grade and the second quarter grade, there is virtually no second quarter grade that would earn a passing grade for the semester. Only a 100 percent grade for the second quarter would yield a passing semester grade (average of 20% and 100% is 60%, or a D-). The student with a 45 percent first quarter could mathematically earn a C (70%) for the semester if she has a second quarter grade of a 95 percent, though it is unrealistic: Not many students can so drastically improve their performance so quickly. The student is well aware of this unlikelihood and sees no path toward redeeming her low grade of first quarter.

A student who has an unexcused absence on the day of an exam isn't allowed to take the exam when she returns, a student with too many errors receives a failing grade on a project, and a student who fails a quiz or two has to score that much better on the next unit. Teachers are familiar with the psychological and behavior trends of many struggling students: They begin the year ready and open, but every mistake and failure chips away at their openness and engagement. With each mistake or failure, the mathematical likelihood of success wanes, and each student's reservoir of psychological resilience is drained. These students become less likely to volunteer, or come to class less often, or leave larger portions of assignments blank. For the students who have experienced unredeemable failure in school for many years and in many ways, the half-life of their engagement can be astonishingly brief. Teachers become frustrated and angry when students with low averages refuse to participate or are disruptive, but when prior mistakes and failures render success impossible, what would we expect? Teachers never give up on students and do their best to find powerful ways to motivate students by creating hands-on, relevant, and creative lessons, but it all may be for naught if we don't motivate them by how we grade. We need to show them that no matter where they start, and however many times they fail, success is possible. Otherwise we take away hope.

What would it look like to support hope and redemption in our classrooms through our grading practices? We've described several already as representing other equitable grading pillars. For example, we would accept that mistakes will occur in the learning process and precedent to success, so would consider a student's most recent performance (chapter 8), we wouldn't lower a grade for cheating or copying but would identify alternative consequences (chapter 9), and would exclude homework from being included in the grade calculation, thereby making homework and other formative assessments about practice and mistake-making (chapter 10). Mistakes would be normalized, with a message of "Of course you're going to make mistakes. You're learning—what else would you expect to happen?" Teachers would solicit not only the right answer but would request students to share out their mistakes: "Who wants to share and explain their mistake? Who else made a similar mistake? What did the mistake teach you?" Students would be asked to share their mistakes with each other: "Share with your partner the mistake you made on the assignment that was most helpful to your learning."

There would be an overarching message: Mistakes are necessary for learning, and making them doesn't limit your possibilities for success, or worse, ensure your failure. Mistakes lead to redemption. Mistakes are not only normal for learning, but they *lead to success*. Mistakes aren't the end of learning—they are the prelude to learning. Teachers who use these practices give struggling students more hope, reinforce a growth mindset, and build stronger relationships with them, all of which motivate students to persevere toward success. This chapter will address three additional grading practices that build hope and a growth mindset by allowing mistakes to lead to success: minimum grading, changing the grading scale, and allowing retakes and redos.

Minimum Grading (A Revisit)

In chapter 7, we addressed the mathematical inaccuracy of traditional grading, showing that the 0–100 scale is disproportionately oriented toward failure. With 59 points representing failure—nearly two-thirds of our scale—it's easy for students to get overwhelmed, dispirited, and resigned when their early performance is below passing. As explained in that chapter, one way that teachers, schools, and even entire districts have provided more hope is to overcome the mathematical unsoundness of the 100-point scale by establishing a "minimum grade" of a 50 percent as the lowest percentage a student can earn. Even though that grade "floor" of 50 percent is still an F (50%–59%), it allows students to recover from early failure. A student with a first quarter grade of 40 percent doesn't need to have a transformational (and highly unlikely) turnaround in quarter 2 to pass the semester course; they merely need to improve from an F (50%) to a C (70%) to earn a 60 percent D—a still difficult, but much more attainable, achievement. The minimum 50 percent actually corrects the deflation that occurs when we use the 100-point scale. A 50 percent is still an F; it just makes the distance to raise a grade from F to D the same as to raise a C to a B. We learned about how the minimum grade makes the 0–100 scale more mathematically sound.

Now that we're exploring our Motivational pillar, what is the effect of the minimum grade on motivation?

It's worth revisiting chapter 7's Carifio and Carey's (2013) study, the largest study to have researched the impact of minimum grading. As a refresher, researchers studied a large Massachusetts district that established a 50 percent as the minimum grade a student could earn in the first quarter of a semester-long course. They analyzed the district's 343,000 grades awarded to nearly 11,000 students over a seven year period. Contrary to the fears of teachers, widespread and undeserved passing did not occur. Only a tiny subset of the students who received the 50 percent minimum at the quarter (140 per year out of 50,000) passed the course at the semester. These students who benefitted from the policy were found by the researchers to have had early and "intermittent" performance failures—who perhaps had some significant short-term challenges that interfered with their learning. Because of the minimum grading policy, this small subgroup of unique students were able to overcome early failure, which would have been impossible under the traditional system.

Rather than put all failing students in the position of "hopeless failure," the district gave them hope. The researchers found,

> *Minimum grading actually empowers teachers and schools rather than disempowers them, as it lessens, dampens out and neutralizes most of the negative aspects of grades and grading in school learning and in the behavioral processes while creating a climate of caring, hope and support, particularly for those students whose growth and development will most probably always be an intermittent and somewhat chaotic process and path. Minimum grading is a first step and key component in creating a culture of compassion and caring in a learning organization, classroom or school. (p. 24)*

Minimum grading does something larger than compensate for the mathematical unsoundness of our 0–100-point scale. It motivates students by offering them an opportunity at redemption; it communicates to them that success is possible even when there is early failure. And it can provide the same opportunities whether we apply to a quarter of a two-quarter course, for the first half of a quarter-long course, or to any and all assignments.

Before moving on, it's worth sharing one more fascinating finding of the researchers that wasn't mentioned in chapter 7. The researchers compared the state test scores of the 1,159 students who benefited from minimum grading to the state test scores of students who passed both quarters of the semester (in other words, who didn't need the minimum grade policy) and found that the students who received minimum grades *outperformed their peers who had not received the minimum grades*! Could it be that some of our students who have early failure and give up because of the 100-point scale actually have higher academic potential than we realize?

In my experience, despite how much this all resonates with teachers, they still worry about motivation—that the 50 percent creates a perverse incentive for students to opt out of the coursework because a minimum score gives students "something for nothing." Teachers are surprised when the minimum grade of 50 percent doesn't lead to widespread unearned passing or to students no longer working. In fact, often the opposite happens:

"I took a little while to not put zeroes in [the grade book]. I realized minimum grading didn't really change student motivation. I didn't lose kids. They were still working for me because they were sitting at a 53% or 55% or something, and I had fewer discipline issues. That was the biggest eye-opener for me." (Anne, high school world languages teacher of twenty-three years)

The minimum grade is not inflation, and it's not teaching students to be unmotivated. It's restoring mathematical accuracy and it motivates struggling students because it preserves the possibility of redemption and success.

By contrast, using low grades as punishment doesn't motivate students; it erodes their motivation. Students with low grades feel helpless and disempowered, blame themselves, and lose hope (e.g., De Castella et al., 2013; Guskey, 2011). A response of helplessness is in fact a very rational response when a series of zeros can render the grade unsalvageable. As Natalia, a middle school student, explained, "I have a lot of Fs, and in classes like math, I'm like, 'I'm not going to be able to get my grade up,' so I just kind of quit toward the end of first quarter."

Renaming Grades

As explained back in chapters 2 and 3, we use abstract symbols—the A–F scale or numbers—to describe student achievement because it has helped us to easily describe students and efficiently organize and sort them.

Here's an example of how a middle school sought to increase motivation by renaming the levels of performance in its grading scale. Rather than use a 0–4 or A–F scale, the school titled its levels as the following:

- Exceeding Standards

- Meeting Standards

- Approaching Standards

- Not Yet Met Standards

- Insufficient Evidence

Replacing letters and numbers with short descriptors gives the teacher and the school the opportunity to make their expectations and their beliefs about student learning more explicit for students. They can dispel some of the baggage and abstract symbolism of letter and number grades, and by doing so, can motivate students to look at their performance and themselves differently.

What were formerly the C and D level of performances are "Approaching" and "Not Yet Met"; the underperforming student is assumed to be in an active process of eventual success. Note also that in this school, missing or incomplete assignments or assessments result not in an F; the lowest grade isn't really "low" at all. "Insufficient Evidence" connotes that a description of achievement is not possible because the student did not submit work or was absent during a summative assessment. As opposed to the message a teacher sends when they assign a zero or F, this grade communicates that the teacher is currently unable to ascertain whether the student met the standard, and therefore the student receives no grade rather than an inaccurate grade. The motivating message is that the student has more to share, that more is possible.

In most grading software programs, teachers can substitute abbreviations for the traditional letter grades. For example, in the example above, the school has abbreviated the level names with the letters E (Exceeding Standards), M (Met Standards), A (Approaching Standards), N (Not Yet Met Standards), and I (Insufficient Evidence). Like all changes to traditional grading, this renaming of grades requires support, communication, and education of students and families. When necessary to communicate student grades for transcripts or external reporting, the school can easily convert the descriptors to letters or numbers. Until it's necessary to convert to the traditional "language" of grades, many schools have found that the seemingly cosmetic change from the letters of grades bolsters the school's internal culture of a growth mindset in which *every* student is on a trajectory toward eventual academic success.

Retakes and Redos

Learning depends on mistakes, but only when there's a mechanism to review mistakes and an opportunity to correct them. Students must fix their errors and give it another try until they succeed, which means we have to offer them that next try, those additional learning opportunities that come when students retake or redo an assessment. As we'll see, students are motivated to keep learning if we let them—if they have the chance to redeem themselves and show improved performance. May, a high school world languages teacher for twenty years, was surprised at how her students responded to retakes, when she gave them hope:

"I used to think I wouldn't see a lot of progress in students who get low grades, but by allowing them to redo as many times as they wanted, they actually had the confidence to come back and think, 'Oh. I could actually get a good grade in this class.' They're willing to put in more effort because as they redo tests they're seeing that they can do the work. They seem to respond more positively to the learning process. They're not giving up."

From my work with hundreds of teachers, retakes raise many questions—theoretical, technical, and even psychological. We'll start with some approaches that I've found teachers frequently use, and then address some concerns that teachers often raise.

Retakes: Frequent Approaches

What Does a "Retake" Mean?

A student, after she's taken an assessment and receives the results, is allowed another opportunity to demonstrate her understanding.

What Circumstances Would Justify a Retake?

When a student performs poorly on an assessment, there likely are three possible causes:

1. *She had some interfering event or condition that impeded her from performing her best.* For example, if she comes to school ill on the day of the test or was ill the night before, she is unlikely to accurately demonstrate her knowledge. If she is experiencing a challenging or traumatic situation outside the school, such as her parents' divorce, or gunfire, or an ill younger sibling who was up all night, her low performance on the assessment will mask her true understanding. In these cases, the retake, if it occurs after the interfering health condition or difficult situation is over, permits the student to demonstrate her accurate level of content mastery.

2. *The format or design of the assessment itself impeded the student from communicating her knowledge.* When an assessment has confusing syntax, unnecessarily complex sentence structures, is too narrowly tailored to a single learning style, or has an error, the retake gives the student as well as the teacher a second chance to accurately assess a student.

3. *The student inadequately prepared or had weak understanding.* Retakes allow students who learn more slowly or need more support to continue learning. For them, the assessment may simply have come too soon and measured their knowledge prematurely. Remember the four students in chapter 8 with different learning trajectories (see page 97)? We established that rewarding students for the speed at which they learn is inequitable because some students start with a stronger education background or receive more support than others. Not all students can learn at the rate we teach them; students learn on different timelines and with different trajectories, and some will need to make more mistakes than others in their learning.

What Score on an Assessment Qualifies a Student for a Retake?

When teachers initially try this practice, some allow retakes only for students who fail or who score below a C level. Those students are most in need of a retake, teachers reason.

But this policy is problematic: What if a student who failed on the first assessment scores a B- on the retake? It doesn't seem right for her to receive a higher score than the student who earned a C initially? A more fundamental question is: *Why would we tell our lowest performing students that they can continue learning through the retake process but deny that opportunity to their higher-performing peers?* Every student should have the chance to continue learning from her mistakes and to show her improved understanding. If a student who scored a B on the initial assessment wants to learn from her mistakes and demonstrate a higher level of content mastery, who are we to stop her? Any and all students should have the opportunity to retake a summative assessment.

Should There Be Retakes on Everything, or for Only Certain Assignments?

Certainly, one could allow redos for formative assessments such as homework, but most teachers constrain the retakes to summative assessments because the logistics of allowing retakes for formative as well as summative assessments can be overwhelming. A summative assessment by definition occurs at the end of the student's learning, after all the practice, support, and intervention has occurred and is completed. (When teachers include only summative assessments in the grade, an equitable grading practice explained in chapter 10, this system becomes moot.)

Let's approach the question of what a student should be able to retake from another angle: When should a teacher stop a student's learning? We might reasonably respond that a teacher should never stand in the way of students continuing to learn. When we give a retake opportunity, a student who showed her learning on a summative assessment and otherwise would have ended her learning then gets to continue learning. Her summative assessment thereby becomes a formative assessment that gives her feedback so she can learn from her mistakes. The retake is now the summative assessment. Whether an assessment is a summative or a formative assignment is up to the professional expertise of the teacher; once more learning will occur, the formerly summative assessment becomes a formative assessment, by definition.

As teachers we may have been taught that whether an assessment is summative and formative defines where the student is in the learning progression, but in equitable grading the opposite is true: where the student is in her learning progression defines whether an assessment is formative or summative.

Let's say a student takes an end-of-unit exam—a summative assessment—and based on her answers, she did not learn sufficient material and skills to receive a passing grade. The teacher has a decision to make: Is the student's learning completed? If yes, it's a summative assessment. But could the student learn from her mistakes on the test, correct her misunderstandings, and improve? In other words, could she continue to learn? If so, then POOF—the teacher can decide the summative assessment is a formative assessment by offering a retake to the student. As with all formative assessments, the student now can relearn material and understand her misconceptions, the teacher can provide intervention and corrective information, and then the student can try again. That retake is now the summative assessment.

If we really want to empower and motivate the student, the decision on whether a summative assessment becomes formative would not be entirely up to the teacher. What if a *student* could decide to continue learning, that after the test she wants to learn more. Would a teacher tell a student that she needs to stop learning? Would any assessment be summative before it absolutely had to be?

In equitable grading we could even transform a formative assessment into a summative assessment *after the fact*. Because an equitable grade accurately represents a student's level of understanding, the teacher may have obtained sufficient evidence prior to the summative assessment—through formative assessments such as class discussions or other assignments or activities—and she could consider that information as more valid than the student's performance on the summative assessment. For example, if a student has a terrible performance on a final exam because of anxiety or other circumstances but the teacher determined that the student showed standards mastery in the review exercise (a formative assessment) the day before, the teacher could make that prior formative assessment into a summative assessment—POOF!—and consider that evidence as more validly reflecting the student's level of content knowledge. The summative/formative assessment division isn't fixed in equitable grading; it's flexible. That flexibility in assessment and deciding what performance is included in the grade gives us more accuracy and students more motivation.

Should the Student Retake the Entire Summative Assessment, or Just the Content She Failed?

If a student showed she learned 50 percent of the material on the first assessment, then what's important is that she learn what she hasn't yet learned (or demonstrated that she has learned): the remaining 50 percent. Therefore, she would only need to retake the portions of the assessment that ask her to demonstrate that corrected understanding. In other words, there's no need for her to redemonstrate what she already showed she's mastered.

This creates lots of benefits—pedagogically and logistically. Students can narrow their focus to what they haven't yet understood and the teacher can provide targeted support. Plus, it's efficient; when the student is reassessed only on content she hasn't yet shown mastery of, it takes less time for her to retake the assessment and for the teacher to score it.

This approach to retakes particularly benefits students with weaker education backgrounds and who receive special education services. For them, learning all the content and showing mastery of it all on a single assessment can be simply too high a mountain to climb. Retakes that are tailored to assess only what a student has not yet mastered allows students to chunk the content into more manageable pieces. Rather than view this "chunking" as a nuisance, some teachers capitalize on it: For example, if a student has shown on an assessment that she still has

50 percent of the content to learn and show mastery of, the teacher might have the student focus on only half of the unmastered content, assess her on that portion, then have her learn the remaining content and assess her on that. The struggling student who in the past saw failure because she learned an insufficient fraction of the content can achieve success through the retake process and learn the content in more manageable learning chunks.

What Happens Between the Original Assessment and the Retake?

When a student gets a low grade on an assessment because of insufficient understanding or inadequate preparation, a second chance by itself isn't likely to result in a different outcome. In these circumstances, summative assessment performance isn't like a dice roll where if we don't get a good roll we just need to roll the dice again. However, we shouldn't be surprised when low-performing students want the retake with no additional preparation; students who historically haven't done well in school may believe that their best chance of success is through random luck. The key to improving performance on a retake, of course, is that a student learn (or relearn) material that she didn't successfully learn initially. Before allowing a student to retake an assessment, many teachers require the student to attend tutoring or otherwise demonstrate to the teacher that she has made sufficient improvement and will perform better on the retake. Otherwise, the retake is a fruitless exercise for the student and a waste of time for the teacher, who has to create, proctor, and correct it.

Many teachers believe that if students are going to learn from the mistakes of their first assessment, they need to be more explicitly aware of their misunderstandings and misconceptions. As part of the retake process, teachers devise error analyses, reflections, and correction exercises that focus the student on the errors she made on the assessment. See **www.gradingforequity.org** for examples.

While some teachers create tutoring exercises to target particular gaps reflected in the initial assessment, other teachers who offer retakes identify the previously assigned homework or classwork assignments that would address students' gaps. Before the assessment, did the student complete the assignment that was intended to build that skill or reinforce that content? If so, were mistakes in the assignment overlooked or uncorrected? Teachers may require students, as a prerequisite to retaking an assessment, to complete or redo any homework or classwork assignment about topics or skills that the student did not successfully master on the assessment. Even though equitable grades do not include a student's performance on formative work, recording the student's performance on homework and classwork (as suggested in chapter 10) provides valuable information to explain the summative assessment performance and to identify what the student needs to do before the retake. If a student showed poor performance on the summative assessment because she chose not to complete homework assignments, or copied them, she now has the opportunity to learn the material. If she didn't understand certain assignments or didn't learn from them the first time, she can redo those assignments and receive additional support. When the student completes the assignments and shows the teacher that she is ready to demonstrate improved performance, the student can retake the test. In this way, a retake isn't another spin of a wheel; it's a chance to continue learning and earn the rewards of that continued learning after additional learning and preparation.

The harmony between formative practice and summative evaluation, and the benefits of not including homework and classwork in the grade, are now clearer. Students build a connection that traditional grading has fragmented: Homework and classwork prepare students for the assessments; not doing them, copying them, or not fully utilizing them causes lower scores on the summative assessment. If a student did not complete homework designed to practice and learn certain content, and failed to show mastery of that content on the summative assessment, then it's clear that the homework should have been completed—it would have improved the student's preparation for the assessment—and in order to retake the assessment the student needs to do what she should have done. She's learning that homework was designed for no other reason than to benefit her.

What Assessment Designs Best Support the Retake Process?

With retakes, students need only demonstrate knowledge on the content they weren't able to on the initial assessment, which means that both the teacher and the student need to identify that content. Unfortunately, we traditionally organize tests—the predominant form of a summative assessment—in ways that make it difficult for us to pinpoint a student's content weaknesses. Often, we structure tests by the type of question. A typical test might have this question sequence: true/false, followed by multiple choice, then fill-in-the-blank, then short answer, and finally essay. It's as if there is a Maslovian hierarchy of questions, beginning with the simplest cognitive requirements and gradually increasing. This common design can obscure information that is critical for identifying students' content strengths and weaknesses—information essential to the relearning and retake process. To understand what content a student needs to relearn and retake, we must disentangle the questions; for example, we assessed kinetic energy in true/false questions number 2 and 4, multiple choice question 7, fill-in-the-blank questions 15 and 16, while we assessed students' understanding of momentum in true/false questions 1 and 3, and multiple choice questions 6 and 8.

If we instead organize our test not by the type of question, but by the topic or content standard, retakes become so much simpler. In other words, if the first eight questions on a test, of whatever combination of question types, assess a student's understanding of kinetic energy, the student's answers to that cluster of questions will tell us whether a student hasn't yet shown competence or mastery of that content and needs to retake that section. An additional benefit of organizing tests by standard or topic is that students can more easily navigate the test; we've lightened the cognitive load that could interfere with them revealing what they know.

Should Retakes Be Optional or Mandatory?

Teachers initially may treat retakes as an option: It's up to the students to choose whether to take advantage of the opportunity. For those of us new to offering retakes, this is a common starting place.

What often follows is predictable, frustrating, and problematic: The students who choose to retake are often the higher-performing and more motivated students, the ones who scored a B or even higher on the initial assessment. Teachers are disappointed that the failing students—the students who need the retake, who would most benefit from it—don't take advantage of the second chance. Why, teachers wonder, do the students who don't need the retake want it, and those who need the retake don't seem to want it? If it's any consolation, the same dynamic happens in college: Lower-performing students forgo opportunities for support, while higher-performing students take advantage of supports (Moore, 2008).

A reason the students who score an A or B take advantage of the optional retake is no surprise: They usually are students who have experienced years of success in school and have positive feelings about teachers and learning. They likely have more confidence in themselves as learners, and trust that the school as an institution is there to support them and that teachers are there to help them. Retakes reinforce their positive feelings about schools and learning. And mathematically, a high score is within reach; with only a small amount of content to study and retake, the improvement process is relatively easy and brief.

For the student who performed at the D or F level on the initial assessment, her situation is starkly different. To her, the distance to success is so vast it can seem inaccessible. If she has failed previous assessments, over multiple years in multiple courses, her failure on your assessment may have reinforced her fixed self-concept as not cut out for your subject or school. She may have experienced so much difficulty in school over the years that she perceives the school as indifferent to her needs at best and, more likely, hostile to her and her community, epitomized and reinforced by the failure on your assessment. Under these circumstances, why would the D and F students choose to subject themselves, *voluntarily*, to an additional assessment and possibly a second failure? When offered a retake of a test, her choice is likely to be to avoid it at all costs, and why would we really expect otherwise?

Realizing this, many teachers believe that the way to motivate lower-performing students to retake is to find ways to overcome students' negative feelings. We leverage our personal relationships with students ("Let's work together after school and then have you retake the exam."), persuade them ("Give me thirty minutes after school on Wednesday to prepare and thirty minutes on Thursday to retake only the questions you missed, and I can almost guarantee that you'll get a higher score!"), create incentives ("I'll give you 10 bonus points on your participation grade if you retake the exam."), and bolster their confidence and reaffirm our high expectations

("I am sure beyond a shadow of a doubt that you know this and can do better on a retake!"). Sometimes we succeed, with some of the students.

Our crucial question is whether making the retake voluntary—allowing lower-performing students to opt out—is equitable. It's not.

Retakes are equitable only when they are *mandatory*.

Here's why: My parents both graduated from college, were very engaged with the school and aware of my progress, had a solid relationship with me, and were able and comfortable talking with teachers about any concerns or advocating on my behalf. If I received a low score on a test and my parents knew that my teacher offered retakes, it wouldn't be up to me whether I wanted to retake the test. The only option my parents gave me was *when* I would retake it.

Many educators have had similar experiences, as do many of our students. But too many of our students don't have that experience and instead have caregivers who are stretched too thinly or speak a different language than those with power in the school, or who have poorer relationships with their children, or are less comfortable with the school because of their own negative experiences with school and learning. For any of those reasons, students could feel no mandate to retake.

This is our equity issue: Should whether a student retakes an assessment depend on her caregivers and other life circumstances outside her control? Of course not. Every student deserves to have an adult in her life who pushes her, who cares for her enough to expect her to continue learning and to advocate for or provide the support she needs until she's successful. That means that when caregivers aren't able to do or be that, for *any reason*, educators have to be that for those students. When we make a retake mandatory for underperforming students, we're telling them that they can't get away with that underperformance, that failure isn't okay, and that we know that it's just a matter of time and effort before every student shows mastery. In other words, we care enough about them that we won't let them fail, and we won't let them avoid learning. It's being a warm demander (Delpit, 2006). Wormeli (2011) writes, "Maturation occurs in the fully credited recovery from unsuccessful attempts, not by labeling those attempts as failures. If our mission is to teach so that students learn, we don't let their immaturity dictate their destiny. Irresponsible, forgetful, and inattentive students need us to be in their face more, not less" (p. 26). Students recognize that when we require them to succeed, we're saying something about what we believe about their potential and how we feel about them:

"If you had a C- or lower, my science teacher would write a slip for you to come in at lunch. You would get your food and she'd work with you until you got your grade up above a C-. If you didn't come, she'd give you a [disciplinary] referral. I liked it. It shows that she cares about all of her students, and she doesn't want any of them

to fail. That also helps to motivate the students in other classes: 'If I do my work in this class and I'm getting my grade up, what if I could do it in my other classes?'" (Bryan, middle school student)

How Do I Record Retakes in the Grade Book?

If we enter both the original and the retake score(s) into our grade books, the software will average the scores, thus yielding an inaccurate and therefore inequitable representation of a student's level of performance. Therefore, how a teacher records the retake depends on what story the teacher and student want to be able to tell:

1. If the earlier, lower score doesn't matter, you can simply overwrite the original score with the retake's score.

2. If you want to preserve the original score to help both you and the student to describe her growth and progress, you and/or the student can keep a record of initial scores independently of the grade book—in a tracker or separate spreadsheet—and the retake score is entered into the grade book.

3. If you want to preserve the original score but would rather not keep the data in two separate places, grade book software often allows a comment to be entered for a student's score on an assignment. The teacher can replace the original score with the retake score and create a comment for that score that includes the original score.

4. If you want to preserve the original score and it's important that both scores are easily visible in the grade book, you can enter the retake test score as an additional "assignment" but tag the original score so it isn't included in the final grade calculation. Another option is to enter a retake score that embeds within it the original score. For example, if the student scored a 75 percent on the first summative assessment but scored an 89 percent on the retake, the score in the grade book could be 89.075 percent. The retake score overwrites the original score but the original score is captured without any significant mathematical impact on the grade's accuracy.

After the Retake, What Score Should Be Entered Into the Grade?

Some teachers believe that there should be a "grade ceiling" on a retake—for example, that a student who scored a D on the first test shouldn't be able to get higher than a C on the retake. However, this penalizes students who learn more slowly and inequitably punishes students who have a weaker educational background or fewer resources, or who just need more than one attempt to demonstrate understanding. Establishing a ceiling grade on a retake creates the same mathematical inaccuracy and demotivation as averaging: If a student showed a higher level of content mastery on a retake, then to do anything but report that grade would be inaccurate and inequitable.

What If a Student Scores Lower on the Retake?

If teachers, before providing the retake, require a student to prepare and demonstrate that she will improve her performance, this shouldn't happen. But if a student does score lower, the teacher needs to decide which score is the more accurate. Did the student really just get lucky the first time so the retake score is more reflective of her level of content knowledge? Were there aggravating circumstances for the retake which rendered her score a less valid measure? Was the cognitive or linguistic complexity of the retake so challenging that it prevented the student from showing her learning? Examining the causes of the lower performance will reveal the right solution to ensuring that the grading is equitable.

Retakes: Common Concerns

Do We Really Want to Open the Door to Retakes, Much Less to Normalize Them?

In truth, the retake door is one most of us have opened many times. At one point or another, every teacher has had the experience of a student sheepishly, apologetically, and sometimes with shame, asking for a retake. Maybe her younger brother was up all night with a fever, or the electricity went out, or there was police activity, or any number of situations that interfered with the student being fully prepared and that made it hard for her to do her best on the assessment. Or she felt that she still had so many questions and didn't have a chance to have them answered. When we heard the disclosure, we appreciated that the student opened up to us and maybe even felt a deeper relationship with them. Although we might have been a little hesitant because we knew that it would mean bending the rules and creating extra work for us, we allowed the student to retake the assessment. We knew it would give the student a chance to show her full potential and would give us the grade that we knew she deserved.

And for every student who tells us about a difficulty in her life or shares her vulnerability, there are countless other students who don't. They don't trust us, they're embarrassed, they don't have enough English fluency, or they fear that there would be repercussions for their family. Maybe they worry that we wouldn't believe them or would be dismissive, or they fear how we'd treat them or who we'd tell. As Cynthia, a high school student shared,

> *"As a student–athlete I've always been taught, 'You should prioritize; you should get the work done.' But in instances where something is going on at home or with you, then I don't feel comfortable at school to tell the teacher, 'I didn't do it' or 'I'm not prepared because of this reason' because it creates anxiety. There's also this fear of 'Are they going to believe me?'"*

Maybe some students believe their personal circumstances aren't our business, and they might be right. For any number of reasons, some students are silent and therefore are not receiving our largesse in allowing retakes or extensions. They're therefore not getting the retake opportunities even though their circumstances may just as adversely prevent them from sharing their full potential on the exam. It's inequitable to offer retakes to those students who have the courage, confidence, relationship with us, trust, and language, and not to those that don't have those qualities. To be equitable, retakes shouldn't require the student to provide an excuse or justification, or to have sufficient confidence, language skills, or a relationship with us, and we don't want students to feel sheepish or embarrassed for that request. Retakes should be available whenever a student wants to improve her performance.

Is a Retake Having the Student Just Do the Same Assessment a Second Time? Wouldn't Any Student Score Better the Second Time?

The first pillar of equitable grading is that the grade accurately describes a student's level of content knowledge, and therefore the assessment needs to be one that yields a valid reflection of that knowledge. That means that whether the assessment is modified or not for a retake must be driven by a teacher's answer to the question: What will most accurately capture student understanding? If a student has to write a research paper as a summative assessment, rewriting the paper with the original requirements and prompts may yield valid information about a student's skills, while on a math test retake the questions might need to be changed to accurately assess the student. Some teachers decide to increase the complexity of the response format in a retake; multiple choice questions on the initial test become questions that require paragraph responses on the retake. Modifying the design or format—assuming that doing so does not interfere with the student communicating her knowledge—may both accurately assess student knowledge and create an incentive for the student to do her best on the initial exam rather than rely on the retake (see below for more on this aspect of retakes).

Could I Be Stuck Giving Retakes on Chapter 1 Until the End of the Term?

If a student's mastery of the content is important for success on future content, then you might want to give retakes until students have demonstrated necessary understanding. However, there are other options that teachers use to streamline the retake process.

Here's how. In every course, content builds somewhat cumulatively over the term. Quizzes cover segments of a unit that, combined, are assessed in its entirety on the unit exam; unit exams cover material that is assessed cumulatively on the semester or final exam. In English courses, writing skills spiral, and in math classes, the early skills support operations later in the unit or semester. In disciplines with more discrete and independent content units (such as science, social studies, arts, some electives, and PE classes), some essential skills and concepts spiral across different content.

For example, the skills of critically analyzing primary documents (social studies), applying the scientific method (science), and understanding composition (art) develop through their application to different content units.

When this is the case, Dueck (2014), in *Grading Smarter, Not Harder*, suggests "double-dipping" assessments (pp. 108–109). Rather than offer a retake for every quiz or test, a teacher designs each summative assessment through the term so that it can measure prior content, either in separate sections in the assessment or by integrating current and earlier content. In this way, a student's performance on an assessment can provide evidence of the student's up-to-date learning and the teacher can overwrite the student's performance on an earlier assessment. Each assessment can serve as a "retake" of prior assessments. This strategy achieves the same goals of a retake but can be more efficient for both the teacher and the student.

Teachers who use a "double-dipping" assessment strategy often find that they need to make some changes to their assessment design. Tests need to be structured so that a teacher can identify a student's mastery on earlier content so that she can replace earlier, lower scores with improved scores. The unit exam functions as the retake for previous quizzes, and quizzes can function as formative assessments to help students to identify and address weaknesses before the summative assessment. Students become motivated and invested in using quizzes as a learning tool and treating summative assessments as an opportunity for redemption.

If Second, Third, or More Chances Are Allowed, Could a Retake Process Go on Forever?

The course term is going to end at some point, and summer break will come. There has to be some finality to the grade, even if just for logistical purposes and our sanity as educators. We have a lot of content we're responsible to cover, and past assignments can become stale and even moot in light of more current content. At the same time, let's admit that the demarcations of student learning during the school year—when it's time to end chapter 4 and move to chapter 5, or when the semester ends—are artificial and generally arbitrary. Just because a unit "ends" and a new one "begins" (or first quarter ends and second quarter begins) it doesn't mean that learning earlier content will, or must, no longer occur. To allow for all students to succeed, particularly those who face the most challenges, have the weakest education backgrounds, and learn at slower rates, we will need to allow students to continue learning beyond the traditional and externally imposed deadlines. There's no reason why we need to truncate learning if a student wants, or needs, it. Even when deadlines aren't decided by teachers in classrooms, but by school or district administrators, perhaps we can prevent even those arbitrary markers from limiting student learning. Most schools and districts allow grade changes after a semester is over, so doesn't that explicitly allow, perhaps invite, a student who wants to learn unmastered material to continue learning beyond the term and have her grade reflect that learning? Who are we to stop them?

How Do Retakes Affect Students With Test Anxiety?

When students experience stress, their brains function less effectively and their performance drops—anxiety prevents their brain from accessing all of their executive functions and memory. (See also, Hammond, 2015.) Without retake opportunities, everything depends on a single "performance event"—the summative assessment—regardless of all of the circumstances that can impede a student from accurately demonstrating her learning. Even when summative assessments are heavily weighted in the grade, retakes can be the antidote to test anxiety. With retakes, a student always has another chance, and knowing this can decrease her stress on the assessment and actually increase her performance. Because it changes the stress and pressure of assessments, allowing retakes can fundamentally change the test atmosphere, and therefore the overall learning environment, of the classroom, as Elisa, a high school physical education teacher for thirteen years, found,

"One of the children asked, 'You're giving me another chance? Really?' Not only did the students increase their overall average in my class, but we built a more positive relationship. Some of them were the 'bad,' 'lazy,' type that have been labeled, or mislabeled, I should say. They ended up being my best students. I really think it's because of this redo policy. They found me to be a teacher that wanted them to be successful, who didn't want to just put in a grade and be done with it."

Plus, retakes allow the *teacher* a second chance as well. If the initial assessment was imperfectly designed, with linguistic demands or response formats that impeded the teacher from accurately assessing students' knowledge, the retake gives her another opportunity to do that, which can reduce the pressure on teachers to design the perfect summative assessment. Teachers have found that the *retake opportunity can ironically make retakes less necessary*: Students, knowing that they can always get a second chance, relax during the initial assessment and produce a much more accurate performance of their knowledge and skills.

How Will We "Force" Students to Retake?
(We Can Lead a Horse to Water but We Can't Make It Drink)

The answer: We can provide a salt lick that makes the "horse" very, very thirsty. Some teachers embed retakes into the class period to make the retake very convenient and students don't have to stay after school. Entire schools create structures and cultures that make retakes easier logistically for both teachers and students and normalize retakes as a part of learning. For example, some schools create "intervention blocks" or even schoolwide retake sessions into their calendar. On those dates or blocks of time, every student in the school—whether she is trying to increase her score from an A- to an A or from an F to a D—retakes an assessment. To ensure that the retake day is a success, the prior day every student attends a tutoring session in that subject to learn from her mistakes and prepare. For the most struggling students, additional support sessions are scheduled. In other words, everyone retakes an assessment and improves their performance, and everyone is set up for success. We can build a community for our students that doesn't just say that mistakes are normal and expected but shows that we learn and grow from those mistakes; that all of us not only are capable of success, but we each can achieve success through preparation and multiple chances: "Culturally responsive teaching makes academic success a non-negotiable mandate for all students and an accessible goal" (Gay, 2010). In equitable classrooms, unredeemed failure is simply not an option.

Won't Students Just Take Advantage of the Retakes?

Many teachers fear that if students know that every summative assessment is followed with a retake, students won't take the initial assessment seriously; they'll treat it as "practice," which will undermine the validity and integrity of the initial assessment, to say nothing of how it will frustrate the teacher. What actually happens, however, shocks teachers, including Elisa: Students continue to take the first test just as seriously even knowing there are retakes.

"My fear [with a redo policy] was 'Are they going to try their hardest the first time if they know that they would be able to redo it for a higher grade?' But I didn't run into that problem. The kids did well the first time. It's kind of weird to explain because you would think the opposite, like they wouldn't try. The first time around, they tried harder. I think it was because they knew, by me giving them a second chance, that I had faith in them that they knew the material and would do well, that at the end, they could do it. That was the whole idea."

Why? When students know that the teacher cares enough to give retakes, she's expressing high expectations that everyone can succeed despite mistakes. Plus, it's not as if students like taking summative assessments; they would generally prefer to perform their best the first time if possible. Plus, a retake requires additional time in and out of school for preparation and to do the retake, students are motivated to perform before the retake. Consider also that there are some students who actually need the initial assessment to learn—it helps them more clearly understand the content expectations and their gaps. That's why so many people in the adult world use practice tests to prepare for high stakes exams.

Do Retakes Prepare Students for the Real World, Where There Aren't Retakes?

Another common concern is that retakes make learning "soft," that it provides students with too fluffy a cushion compared to the "real world," where there are no retakes or redos. In the professional, adult world, do we get second chances?

We sure do—all the time.

The person taking your order in a restaurant can send it back to the kitchen to be corrected, the painter who forgets to apply primer can remove the paint and start over, the teacher whose first period class doesn't go well can change things for second period and can even come back to first period the next day and reteach. The software programmers who make a coding error later send a patch. Sure, there will be extra time and resources spent in all of these examples, but that's no different than requiring the student to spend time after school to study and prepare for the retest.

Of course, sometimes professionals only get one chance: the lawyer who has to argue her case before a jury, the saleswoman who pitches her product to a potential buyer, the doctor who has to remove a ruptured appendix, the runner competing in an Olympic race. In all these examples of having only a single chance, before the high stakes performance they practice, get feedback, and practice many more times.

Plus, most professionals, prior to entering their fields of expertise, have to first demonstrate competence on assessments of proficiency—bar exams, medical boards, nursing exams, teacher credentialing, and many more—and *all* these assessments allow second, third, even unlimited chances to pass, with no penalty or prejudice. Even the lowly driver's license is a test of proficiency that allows multiple retakes. On all of these assessments, a failure only postpones the rewards of passing. They may require some additional cost and time to prepare more effectively, but with no consequence to the person's privileges when she ultimately demonstrates competence. With our students years away from the demonstration of professional proficiency (and many students years away from even the driver's license), isn't mastery of our curriculum and skills, even if it takes multiple tries, truly the best preparation for the professional world? This competence is surely better preparation for college and the professional world than the alternative—that a student fails the assessment and the course because she didn't demonstrate sufficient learning in her initial assessment attempt.

In another surprise to teachers who implement retakes, the number of students retaking tests often *decreases over time*. In the traditional approach to summative assessments, students who don't learn material sufficiently just move on to the next unit (and don't get a chance to address their misconceptions and cure a low grade). As a consequence, the new content, which likely builds on the previous content, becomes even more difficult and those students' grades and confidence continue to drop. If instead students are able to relearn the first unit's material, they have a foundation that better prepares them for future content, have confidence in their competence, are more motivated to attain and demonstrate this competence, and have less need for retakes in the future. Plus, in the retake process, teachers, through guided support and tutoring, model for the student how to study more effectively. Students learn to better prepare for initial assessments.

Additionally, retakes can support students learning time management and priorities, skills that are essential to success in the "real" adult professional world. As a high school student explains,

> "It's my sophomore year, and half my classes are AP classes, and there's a lot of things going on with sports and clubs, so it's hard to manage your time. My AP World class teacher assigns a load of notes and homework each and every night, but there are other classes. It's like, 'Hey, you're not my only class. I have five other classes that I need to manage and keep up, too.' With retakes, it's like, 'It's okay if I bomb this test, I have time to make it up.' You're only one person and you're expected to learn six different subjects, so retakes give you that cushion. It's like, 'I have my priorities now. This test is not one of them, but I can worry about it after I clear some stuff up.'" (Jocelyn, high school student)

Not only does Jocelyn use retakes as a way to feel less stress with her ambitious slate of classes, retakes allow her to demonstrate her full potential.

Setting the Professional World Aside, Do Retakes Prepare Students for College?

We may remember college as a place where the competition is fierce and professors give impersonal lectures to large classes. Most of us don't recall the word *retake* ever being a possibility. Are we just setting up our students for failure in college?

What if college is different than how we remember or characterize it? What if college professors actually want students to perform their best so that a student's performance on assessments is the most accurate reflection of her content and skill knowledge? What if professors allowed retakes?

It turns out that professors *do* allow retakes. Although not yet the subject of a scientific study, every professor I've ever asked has said that they would allow a student to retake an assessment if there were circumstances that prevented the student from scoring her best the first time.

If this is true, why do many of us have such a different impression of college? What could be going on is that we actually had retake options but *weren't told* that we just needed to ask for the opportunity. It's an example of "veiled" information about how to be successful that we will discuss in the next chapter. We, especially those of us who are first in their families to go to college, might have been intimidated and afraid of professors and didn't know that we could have a relationship with them in which they prefer us to be successful and want to report our best and most accurate score. Viewed from this perspective, by normalizing retakes we may actually be helping students to learn an essential skill of self-advocacy. Rather than say, "In the real world you only get one chance," perhaps our most truthful and most helpful message should be "In the real world, retakes are often available; you just might have to ask for them and put in some additional work."

Finally, it's worth considering that in our current adult professional world, a world with persistent historical inequities, certain groups actually get fewer redos or second chances than other groups. Women may get fewer chances than a man to impress the boss, and someone who speaks English with a Spanish accent may not get the same leeway to err as the native-born speaker. There's overwhelming research that if you're African American or Latino, you're more likely to get stiffer punishments than whites who commit the same infraction, who may not get a warning or light consequence—whether in the workplace (e.g., Greenhaus, Parasuraman, & Wormley, 1990), school (e.g., Lhamon & Samuels, 2014), or criminal justice system (Alexander, 2012)—and therefore do not get a redo or second chance. To best prepare the students who will likely face discrimination, should we want to replicate that world in our classrooms?

Of course not. Let's instead give our students who have been historically underserved—who in their real-world experience racism from institutions as well as the people who work within them—a learning environment free from that treatment. We don't serve our historically underserved students by replicating the inequities that caused them to be underserved, but by creating the most equitable community—and most equitable grading and assessment system—we can. Let's allow multiple chances for success on our assessments to anyone who can continue to learn and improve. And that means everyone.

Summary of Concepts

1. Extrinsic motivation techniques in traditional grading aren't just ineffective; they undermine intrinsic motivation, which is critically important in learning. In fact, our most struggling students have received years of low and failing grades, and for them, traditional grading provides little positive motivation. Instead, they frustrate, dispirit, and confirm students' academic inadequacies, so much so that those students could be considered "motivated to fail" by grades.

2. Equitable grading practices allow and even encourage mistake-making as a means for learning. To do so, classrooms must create opportunities for redemption in which students can correct their errors and misunderstandings. Minimum grading and renaming grades to communicate a growth mindset are two examples.

3. Implementing procedures for students to retake and redo summative assessments, and considering the more recent (and therefore more accurate) score, motivates students to learn from mistakes and to increase their competence and understanding.

4. There are many options and complexities with implementing retakes. Some decision points include what qualifies a student for a retake, when and how they will be offered, for how long students can retake, and who decides and develops the retake's content and assessment design to ensure validity. Retakes are only truly equitable when they are required, not just optional, for students who show less than mastery of course content. Making this decision can test and confirm a school's commitment to equity, although this decision can raise challenging questions about the school's commitment to equity.

Questions to Consider

1. When in your professional life have you been given a "redo"? Who offered it to you, and why do you think you got that second chance? What did it feel like to receive it? What happened before and during your second chance? How did it benefit you? Was there a time when you were asked to demonstrate competence and weren't given a second chance? Why weren't you given that chance? Did you ask for it, or believe that you could?

2. For Teachers: How much of a motivator is hope? How much do you notice a change in student behavior and motivation, particularly among lower-performing students, before the first assessment of the term compared to after they have received the scores of that first assessment? At the beginning of the term versus after the first progress report or report card (when they receive their first formal low grade)? How could offering redemption via retakes, weighing more recent performance, minimum grading, or 0–4 scales throughout the term affect motivation?

3. For Teachers: How would the commitment to mandatory retakes align or conflict with your school's vision? What would have to change for your classroom or your school to commit to mandatory retakes? What would make it difficult? What could your school do to make it easier to make retakes mandatory?

CHAPTER 12

Practices That "Lift the Veil"

- **Rubrics**
- **Standards Scales and Tests Without Points**
- **Standards-Based Grade Books**

In this chapter, we will answer the following questions:

1. What can transparency look like in equitable grading, and how does it motivate?

2. How are well-designed rubrics an important element of equitable grading? How can they be used to motivate and empower students? How should performance on a rubric be translated into an equitable numerical score?

3. How does the use of points to score assessments make student performance less transparent? What are alternative ways to evaluate that more transparently assess and describe student performance relative to a standard?

4. What are standards-based grade books, and what makes them more equitable?

Driving Principle: *The way we grade should be so transparent and understandable that every student can know their grade at any time and know how to get the grade she wants.*

A student can hit any target that they can clearly see and that doesn't move.
(Stiggins, Arter, Chappuis, J., & Chappuis, S., 2004)

The Veils in Our Schools, and "Hostile Attributional Bias"

Schools are complicated places, to put it mildly. To succeed there, a student has to understand and navigate multiple systems and structures: appropriate clothing, codes of conduct, daily or weekly schedules, class websites, course sequences and prerequisites, themed programs, GPA calculations, unexcused versus excused absences, and tardy policies to name just a few. While a school's many systems are explained in school handbooks, many rules and procedures aren't included and may not be formalized at all: How do I catch up after an absence? Can I switch out of or into a class? How do I ask a teacher to slow down the pace? Where do I go if I think something is unfair? What do I do if I have an after-school conflict between two activities?

The complexity of a school's formal and informal rules advantage the students and families that our schools were originally built to serve: those with higher education backgrounds, native English speakers, and the well-to-do. These more privileged students and their families not only are better able to understand and navigate the formalized and written policies (which are often written only in English and at an advanced reading level), but because they are more likely to have generations of experiences in schools as well as greater financial means, they are better able to access, respond to, and take advantage of the unformalized rules. Less historically privileged students and their families—those of color, immigrants, and low income—are at a clear disadvantage, being without the language, resources, and experiences (and therefore often without the confidence) to navigate the school's rules and requirements. The less visible and formalized the rule, the greater their disadvantage.

In response, schools understand that to be equitable they need to "lift the veil," to make the rules visible and explicit: student handbooks offered in multiple languages, caregiver education events throughout the year, and communication through snail mail, email, phone, and text "blasts." To be equitable means that all students and caregivers have equal information, access, and opportunity to successfully navigate the school's systems and structures. Grading is motivational when it not only builds in the opportunity for redemption, but also when the "targets" for academic success are clear, don't move, and the path to hitting those targets are explicit for all.

This may not seem very radical: Teachers want to make their grading transparent so that every student understands how the grade is earned. Teachers create detailed syllabi, sometimes in multiple languages, distribute frequent progress reports, and many schools use grading software that students and caregivers can access through an app to get up-to-the-minute updates on grades. We believe that through these efforts to make our grading transparent, we level the playing field, empowering all students with the knowledge they need to earn the grade they want.

Unfortunately, as we've come to realize through previous chapters, our grades aren't very transparent, and can be more obfuscating than clear. First, we've seen how our traditional grading confuses precision for transparency. In chapter 4, we learned how category weightings in grade software calculations are often so complicated that grades become nearly impossible to understand and therefore can seem mysterious and arbitrary. Secondly, defining achievement simply as the acquisition of points, regardless of whether from completed homework, extra credit, tests, classwork, participation, attendance, or any other point-earning act, we hide what academic success requires. The extremely complex algorithm of weighted categories combined with the fungibility of points within and across those categories makes it virtually impossible for a student, and probably also for the teacher, to know exactly how a grade is calculated, much less how to improve a grade, making the path to improvement seem not just hidden, but unavailable, to many of our students. Added to this confusion is our traditional grading's clumsy and unhelpfully vague communication of student performance. When a student's grade reflects a potpourri or hodgepodge of academic and nonacademic criteria, it is impossible to know what a grade represents, and it becomes useless as feedback.

As a result of all these dysfunctional elements of our inherited grading systems, when students want to know why they have a low grade or what they can do to raise it, we ourselves sense the inadequacy of our grading to describe academic performance. Our responses can sound overly simplistic: A student should have "studied more" or "taken the class more seriously" or "paid attention more." It is no wonder that students interpret grades as a referendum on who they are rather than what learning they demonstrated. Boud (1995) unflinchingly suggests that our use of this kind of vocabulary not only sends a brutally harmful message to students, but is an evasive sleight-of-hand:

> Too often we fail to make absolutely clear the distinction between giving feedback on a specific product which has been produced by a person and judging them as a person. We write and say things which can readily be taken as comments about the person rather than their work and in doing so we link in to the doubts and uncertainties which they have of themselves and our remarks are magnified at great cost to the self-esteem of the persons concerned. . . . [T]hey come easily to hand; they help us avoid having to engage with the substance of what we are commenting on and they give the impression that we are concerned with quality and standards without anything of quality being said. (p. 6)

When we use language reflecting the points-as-achievement universe, we are no more transparent; grades provide no guidance to students other than reflecting how well they have taken advantage or squandered point-accumulating opportunities:

"If only you had turned in that classwork . . ." or "If you had gotten a few more points on the unit test . . ." or "If you had been more focused and earned more daily points . . ." Unsurprisingly, when students talk about their grades, it's using the same limited vocabulary: "If only I had gotten a few more points I'd have scored a 90 percent instead of an 89 percent " Grades become simply a number that was reached or not reached, who knows, or cares, how.

This ambiguity in expectations can lead to confusion, disempowerment, and even mistrust, particularly when that ambiguity increases the teacher's power and the potential for abuse. Yeager et al. (2013) writes that this mistrust can undermine motivation, particularly for African American students even when controlling for socioeconomic status and education, who "may wonder if the teacher's criticisms signal a genuine desire to help or a bias against their racial or ethnic group.[1] When ambiguity is high, students may use their chronic trust, or lack of trust to go beyond the information given and infer the motives of the evaluator." Yeager continues by defining "hostile attributional bias":

> *Children raised in aggressive contexts learn to expect hostility against them and thus interpret ambiguous provocations as intentional . . . Likewise, mistrust could arise from minority students' growing awareness of the significance of race in school and society. This in turn could lead them to see bias as a possible factor motivating their teacher's critical feedback. . . . It is not the case that African Americans lack motivation in school. Rather they understandably may be uncertain as to whether they should invest their effort and identity in tasks where they could be subjected to biased treatment.*

> *Perhaps for White students there is less attributional ambiguity because they are not visibly stigmatized, permitting them to take a teacher's comments at face value and recognize that they are concrete and peppered with encouragement. That is, chronic mistrust has less of an opportunity to color their interpretations. By contrast, African American students' visibly different group membership may cause them to question a teacher's intentions. The resulting ambiguity may leave relatively greater opportunity for mistrust to filter their interpretations. (p. 17)*

If we want to fulfill this second Driving Principle for our Motivational pillar—The way we grade should be so transparent and understandable that every student can know her grade and know how to get the grade she wants—to make our grades equitable and empower all students, particularly recognizing the disadvantages of historically underserved students, we can't describe success in the vague and misleading vocabulary of points, percentages, and platitudes of needing to "focus more."

---

[1]While Asian Americans have been found to show lower levels of trust relative to whites in national surveys, Latinos have been found to mistrust at rates almost as high as those among African Americans, and "racial trust gaps" persist even when controlling for income and education.

What if the way we graded supported students to think about their grade in terms of what knowledge or skills they had mastered? What if, instead of talking about their grade in the language of points, students said, "If only I had mastery of the application of kinetic energy, not just how to correctly use the formula in an equation, I'd have earned an A"? And what if, knowing what they hadn't yet mastered, students could identify what steps they needed to take to get the grade they wanted? In other words, what if the way we thought about transparency wasn't an explanation of percentages and points, but about students knowing what level of content knowledge constituted each level of achievement?

We have to pull back the curtain, to share with our students exactly what we expect them to know and do—not just that they do our homework and follow our directions, or that tests are worth 60 percent and they scored 94 points out of a possible 125. To engender their trust in their teachers and their schools, we need to reduce ambiguity, to leave less to students' interpretations of the motives behind our grading and feedback. We must use grading practices that help us to reduce our accidental and inadvertent ambiguity, because when our expectations for academic performance are vague to us, we give our students less confidence in our judgment and less trust that our judgment is fair.

Part of the challenge in this Driving Principle is that many of us educators haven't ever been trained to define our grades in terms of academic achievement: What makes an A if not simply 90 percent of the points? For some of us, the honest answer may be that we don't know what qualifies a student to receive an A other than accumulating a high percentage of points according to our grading software. We've been stuck in the points-as-achievement universe where points or percentages define the grade. The questions we need to explicitly answer are "What would a student have to show, or fail to show, in her understanding of a concept, to warrant a C? What quality of work do we define as A quality?" To do this hard work, we will have to define what students must demonstrate to prove they have learned, or what mistakes identify that they haven't learned.

Boud (2000) writes,

> *Grades or marks are a form of code familiar to teachers, but which acts as a barrier to student understanding. Rather than have teachers encode their comments into a symbol whose meaning is not shared only to have students attempt to decode this symbol to gain feedback, better to minimise the translations required between comment and reception. "Say what you mean" is a characteristic of good feedback. Grades always say more or less. More in the sense that they place a weight of classification on a piece of work which binds the learner to the classification, less in the sense that grades cannot point effectively to the specifics of what can be undertaken for improvement. (p. 6)*

Tackling this work—making grades "say what we mean" with details, specificity, and transparency—means that we will have to lift the veil from over our own eyes, to articulate for ourselves what students should learn and what that learning looks like beyond broad adjectives and *independent* of points. If we can describe the equality of work or understanding each grade represents, we will have lifted the veil—targets will be clear, and therefore, attainable. Every student can hit a target as long as she can see it and it doesn't move.

Rubrics: What Are They, and Why?

Perhaps the most effective and pedagogically powerful ways to lift the veil on our academic targets is through rubrics. A rubric describes how a piece of work or a performance will be evaluated—the specific criteria as well as what constitutes distinctive gradations of quality for every criterion. Here is a simple rubric that a physical education teacher used to evaluate students' skills at the end of a basketball unit (the acronym BEEF is a reminder of the proper shooting technique: **B**alance, **E**yes (on target), **E**lbow in correct position, **F**ollow-Through):

	1	2	3	4
PASSING	Student does not attempt to pass the ball to a teammate during a game of basketball.	Student is able to pass the ball but not yet with accuracy. The teammate has to move more than 5 feet to receive the pass.	Student is able to pass the basketball accurately to a teammate in a game of basketball.	Student is able to pass the ball accurately between two defenders.
DRIBBLING	Student does not dribble the ball and constantly walks or runs with the ball in hand.	Student dribbles the ball at times with two hands.	Student is able to dribble the ball with one hand at a time.	Student is able to cross over a defender and break ankles.
SHOOTING	Student does not attempt to shoot the ball at all during a basketball game.	Student executes some of the letters of BEEF on shots taken during a basketball game.	Student is able to execute all of the letters of BEEF consistently during shots.	Student is able to execute all of the letters of BEEF consistently during shots and is able to make all or most shots.

For each of the basketball unit's skills, the teacher evaluates student performance on a scale of 1 to 4. Later in this chapter, we'll address some effective approaches to scoring rubrics; using a 4-point scale, as this teacher did, is a good start. For more examples of teachers' rubrics across subjects and grade levels, see gradingforequity.org.

Ordinarily, the only target for students on an assignment is to get the most points, to follow the teacher's instructions the best they can. Students can get feedback, and the students in families with a stronger educational background can use their experiences to identify what makes a performance on an assignment "good enough," but the target of exactly what makes an assignment an A versus a B is largely hidden in the teacher's mind. What makes rubrics such a valuable strategy for equitable grading is that what distinguishes one score from another is explicitly described. With a rubric, the teacher's considerations and definitions of quality are now made manifest for everyone to access. The students don't have to guess or infer how to succeed.

The rubric "democratizes" the power to evaluate. In traditional grading, the teacher is the only "expert," the only one with the knowledge, information, and ability to determine the quality of a student performance. Students are beholden to the all-knowledgeable teacher's judgment and become dependent on that judgment. "Is this good enough?" "How did I do?" are the questions teachers must repeatedly answer, because *no one else in the classroom can.* Rather than be passive recipients of grades who must depend on the unassailable and opaque, but determinative, judgments of their teachers, rubrics share information and power. Rubrics equip students to self-assess and even to peer-assess work, empowering them not only to know exactly what grade they will get, but exactly what to improve in order to earn a higher grade. The teacher is sharing with students exactly the recipe for success, and although students might need varying levels of support to properly "cook," they know exactly how that work will be judged.

Traditional grading is embedded with ambiguity, including what qualifies as an A, and we know that the more ambiguous the situation, the more likely that implicit bias will operate because a teacher's "background experiences and automatic associations shape his or her interpretation of the scene" (Ogletree, Smith, & Wald, 2012, as cited in Staats, 2014, p. 53).

Rubrics make grading so much more straightforward and bias-resistant, relieving the teacher of the worry that her evaluation of student work won't be objective: giving a higher grade on student work that has nicer penmanship, more "glitter," or other qualities that aren't relevant to the evaluation of student knowledge and that often inequitably reflect a student's resources or supports, but that nonetheless often influence a grade. Rubrics can protect us from bringing our implicit biases about students into our evaluation, and because the rubric shows exactly what we are using to evaluate students' performance, it engenders more confidence in the students that the teacher isn't judging their performance by anything *other* than what is on the rubric.

Rubrics also help teachers make sure that our evaluations are consistent: When we have dozens of students' assignments to grade, perhaps the first papers in the stack are judged one way, but by the twentieth or twenty-fifth paper we make shifts in our evaluative lens. Perhaps we find trends in student mistakes and we grade the rest of the stack more leniently, or we realize our expectations were too low and we evaluate papers further in the pile more stringently.

Finally, what makes rubrics so valuable is also what can make them challenging to construct. Rubrics require us to identify and articulate how student work will be graded, as well as the different gradations of quality that will earn each grade, with the goal that anyone who uses the rubric will make a similar judgment about the work. Rubrics force teachers to "up our game," to be more thoughtful and objective in how we define what we expect from students, and to be held accountable to those expectations. It forces us to share the target, to describe what it means to hit the target and what it looks like to fall short; it ensures that we leave that target where it is so that everyone can hit it. Rubrics don't just make students more accountable to high-quality work; they hold teachers to their expectations:

"I like rubrics. They hold the teachers accountable because both the student knows what the teacher wants and the teacher has to actually think about how they're going to grade something, instead of just throwing an assignment out and saying, 'Do this today.' I feel like the teacher puts more effort in on the grading side and grading the assignment, so there's more effort from both sides." (Damian high school student)

In all these ways, rubrics increase the accuracy and bias-resistance of our grading and motivate students by giving them more trust that their teacher will treat them fairly.

Scoring Rubrics and Grade Book Entries

Beware: Incredibly detailed and clear rubrics can result in inaccuracy and inequity if teachers accidentally apply the flawed mathematics of traditional grading addressed in chapters 7 and 8: using the 0–100-percentage scale or averaging.

A common mistake teachers make is to calculate the rubric score as a ratio—the number of points a student earned in each criterion divided by the total number of possible points across the entire rubric. In chapter 7, we learned about the mathematical unsoundness of the 0–100 scale and how it is disproportionately and inequitably oriented toward failure. If we apply a ratio to the rubric scoring, we're converting our score into a 0–100-point scale with all its inequities and inaccuracies. This mistake of turning a rubric score into a ratio is an extremely common pitfall for teachers, reflecting how deeply pervasive and unconscious we are of our inherited, yet unfair and mathematically inaccurate system, of grading.

For example, in the basketball rubric, a student can earn between a 1 and 4 for three different criteria, and let's assume that meeting the standard is demonstrating skills at the 3 level. If we apply the mathematics of traditional grading, we total the number of points the student earned divided by 12 (4 points possible for each of the three criteria). If a student scored at the 2 level in all the categories, signifying that she nearly met the standard in every area, her total score would be 6 points earned out of 12 points possible = 50 percent, which translates into an F. Nearly meeting the standard in every skill area shouldn't result in an F. In fact, if she met the standard with a 3 in one skill and earned 7 points, she would still have a failing grade (7 divided by 12 = 58%). When we integrate the 0–100 scale with its disproportionate alignment toward failure, we get more, and undeserved, failures. To solve this problem and avoid warping our intended grade, we should never introduce the 0–100-percentage scale into rubric scoring, which means we should *never total scores and apply a ratio calculation to a rubric.*

Here are four alternative approaches to derive a rubric score:

1. Average the scores (mean), identify the most frequent score across the criteria (mode), or order the scores of criteria from low to high and take the middle number (median). In other words, define the student's performance on the rubric according to professional judgment and mathematically sound considerations. Then, having generated a single number, translate that number directly into a grade using a GPA-like translation table (see page 82 in chapter 7).

2. Record distinct criteria as separate grades in the grade book to ensure clarity and transparency. Are multiple standards assessed by the rubric such that a single score would blur important distinctions and give unclear feedback? Would entering separate scores into the grade book for different criteria or clusters of criteria provide clearer descriptions of student achievement?

3. Decide the value of each criterion and weight each appropriately. Is each criterion of relatively equal weight or are some criteria worth more than others? For example, in calculating the overall grade, teachers can "double-weight" a criterion—calculate the average score and count the most important criterion twice. A criterion can be the "floor" or "ceiling" of the overall grade regardless of performance on the other criteria. For example, the teacher of the basketball unit could decide that dribbling is the most important of the three skills, and that a student couldn't earn an overall score that is higher than her rubric score on this specific criterion. In other words, the teacher could communicate that no matter how well a student shoots or passes, her proficiency at dribbling has to be of high quality to earn a high grade for the unit.

4. Score criteria but don't include those scores in the grade. Rubrics can be part of classroom community of feedback (see chapter 13). For example, the rubric could include a fourth criterion—Teamwork—which the teacher could score only to give feedback and to help the student see the relationship between those behaviors and her rubric score.

Using Rubrics to Empower Students

When a rubric explicitly describes the teacher's expectations, it fulfills the first criteria of our Motivation pillar's Driving Principle to "Lift the Veil": making a grade transparent and understandable. But the real power of the rubric is in how it achieves the second element: Every student can know her grade at any time and know exactly how to get the grade she wants. Zora, a high school student, perfectly captures this idea: "A rubric is almost like an instruction manual on how you complete an assignment properly." In contrast to perceiving grades as something arbitrary that the teacher assigns based on mysterious factors or personal feelings toward the student, a rubric gives the student power and agency over her performance. When the veil of the teacher's expectations is lifted for students to see, the student can self-assess her work, set a goal for herself, and know exactly what it will take to reach that goal. Rubrics foster a growth mindset because everyone can identify her own current achievement and can identify her next step.

However, because rubrics are complex evaluation instruments, and because so many students have never been asked, or allowed, to be evaluators, they require lots of assistance with comprehending and using them. We can't just hand out a rubric and expect students to understand it. Here are a few rubric scaffolding techniques:

- Focus students only on a single criterion rather than all the criteria at once, and then add criteria as students become familiar with the task and learn how to apply the rubric.

- Ask students to translate the rubric into student-friendly language to identify what distinguishes each level of performance within a criterion.

- Have students find specific connections between the instructions for a project and its rubric to help students recognize the relationship between both documents.

It's also important to "calibrate" interpretations of a rubric to ensure that the teacher and students apply the expectations of the rubric similarly. Just as evaluators of standardized essay tests calibrate so that they all have consistent scoring, teachers calibrate with students to ensure that they clearly understand and don't misinterpret the rubric to be either unrealistically demanding or too forgiving. Students individually or as a class can be asked to evaluate a student work sample so the teacher can assess the students' interpretations of the rubric and adjust them to match her own. Calibrating a rubric with students also affirms you are immunizing your grading against biases and irrelevancies because students will see that their grade will be based only on the criteria in the rubric.

Jasmine, who has taught middle school art for two years, calibrates expectations before they begin each project by having her students evaluate a project sample from prior years using that project's rubric. After every student individually assigns scores to the same sample project, she requires that the students come to consensus on the scores for that sample, first in small groups and then as an entire class. Students share different opinions and debate those opinions, often passionately, by referring to evidence in the project and the details of the rubric. This exercise helps her to ensure that the entire class has a common understanding of the rubric's expectations and students can apply that common understanding when they do their own project. It also reveals ambiguities and weaknesses in her own rubric, and she can make corrections before students begin the project.

Jasmine has found an interesting piece of data from this exercise: The more students argue among each other (gauged by engagement, volume, passion) in their process of coming to consensus, the better performance the students have on that project. Jasmine theorizes that the students' performances increase because the act of arguing deepens their understanding and internalization of the rubric contents. Because of this, she even finds ways to facilitate more "arguing" during calibration activities. Teachers dread students arguing about whether we awarded enough points on a test answer or a project, but what if that arguing could actually improve their performance?

Expanding feedback beyond the traditional teacher–student assessment relationship—the student does something and the teacher tells her how she did—is difficult. Dislodging the locus of assessment authority from teachers and transferring it to students (peers and the self) can be unnerving for everyone. But imagine the benefits: No more students asking, "Is this good enough?" or "How do I get a better grade?" We teachers are responsible for assigning a grade—no one else does, or should, have that authority. However, in determining the quality of work or what needs to be improved, we aren't the only ones who can do that. Arguably, if we're really going to empower our students as learners, we can't be.

"Lifting the Veil" for Tests: The Opacity of Points

We can imagine how rubrics make teachers' expectations transparent for certain types of assessments—lab reports, essays, arts or sports performances, projects, and other presentations. But what if we assess student knowledge with a test, with multiple choice questions, short answers, extended responses, and diagrams? Most of us try to make our expectations transparent with a Review Sheet that includes a list of concepts and skills that will be covered in the test or quiz. We tell students, "Study these topics as best as you can and you'll get a good grade on the test." But could we be more transparent? Could we lift the veil even more for students and explain exactly what they will have to do to get a specific grade on these types of assessments, or better yet, how to be successful on *any* assessment, regardless of the format or design?

Let's start a few steps back, reiterating the traditional design and evaluation of tests. When we construct an assessment, we make a total number of points available, and for every student who takes the assessment, we count up the points she earns, divide by the number of points possible, which renders a ratio or percentage that falls into our grading scale and . . . presto, we have a grade for that student. A student earned 42 points out of 50 = 84 percent, which translates into a B. We saw in chapter 4 the weaknesses of the "omnibus" grade that collapses disparate information into a single grade, revealing almost no helpful information about the student. We'll see how our common use of points to score and measure achievement replicates the inequities of omnibus grading on a smaller scale and explore a much more equitable approach: student scales.

Suppose three students earned the following on a test that assessed multiple standards:

	PART 1: STANDARD 1 (20 PTS POSSIBLE)	PART 2: STANDARD 2 (20 PTS POSSIBLE)	PART 3: STANDARD 3 (20 PTS POSSIBLE)	TOTAL SCORE
Miguel	8	20	20	48 / 60 = 80%
Olivia	16	16	16	48 / 60 = 80%
Kamryn	20	20	8	48 / 60 = 80%

All three students earned the same number of points, and therefore the same grade, but demonstrated very different performances. Miguel and Kamryn deeply understand two of the three topics and know little about the third, but they earned the same number of points as Olivia, who has reasonably competent knowledge of all three topics. If each part of the quiz addresses a distinct standard, then it's deeply problematic if all three students receive the same B–; each clearly has different profiles of what they know and what they don't yet know. If we were asked to identify students for additional support and looked only at composite quiz scores, we would miss the fact that Miguel and Kamryn clearly need support before moving on— Miguel with part 1 content and Kamryn with part 3 content.

The fungibility of points—every point is equal to and can substitute for every other—is a hallmark of traditional grading, but it makes the measurement of student achievement clumsy and misleading. We want assessment scores to clearly represent each student's unique performance in our class—their specific strengths and weaknesses—but points often prevent us from doing this. What's more, accurate information about our students' achievement becomes hidden from *them*—Miguel and Kamryn might think that their 48/60 means they're as ready as Olivia for the next unit, which is simply not true.

Think about what message we are sending: What does it take to earn a B? 48 points. Not only is that unhelpful and, if we want students to focus less on points, counterproductive, but it conceals how to earn a higher grade beyond "score more points"—6 more points on this quiz to be precise. What does that even mean for a leaner? We're not lifting a veil—we're giving students glasses with number (#) signs painted on the lenses.

But what if a grade on an assessment weren't determined by points students earned, but on the quality of their performance? What if the student who knew two of the three topics could be distinguished from the student who knew two-thirds of each topic? To do this, we need to identify a more transparent way to describe students' performances. We want students to understand that a quiz or test grade isn't defined by a numerical score but is a reflection of their level of mastery of the course content, or the course standards. If we don't want students to be surprised or confused about why they got a C+ instead of a B-, the assessment grade has to be something other than an earned number of points or a percentage cutoff. What would this look like?

Beyond Points: Standards Scales

Instead of calculating point totals, we can create a scale with simple descriptors along a continuum of standards mastery (see Marzano, 2011):

GRADE	LEVEL OF MASTERY
A	Exceeded the standard
B	Met the standard
C	Student has key gaps in their understanding of the standard
D	Student is unable to demonstrate B or C levels without assistance
F	No evidence

For each standard, the teacher describes what the student would demonstrate to qualify for each level of mastery. The teacher identifies the B level by describing exactly what it means for a student to meet the content standard, the C level describes performance that reveals students' common misconceptions or knowledge gaps, and the A level describes the advanced application or analysis of the content standard the student would need to demonstrate. Note that the D level description explains that the student can show C or B level performance but only with support and scaffolding, which encompasses all student performance below a C and sends the motivational message that meeting the standard is possible for all students; it's just a matter of time and practice. An F is only earned when there is missing information.

Teachers, as content experts, have a conception of what constitutes competence on a standard. After all, we teach curriculum, assign homework and classwork to learn and practice content, design assessments to measure content knowledge, and provide feedback. We know conceptually what it means to demonstrate competence on the standards we teach. Ordinarily, the traditional approach to evaluation privileges students who have had more academic success, who can better "read" the signals of the teacher, or whose caregivers have a stronger educational background. Creating a scale for a standard forces us to move beyond applying a "knowing it when we see it" definition of competence, and instead to articulate that conception, to make it transparent to everyone in the classroom. Standards scales, like rubrics, ensure that we honestly and thoughtfully have defined what matters to us, and that we aren't inadvertently bringing biased assumptions or hidden expectations to our evaluations.

This work to create scales for standards isn't easy. It requires a deep knowledge of the content and of students' common prior knowledge and misconceptions, and teachers should create standards scales with department or grade-level colleagues and pool their resources and experiences. Fortunately, there are also a handful (and growing) number of online resources that publish scales of standards. (See grading forequity.org.)

The Effects of Standards Transparency

Once teachers establish standards scales, they begin to shift how they approach assessments—their purpose, design, and grading process. Rather than create a test oriented so that the total points add up to 100, or even establishing points for each question, teachers design assessments with the sole purpose of being able to accurately identify a student's level of achievement on a standard. The teacher must decide which assessment strategies or design—project, multiple-choice questions, essay, for example—will yield the most complete evidence of a student's understanding, and the number of questions or tasks on the assessment is the minimum number that the teacher believes necessary to elicit the student responses that allow the teacher to accurately describe a student's level of mastery. Assigning points to questions becomes unnecessary. A student doesn't earn a ratio of overall points earned divided by possible points. Instead, the teacher reports the student's level of achievement on the standard tested: "You have earned a C+ on the immigration standard based on the totality of your performance on the assessment: because you did not yet demonstrate knowledge of both a government and a public response to immigration."

Standards scales change more than assessment designs; they can transform the language of learning and achievement in a classroom. First, rather than defining student achievement in terms of a percentage score or total points ("You scored 98 out of 125, or a 78 percent on the assessment."), a student's performance is described in terms of the standard: "You have met the immigration standard for Irish immigrants but haven't yet demonstrated all of the elements of the standard for Mexican immigration, or the comparative response to their immigration." Secondly, because the expectations on a student scale are detailed and transparent, teachers report that arguments over whether a student has demonstrated sufficient learning becomes a thing of the past. What students must show and do is explicit and not ambiguous. There is no more arguing over points ("Why did I only get 2 out of 5 points for this question?").

Joanna, a middle school math teacher, shares a standards scale with students when she begins a new unit. Throughout that unit, she often refers to that scale and the different levels of mastery by which students will be evaluated. In fact, she even includes the scale on the quizzes and summative tests. By making her curricular goals and performance expectations so transparent, she not only demystifies her plan learning and the path to success, but she equips students to self-assess their progress and enlists them to self-identify learning gaps. As a final question on Joanna's assessments, each student must self-identify her level of standards mastery. For Joanna, the transparency of expectations has transformed the discourse of the classroom—what learning means, how it is described, and how it is evaluated. Rather than students seeing their achievement in terms of point accumulation, agnostic about how and indifferent why they accumulate points, students reconceptualize their own achievement, progress, and goals and see themselves on a trajectory of learning with clear descriptions of each step along that path: "In this algebra unit, I still need help remembering all four computations of the FOIL method, but once I can do it myself, I'll be at the standard." Lifting the veil for the requirements for success makes success possible: A student can increase her level of achievement by "moving up" the standards scale. Plus, students being able to describe their current level of achievement and the next level gives them ownership and empowerment over their grade, a stark contrast to our traditional system.

Standards-Based Grade Books

Once we describe the levels of performance for each standard, and decide that our grades will consist only of student achievement against those levels of performance, how can our grade book facilitate this approach and allow us to track and report each student's level of achievement for every standard? Traditional grade books are organized by listing every assignment and assessment chronologically, each with its own score entry (points earned out of points possible) and tied to a category ("Homework") with its own percentage weight. By contrast, grade books designed to reflect student performance on standards have a much simpler, and therefore more transparent and comprehensible, organization.

Take a look at a portion of the computer grade book that Kelly, a middle school English teacher for five years, uses:

Reporting Term: Q1

Students (33)	(Q1) Final Grade	Standards						Assignments			
		RI.6.1 Textual Evidence 8/8/2016 pts: 4	RI.6.2 Central Idea 8/8/2016 pts: 4	RI.6.4 Meaning of Words 8/8/2016 pts: 4	RI.6.6 Point of View 8/8/2016 pts: 4	RI.6.9 Compare and Contrast 8/8/2016 pts: 4	Conventions 8/8/2016 pts: 4	RI.6.1 Worksheet 1 8/10/2016 pts: 4	RI.6.1 Role-play 8/12/2016 pts: 4	RI.6.1 Essay #1 8/16/2016 pts: 4	RI.6.2 Essay #1 8/16/2016 pts: 4
Student 1	B–	2.5	3	3	2	2	2	2	2	2.5	2
Student 2	B	3.5	3	3	2	3	3	0	0	3.5	2.5
Student 3	C+	2	3	2.5	1.5	2.5	3	3	4	2	2.5
Student 4	C–	1	1	2	1	2.5	2	0	0	1	1
Student 5	C	2	2	1	2	2.5	2	3	2	2	2
Student 6	C	2	1.5	2.5	2.5	2	3	3	2	2	2
Student 7	C–	2	2	1	1	2	2	0	0	2	2
Student 8	C+	3	2.5	1	1	3	3	3	3	3	2

The first five columns (RI.6.1 through RI.6.9) are the English standards Kelly plans to teach in Quarter 1; the Conventions column is an additional standard Kelly included to measure and report; and the last columns on the right are the first four assignments of the term—the first a homework worksheet, the second an in-class role-play, and so on—with each tagged to a standard. Each column has a maximum score of 4 points. All the standards columns are dated 8/8/2016, the first day of the term, and the assignments are dated when they occur.

Before the term began, Kelly populated the first columns with the standards she anticipated covering. When students completed the first assignment on 8/10/2016, she entered their level of performance (0–4) on the standard addressed by that assignment. When students completed the second assignment on 8/12/2016, and the essay assessment on 8/16/2016, she entered each student's level of performance. She then considered the three pieces of data related to standard RI.6.1—two homework assignments and an essay—and, based on the scale for that standard, manually assigned a level of mastery grade in the first blue column: the student's performance on that standard based on the evidence so far. Because the essay also assessed standard RI.6.2, a standard that she hadn't yet taught, she chose not to manually enter the data into the standards column for RI.6.2, but only entered it as a second score for the essay. This process extends throughout the term: With subsequent additional evidence (tests, quizzes, projects) of the students' achievement, she manually updates the grade on each standard when the evidence persuades her that the student's level of mastery has changed. And here's the kicker: Because an equitable grade should reflect only a student's performance on these standards, the data in the columns of students' performance on the standards and the Convention column are the *only elements included in the grade, collectively weighted at 100 percent.* All of the data of a student's work in the class—homework, classwork, behaviors, and even summative assessments (far right)—are not incorporated into the grade calculation through complex formulas as they are traditionally. In Kelly's standards-based grade book, *all assignments and assessments are weighted at 0 percent of the grade.* The information from her assessments, whether they be formative or summative, are assessed against the standards and their performance levels, and then Kelly applies her professional judgment to manually enter the most accurate and current description of the student's performance.

Let's look at two students from Kelly's class. Student 3 showed proficiency of the standard RI.6.1 on the homework (earning a 3) and in-class assignments (3) but showed a low performance on the essay assessment. Rather than being forced to incorporate all three scores through a complex calculation of weights and averages, which is what happens to teachers in traditional grading, Kelly applied her professional judgment to decide that the essay assessment score was a more valid representation of Student 3's performance level on RI.6.1 than the homework and in-class assignments, and therefore manually entered a 2 in that standard's column. For Student 2, who did not turn in the homework assignment and was absent during the role-play assignment, Kelly entered zeros for those assignments. But because that student demonstrated proficiency and somewhat exceeded the standard (scoring a 3.5 on the essay assessment), Kelly entered that score in the standard's column. The student's absence or missing assignment weren't incorporated into the grade, although Kelly did report the absences and the school reached out to the student's caregiver. If Kelly would have been forced to include the absence or missed assignment, the grade would have been lower and misrepresented the student's academic performance.

The standards-based grade book does not depend, and is not determined by, the calculations of any software; instead, the teacher manually enters every grade. When entering a grade for a standard, the teacher gets to make an important decision that teachers are rarely asked and able to make and get to apply an expertise that she has rarely been expected, asked, or able to exercise: The teacher must consider which evidence is valid and what is the student's most accurate and current grade. What level of achievement did the student demonstrate on the recent essay test compared to their essay test of a month ago, and which is more valid? Did the student do poorly on the multiple choice test but show through multiple classroom activities and in-class assignments that she demonstrated competence? Teachers become obligated not to the mathematical calculations of the grade book software, but to ensure that they are getting accurate measurements of a student's performance on the standards rubric. And if the teacher determines that an assessment impeded the valid measurement or misrepresented the student's achievement, then the teacher can consider the assessment accordingly. It may seem a radical and almost transcendent approach to assessment, but it boils down to the same essential questions recommended by Ralph Tyler (1949), an educator who played a key role in the development of educational evaluation and assessment, in the mid-twentieth century: (1) What should my students learn and be able to do? and (2) What evidence will I accept to verify that learning?

The traditionally complex and opaque calculation of grades is replaced with a simple manual entry according to a transparent rubric. Manual entry of a student's performance level, rather than inputting numbers into a calculation, might feel like we're inviting subjectivity, but we mitigate this with clear rubrics, standards scales, and calibration with our colleagues and students. Traditional grading drives a teacher to use "grade hacks" (chapter 4) so that final grade calculations conform to her professional judgment. Teachers find that, after initial worries, grading this way is tremendously empowering and capitalizes on their professional expertise. With standards-based grading, a teacher applies her judgment directly, evaluating student evidence against the teacher's defined levels of student mastery. Teachers become obligated not to the mathematical calculations of the grade book software but to explicitly stated descriptions of what students must demonstrate to earn the grade they want.

Beyond sheer simplicity, which cannot be emphasized enough as we compare this to the bean-counting and impenetrably complex calculations of our current grade books, entering an achieved level of mastery on a standard based on the totality of evidence of that student's performance can have numerous benefits to the learning process. The teacher can more easily identify trends in her students' achievement and can spot which students need additional support for which standards. By a simple glance at the standards columns of her grade book, Kelly can pinpoint what concepts to reteach, how to group students by weakness and strength, and determine what skills need additional practice.

We're truly lifting the veil, telling students exactly what they have to do to succeed. Some teachers are initially uncomfortable with this transparency, but there's no better evidence that there's something wrong with the game of school if we're uncomfortable with students knowing how to play it. We can't fear students understanding our grading system; in fact, we want them to, for that will give them the most faith and trust in us and the school, especially when they see how they can control their own grade. They haven't yet met the B level for one of the standards? They just need to demonstrate that they've improved and can meet it, perhaps by redoing an earlier assessment. This opens entire new worlds of assessment and student ownership. Kim, a high school English teacher for seventeen years, allows students to propose their *own* method of demonstrating achievement on a standard:

"Some students want a teacher-created assessment to demonstrate what they've learned. Other students I give the opportunity to create their own assessments. If they can propose a way to show what they've learned that fits their style and is more accurate, I have no problem accepting their summative assessment. An example of a student-proposed assessment is when a student asked, instead of writing an essay on the themes of Hamlet, if he could write a short film. He created a modern version of Hamlet, written, directed, filmed, and edited by him, and it definitely served as evidence of him getting everything I wanted him to get out of the play."

With standards-based grading, the whole world of teaching and learning is no longer so opaque, mysterious, and unknown. With the veil lifted, the path to academic success is a simple map that anyone—teacher, student, caregiver—can navigate to gauge her own current achievement, set goals, and plan next steps. The expectations for standards mastery are transparent and fixed and enable teachers to assess that mastery and allow students to demonstrate it through multiple assessment sources.

Veils, Rubrics, and the "Real World"

What about the real world, where there aren't rubrics and standards scales for every performance? The adult world is full of veils, so are we coddling our students, setting them up for failure in the world to come? Is this particularly unfair to historically underserved students, who will likely face more veils than our privileged students, and with less opportunity to see behind the curtain?

In chapter 11, we addressed how retakes, an equitable practice that some might mistakenly allege does not reflect the adult world, are actually common when adults are demonstrating competence and often available in professional environments when we ask for them; by normalizing the concept of retakes, we equip and embolden students to ask for them. Similarly, when we normalize rubrics and standards scales, we help students understand that those who will judge us have expectations. If we know what those expectations are, we are more likely to meet them. Rather than making students more vulnerable, we are training them to advocate for transparency, to ask what specifically is expected of them in order to get an A on the college project, to earn an outstanding performance evaluation, or to receive the scholarship award. Even though the students whose families went to college and earn higher-paying jobs may have had the experience to know those expectations regardless of whether a veil is present, for lower-income and less privileged students, we are teaching them to seek clarity about what is expected of them and the criteria for success. Just like the college professor who only needs to be asked for a retake in order to provide it and be more equitable, those who, by not "lifting the veil" inadvertently perpetuate the knowledge gap that prevents some from accessing pathways to success, now will be asked for explicitness about what it takes to succeed. Our students will come to expect, request, and perhaps rightly to *demand* that the hidden become transparent.

Teachers often dread conversations with students and caregivers about grades, who may believe that grades can be adjusted through advocacy and negotiation. What should be an evaluation of the student's performance can feel like a court battle or a guilt trip. Sometimes even the principal or another school administrator engages in that conversation with the teacher, upgrading a teacher's feeling from dread to disgust and frustration.

As we've discussed, not only does this dynamic reinforce an unhealthy understanding of what a grade represents, but it places those students and families who have less confidence, comfort, language, and resources at a significant disadvantage, and injects more potential biases into grading. By contrast, well-constructed rubrics and standards scales, in addition to providing clarity, transparency, and agency to students, make grading less negotiable because there is less confusion, ambiguity, and disagreement about what grade is warranted. Teachers and students have identical and objective information about what each grade represents and how to achieve each level, and with enough calibration, negotiation becomes obsolete. Everything a student needs to know, including how to earn any level of performance she wants, is plain as day. Teachers, students, and their caregivers function as teammates working from the same game plan and set of rules. All veils are lifted, trust is strengthened, and students become hopeful and motivated to succeed.

Summary of Concepts

1. Traditional grading, because of its reliance on points and complex calculations, can seem opaque and arbitrary. Although teachers have conceptions of what they are expecting from student academic performance, these ideas often are inchoate and stay inside the teacher's mind, inadvertently concealing what it takes to succeed and disempowering students. When academic expectations are hidden, grading privileges students whose families have had more access to those expectations, either from prior success in school or in other institutions of power. Equitable grading lifts the veils in classrooms.

2. For any assessment, rubrics are a powerful way to make expectations transparent. Effective rubrics are detailed, clear, and student friendly so that they equip students to be evaluators of their own performance. Rubrics facilitate calibration of expectations not only among students and teachers, but among teachers. Ultimately, calibrated rubrics and standards scales ensure both objectivity and validity, and reduce bias.

3. Scales for standards describe student performance levels, and free the teacher to score assessments not based on points earned but based on the level of standards mastery a student demonstrates. Instead of being dependent on the complex calculations of a grade book, teachers can utilize their professional expertise to determine a student's grade based on a totality of evidence of a student's knowledge across multiple assessment events.

4. A standards-based grade book simplifies what a grade represents and how it is earned, empowering and enlisting students to self-identify areas of strength and weakness, and to know precisely what it takes to succeed.

Questions to Consider

1. Think about your professional career. How have your supervisors made the evaluation of your work transparent, or opaque? How has that transparency, or opacity, affected your feelings of trust, empowerment, motivation, and how you did your job? How could you have gotten more clarity about your supervisor's expectations, and how would greater common understanding between the two of you have changed your feelings and your work?

2. For Teachers: Draft a rubric for an upcoming assessment or select one you've already created and assess it against the "rubric for rubrics" at **www.gradingfore quity.org**. What are ways that your rubric could be more transparent and equitable?

3. For Teachers: This chapter has suggested that teachers need to be the creators of rubrics, but could students create them? Try this constructivist approach: Give students exemplars for an upcoming project, lab report, or essay, and have them identify criteria and the descriptors for different levels of performance in their own words. (Depending on their developmental level and experience with rubrics, they may need scaffolding such as sample criteria or guiding questions.) When they assist with creating a rubric, how does it affect their understanding of the expectations for that assessment, and with this understanding, how does it affect their motivation and performance on that assessment?

CHAPTER 13

Practices That Build "Soft Skills" Without Including Them in the Grade

- **Emphasizing Self-Regulation**
- **Creating a Community of Feedback**
- **Student Trackers**

In this chapter, we will answer the following questions:

1. How are "soft skills" traditionally treated in grading? How is this inherited practice inequitable, and how does it neither mimic nor prepare students for the professional world (sometimes colloquially called the "real world")? What does feedback on soft skills look and sound like in the real world?

2. How can more equitable grading reconnect the causal relationship between soft skills and academic success, and thereby engender students' intrinsic motivation?

3. What is self-regulation, how is it a "sustainable assessment" critical to students' lifelong success, and how can providing feedback independent of a grade build this soft skill?

4. What are ways to create a "community of feedback," and how does this empower and motivate students?

> *Driving Principle: Equitable grading distinguishes and connects the means for learning effectively—the "soft skills," the practice, the mistakes—from its ends—academic success, and utilizes the broad and diverse universe of feedback and consequences, of which only one part is a grade.*

In this chapter, we'll first define what we generally categorize as "soft skills," and then review the research on whether giving a grade for soft skills improves motivation and student performance. We'll squarely examine a common justification that is made for including soft skills in a student's grade: that doing so effectively replicates the feedback in the real world and therefore prepares students for success in that world. How do teachers often describe the "real world," how much does this portrayal of the real world truly reflect the adult world, and what are the implications for equitable grading? What might be behind teachers' characterization of the real world? Finally, we'll explore some alternative feedback methods for building students' soft skills, including assigning two types of grades, building a community of feedback, and supporting students' reflection, goal-setting, and other self-regulation skills.

"Soft Skills"

Most educators believe that they aren't just obligated to teach students the "hard" academic standards. We must teach students the nonacademic skills and behaviors ("soft skills") that are so important to school and lifelong success. Even if students don't learn all of our course content, they have to learn how to be successful in the workplace, to be responsible and contributing members to a community. Some might even argue that these soft skills are *more* important than the academic content. A discussion of equitable grading is incomplete if we don't address the nagging discomfort the previous chapters may have raised: If equitable grading requires us to include only academic performance in the grade and to therefore exclude student performance on these important and lifelong skills, how do we teach and value these nonacademic skills?

This leads us to deepen our examination of equitable grading's third pillar: Motivational. In this last Driving Principle, we want to distinguish between the behaviors of effective learning and the results of those behaviors and include only the latter in a student's grade in order to build intrinsic motivation for the former.

Let's first define what we mean by "soft skills," often a catch-all description of a wide range of student behaviors that we value in our schools and classrooms. Soft skills can include any or all of the following:

Examples of Soft Skills

- Working collaboratively with peers
- Time management
- Project planning and implementation
- Making good decisions
- Completing responsibilities
- Meeting deadlines
- Negotiating conflict
- Consistent attendance
- Punctuality

- Taking pride in one's work
- Problem-solving
- Thinking creatively
- Perseverance (or "grit")
- Advocacy
- Asking questions
- Completing paperwork
- Making good decisions
- Listening to directions
- Showing respect toward adults and peers

In traditional grading, teachers house this diverse set of data in a weighted grading category called "Habits of Work," or "Citizenship," or "Study Skills," or something similar to denote that these skills are part of the grade but distinct from the academic content. While it's not necessary to create a taxonomy for these various skills, some are clearly more measurable than others. A teacher could evaluate whether a student could meet deadlines by documenting how many assignments were submitted on time, or measure promptness by the number of times a student was tardy. For other soft skills, it's logistically impossible for a single teacher to perceive all the opportunities students have to show these skills in a classroom and then to evaluate the skills. We aren't omnipresent enough to spot every instance in which a student could show respect, omniscient enough to evaluate each occurrence, or immune to our own biased perceptions, and don't have nearly enough time to enter all the data in our grade book. Many teachers therefore enter soft skill data more holistically. Every student might receive a daily or weekly score for soft skills. Some teachers at the end of a term simply enter an overall grade in the Citizenship category based on her reflection on the term or, more realistically, on their most recent and outstanding memories of each student.

Aside from the flaws in our data collection of soft skills, there are several other weaknesses that we've previously addressed: To include soft skills in a grade is to warp its accuracy (remember Tangela and Isabel from chapter 4), occlude its message, and weaken its motivational impact. It also confuses the means for success—the soft skills—with the ends—academic success. As we explained more deeply in chapter 10 regarding homework, we don't want to reward students for doing something because we tell them to. Instead, we want them to learn that soft skills, just like homework, are valuable because they lead to better outcomes. We don't want to motivate students to do homework by giving them a grade for that homework; we motivate students to do homework by grading only the ends of doing that homework—the assessment (which, as we saw in chapter 10, also eliminates the motivation to complete homework independent of its intended purpose to learn: by copying). You do homework in order to perform better on assessments, not because the teacher told you to. Similarly, we want students to manage their time not because we tell them to or just for a grade, but because when they manage their time well they will realize a higher performance. Evaluating soft skills independently of their outcome—giving students points for asking questions or for coming on time regardless of whether those questions or that punctuality lead to better understanding—motivates students to compliantly perform soft skills for the teacher's approval and extrinsic reward, depriving students of experiencing their own sense of *why* the soft skills are important and thereby stunting their internal motivation to develop and use soft skills.

Grading as Feedback

We have to investigate a foundation that supports our traditional practice of grading soft skills: our belief that by grading soft skills we can motivate students to improve them. Is giving a grade for soft skills effective feedback?

Thirty years of research has found that giving students a grade as formative feedback—that is, in the midst of the learning process—demotivates students to learn and reduces their performance (e.g., Black, 2013; Butler, 2008; Butler & Nisan, 1986; Kanfer & Ackerman, 1989; Kluger & DeNisi, 1996; Black, Harrison, Lee, Marshall, & Wiliam, 2004). This is detrimental when we do this for academic learning, but when we grade students during the learning process not only for evidence of their learning but for their behaviors during that learning process, we amplify our role as evaluator, ratchet up the stress in our classrooms, and siphon a student's attention away from mastering the content and toward her individual self-perception, which "inevitably leads to reallocation of cognitive resources" and impedes effective performance (Lipnevich & Smith, 2008). What's more, unlike a student's content knowledge, soft skills are behaviors and habits unavoidably interpreted through a teacher's subjective and biased lens (Can we objectively and impartially evaluate a student's "respect" or "cooperation"?), which means that evaluations of soft skills among our most historically underserved students could have a disproportionately negative impact, further weakening their motivation to learn.

Preparation for the "Real World"

Beyond recognizing how grading soft skills is full of biases and can dampen motivation, many of us find a more heartfelt need to grade soft skills. The research notwithstanding, we may believe that grading soft skills replicates the consequences of the performance of soft skills in the real world. Temy, a high school science teacher of fifteen years explains: "I understand when students don't feel like working today, or they feel depressed or sad. And I know that there's so much going on in their lives. I know that we're trying to be understanding. But if you show up to work and you don't do your job, you get fired." Many teachers, as much as they empathize with their students' lives, share Temy's concern with adequately preparing their students for consequences in the real world.

"In the real world," we warn, "if you hand in a report with typos, you'll lose the contract." "In the real world, if you can't remember key information, the boss will give the work to someone else." "In the real world, if you're late to a meeting, you'll get fired." Shouldn't our grading—the key way we evaluate students—prepare them for evaluation in the world beyond school? Because the idea of grading soft skills is steeped in an argument about adequately preparing our students for the real world, let's critically examine this justification.

First of all, let's recognize that when we assert that the real world is something outside the students' comprehension, a world they can't even imagine, we risk delegitimizing and dismissing their experiences. Their world—of social pressures, caregiver–child dynamics, media influences, physiological changes—is quite "real" to them. For those students who witness or experience violence, psychological trauma, substance abuse, poverty, and home instability, their lives can't be any more real. Ironically, when we suggest that only the world outside of school is real, we devalue the "realness" of school and our own work there. Considering that most of us have spent at least sixteen years of the most formative and consequential years of our lives at school, and that we educators devote our professional lives to the world of schools, it seems strange to dismiss the entire institution and experiences there as not being real and authentic.

So what is this "real world" we reference, presumably to motivate students to work harder or to follow our directions? Often we portray it as a harsh place where there are no second chances, with unforgiving punishments for each transgression, and so we may implement grading practices intending to mimic it. We defend our grading practices that are inflexible or unforgiving as being in our students' best interests—that if we give students only one chance to take a test, subtract points for disruptive behavior or lack of preparation, or reduce a score on an assignment when students submit it late, it mirrors and prepares them for the real world. Adults get paychecks for their work; students get grades for their work. Better to lose points now than money later.

The problem is that the real world is not really like this.

Our current grading practices often provide a clumsy analogy and a misleading picture of the real world. With some critical reflection, we'll realize that the real world—or more specifically, the adult professional world—is much more nuanced in its consequences for mistakes and failure than how we represent it in traditional grading practices.

Let's look at what happens in the adult professional world if I don't demonstrate a strong "soft skill."

If as a teacher I come to a faculty meeting late, hand in a form after the deadline or don't complete it correctly, or don't work well with my colleagues, my principal wouldn't deduct a few dollars from my paycheck, which would be absurd and frankly insulting, and she certainly wouldn't fire me. Instead, my principal could choose from an array of possible responses.

Her first decision might be whether my subpar soft skill is worth worrying about at all: Does my action warrant a response because it significantly and negatively affects my effectiveness as a teacher? In other words, does the weakness in the soft skill affect the goal of my job—the most important of which is to increase student learning? If that behavior doesn't really affect that performance—for example, coming late to a staff meeting—then she might ignore it. If it does affect my performance—coming to my class on time—then she would address it. She also might weigh the impact of my behavior on the larger community of the school—do other teachers start coming late to meetings or does my difficulty in working with colleagues damage staff morale?

If my behavior negatively impacts my effectiveness or the effectiveness of our staff, the second decision my principal would make is how to address my weak soft skill. If it's the first time I fall short of expectations, she might talk with me to clarify the rules or ignore it, giving me the benefit of the doubt. The second time she might discretely pull me aside to ensure that I know her expectations and to give me a chance to share my perspective or circumstances. If there begins to be a pattern, she might schedule a formal meeting to ask if anything's wrong, to see if she can help me problem-solve. She might make some specific recommendations or provide support because of something she learns from our conversation; perhaps I have a hard time getting to first period on time because I have to drop off my two children at two different schools, and the principal might adjust my schedule the next semester so my day starts at second period. If I have been providing incomplete lesson plans, she might suggest that my department chair review my plans before I submit them to make sure that they are completed correctly.

My principal might also have a conversation with me to help me understand the relationship between me coming late to first period, or my incomplete lesson plans, and how that impacts my effectiveness as a teacher, and might emphasize that if I want to be an effective teacher I need to make sure I improve those skills. If I am struggling to work well with colleagues, she might ask me about my own perspective of the interactions to see if I recognize my weaknesses before she decides any action. If the problems continue, she might formalize an improvement plan, provide ways that we would check in on it together, and tell me that there needs to be sufficient improvement or it could negatively impact my annual evaluation. If I am part of a teachers union, my representative would become involved at some point to facilitate my improvement and to ensure my principal applies a fair and clear process. If my weakness in a soft skill becomes a long-term pattern without improvement, I might at some point be placed on some kind of probation with additional processes, supports, and clarification of expectations. If the behavior continues to fall short of expectations without sufficient improvement and thereby so significantly decreases my teaching effectiveness, I could ultimately be re-assigned to another position with different responsibilities or lose my job. The preceding paragraphs should illustrate and remind us that for all professions, including teachers, there is a multistage process of feedback with layered, incremental consequences for soft-skill weakness and mistakes.

When the real world is less forgiving of weak soft skills it is at the most elite levels—among the most sought-after professionals and where stakes are enormous—the Broadway performer who forgets her lines and gets a bad review, or the million-dollar contract negotiation that is lost because the lawyer got the date wrong, or the doctor who is sued because she didn't take her time with reading the x-ray carefully and performed surgery on the wrong limb. But realize that those kinds of circumstances with these drastic consequences don't occur until people are well into their professional careers, and they certainly don't happen while someone is in the learning stage of those skills, as all of our students are and will be for many more years.

Interestingly though, at each stage of schooling we find ourselves portraying the next stage of school as harsh and inflexible. Elementary teachers talk about middle school as an uncaring place, middle school teachers describe high school as unsupportive and dog-eat-dog, and high school teachers caricature college professors as being soulless and indifferent to students' individual needs and interests. Of course, middle school teachers are as caring as they come, high school teachers go out of their way to support every student, and college professors are human beings who build individual relationships and differentiate. Just as in the work world, at every level of schooling there are multilayered and diverse consequences.

Our characterization of the real world is more myth and legend than truth.

Why We Invoke the "Real World"

Assuming we find that the real world treats evaluation and feedback in more complex ways, why do we so easily and frequently resort to an unnuanced caricature? Perhaps we think that the fear of a big bad world will spur urgency and motivation to learn, that the spectre of the real world will induce our students to complete our assignments or to take our class more seriously. We might be doing it because we fear what the world will do to our naive and vulnerable students, so the real-world frame is more of a plea than a scare tactic: "Please listen to us, follow our directions, we beg of you, because the real world will eat you alive!"

A more critical sociopolitical critique is that our portrayal of the real world is intended to prepare students for subordinate positions in the economic hierarchy, replicating our own unfortunate experiences in that hierarchy. Many decades ago, Melvin Kohn (1963) found that middle-class parents disciplined their children in ways that promoted autonomy and independent exercise of judgment—characteristics rewarded in professional occupations—while working-class parents used more authoritarian approaches to discipline, emphasizing obedience and punishment, that replicated their work experiences. We teachers may be expressing the conditions under which we experience our own work within school systems, or perhaps we are constructing an overly simplistic version of the types of workplaces we assume our students will enter—lower-skilled occupations in which behaviors of punctuality and compliance are most rewarded.

Hopefully, this examination of how we speak of the real world and its false description of feedback and consequences will help us to refrain from bludgeoning our students with Draconian grading practices and punishments in the name of real-world preparation. How can we be more honest about the world our students will enter after high school and college, and in what ways can we reflect it in our classrooms to authentically prepare them for it?

Whose "Real World" Are We Talking About?

Another issue to keep in mind when we talk about the real world is that this world is harsher and more unforgiving for some students than for others. In the workplace, we know that women in leadership positions are often judged more harshly and given fewer chances than men. Both inside and outside the workplace, African American and Latinos receive less benefit of the doubt for mistakes (or perceived transgressions) than white people (see Alexander, 2012; Greenhaus, Parasuraman, & Wormley, 1990). It's well known that among many historically underserved groups that "You have to be twice as qualified and make half the mistakes as others to be successful." Depending on who is doing the judging and whose behaviors are being judged, receiving less benefit of the doubt can result in accusations, firings, and even worse consequences. Some of us might argue that precisely because the world treats some groups so unfairly, being harsh and less forgiving in our grading practices is actually appropriate, helpful, and in some extreme situations, lifesaving.

The weakness in this rationale is that it presumes that (a) unless we replicate aspects of the unfair world in our classroom, our students will be unprepared for it, and (b) it's better to replicate an unfair world than to reject it within our classrooms. The first perception underestimates our students—students who are from groups treated unfairly deeply understand the unfairness of the world even at an early age. Their families and communities constantly share warnings, experiences, and strategies with their children. The second perception underestimates our classrooms.

Why wouldn't we create a classroom that provides our students with a refuge from the unfair world? Doesn't equitable teaching compel us to treat students more fairly, with more respect and more caring, and love, than the real world? If so, our grading system has to push against the aspects of the real world that are unjust and unfair, that judge people without opportunities for redemption, and that evaluate with harsh consequences rather than offering feedback, dialogue, and support.

Connecting Soft Skills to Academic Success

We know that soft skills directly influence academic performance and future professional success, and for the vast majority of skills and students, we might be able to trace back their low academic performance to a weakness in soft skills. Students, however, might not see that connection because our traditional grading has taught that a connection between soft-skills performance and academic performance exists. Previous teachers may have atomized and isolated soft skills by grading them independently: 5 points for bringing a notebook to class, never mind that not having a notebook makes it harder to participate in a class. We referenced this disconnection between means and ends in chapter 10: When students experience the natural consequences and the causal relationship between preparation, homework, classwork, studying, or any other activity or habit preceding the summative assessment, and the summative assessment itself, they will better understand that soft skills and practice are directly related to assessment outcomes. Mohammed, a middle school humanities teacher for four years, explains:

"I said to the students, 'I understand that you have lives, and I understand you have other classes, so I will accept late work when you can't get certain things done. But, I will be moving on. So, if you don't do the work, you're just piling it up for yourself.' At the beginning of the year, some kids have to learn the hard way; at the end of the quarter, I asked them, 'Isn't it so much harder now?' They learned that lesson, and I kept repeating and reminding them, and the next grading period they were getting things done in a more reasonable time frame. Allowing late work actually was really important for the resource students and students with learning difficulties because they couldn't get things done in time. So, all of a sudden, they had this buffer. These students were actually getting work done, even though they were doing it in their own time frame."

Students who have never been taught the relationship between soft skills, practice work, and assessment performance may treat the absence of soft-skills grades as a license to disregard the soft skills; they won't bring their notebook to class because it isn't graded, will come late to class because no points will be subtracted, won't do the homework on time, or won't participate in a discussion because it's not included in the grade. It then becomes our job to establish, or reestablish, that relationship. Students may need formal reflections: How was your learning affected when you didn't bring your notebook to class, when you came late, when you didn't do your homework when it was assigned, or participate in the discussion? What did you need to do to compensate for that decision? How was your performance on the assessment changed by that decision? Knowing the consequences to your learning, what will you do differently next time so you can show stronger performance on the assessment?

Amid our emphasis on preparation as a necessary means to an end, we have to make sure that we account for students for whom there actually isn't as strong a relationship between specific soft skills and their performance. We have to recognize that many successful adults have weak soft skills; think about Steve Jobs and other innovators and artists, and the quote attributed to Laura Thatcher Ulrich: "Well-behaved women seldom make history." For example, if a student is shy and doesn't ask questions but she performed well on the assessment, it's clear that she was participating through active listening, and she got what she needed in order to succeed. Although a student doesn't do much of the homework, she learns quickly through class activities and scores highly on the test. Even though we might assume that active questioning and contributing answers facilitate learning, or that homework is critical for learning, for a handful of students who learn differently than we might expect, there isn't this causal relationship, and there's no need to punish the means when it doesn't affect the ends.

Of course, even if the soft-skill behavior doesn't negatively impact a student's academic performance, that behavior might still matter. If a student was off-task during group work, their behavior may have limited other students' opportunities to learn even though that student still turned in a high-quality paper. In this case, the student clearly needs feedback on her soft skill, but that still doesn't warrant including it in her grade and therefore warping its accuracy.

Clearly, the issues of soft skills and equitable grading raise a lot of issues to hold in our heads. How can we build students' soft skills without including them in the grade? Let's recall our third Driving Principle for our Motivational pillar:

> *Equitable grading distinguishes and connects the means for learning effectively—the "soft skills," the practice, the mistakes—from its ends—academic success, and utilizes the broad and diverse universe of feedback and consequences, of which only one part is a grade.*

Two Grades: Academic and Soft Skills

When teachers and schools recognize the importance of distinguishing the evaluation of soft skills from the evaluation of academic performance, yet still want to give a grade, some create an additional grade on the report card—for example, a Habits of Work or Citizenship grade. This allows a school to keep the academic grade purely and accurately about academics while still using a formal grade to report on the other skills the school values.

As much as reporting both academic and soft-skills performance separately might seem an ideal solution, it often creates many challenges. Formalizing the soft-skills performance in a grade obligates teachers to collect data to support that grade. Often already overwhelmed with the volume of academic data they collect, teachers now are expected to collect and enter the elusive soft-skills data. How do we collect data on participation, and how often? If teachers decide to include promptness in the nonacademic grade, does every assignment receive two grades—one academic and one soft-skills grade? Secondly, committing to grade soft skills obligates the school to develop common agreements and understandings among teachers about what categories of information go into the academic and into the nonacademic grade; otherwise those grades will be biased and individualized for each teacher. Doing this for academic content is already very difficult for schools; where will they find the resources to confirm common soft-skills expectations? Finally, this solution doesn't really address the deeper problem that giving students a grade for soft skills preserves a locus of control in the teacher, disconnects the work habits and soft skills from the outcomes those soft skills are intended to create, and it creates additional opportunities for many of the inequitable grading issues we've addressed previously: mathematical inaccuracy (averaging soft-skills performance over time versus grading recent performance), implicit biases (subjectively evaluating a student's participation or effort), and opacity of the grade (not being specific, clear, or detailed about what a soft skill is and how students can understand well enough to self-assess).[1]

Therefore, beyond the two-grade solution, which too often only dodges the issue and doesn't significantly reduce inequities, let's explore how students can get meaningful and behavior-modifying feedback on soft skills—both those skills that directly affect a student's academic performance and those that impact others'—without it being included or reported alongside the academic grade. This exploration begins with identifying what is arguably the most important soft skill of the twenty-first century: self-regulation amid a community of feedback.

---

[1] When schools report an academic and a nonacademic grade side by side on a progress report, they face significant pressure to reduce the two grades into a single grade at the time of publishing report cards, calculating GPA, creating transcripts, or on college applications. Some schools choose to weight the academic and nonacademic grades equally; others set up a ratio of academic to nonacademic grades that change depending on the grade level (e.g., ninth grade: academic grade 50% and soft-skills grade 50%; at tenth grade: academic 60% and soft skills 40%; at eleventh grade: academic 80% and soft skills 20%, etc.), but changing the composition of the grade every year makes the meaning of a grade constantly fluid and does nothing to lift veils.

The Twenty-First Century's Soft Skill: Self-Regulation

In our list of soft skills at the beginning of this chapter, we included many—respect, cooperation, listening to directions, meeting deadlines—that are good for students and also make the class function well, also noting that these are similar to the skills prized in the factories of the early twentieth century. Ultimately, we want more from our students—we want them to continue learning and growing throughout their lives to become their best selves. To do this, they need to be adept at self-regulation, which Nicol and Macfarlane-Dick (2006) describe as "the active monitoring and regulation of a number of different learning processes: e.g., the setting of, and orientation towards, learning goals; the strategies used to achieve goals; the management of resources; the effort exerted; reactions to external feedback; the products produced" (p. 2). Students need to know how to set a goal, to identify where they stand in relation to that goal, plan how to reach it, to assess resources that help them to traverse that distance, to respond to formative feedback, and to accurately self-assess, to reflect, and to continuously refine and improve actions until the goal is reached.

In traditional grading, students rarely have the opportunity to build these skills and experience this success. Teachers define the goals, inform students where they are relative to those goals, tell students how to reach them, tell them what to do to improve, and evaluate whether or when they've met the goals. We make our students dependent on our grading for their sense of self-worth instead of teaching them how to feel the joy, satisfaction, agency, and empowerment of achieving a goal. For historically underserved communities, because so much of the decisions that affect them are made by others, they likely have had less agency over many aspects of their lives, and therefore may have had even less experience with this complex but critical soft skill. If we really want to equip students with the skills needed to succeed in the real world, then we must create opportunities for students, particularly students of color, low income, and with special needs, to learn self-regulation, what Boud (2000) calls "sustainable assessment." Just as "sustainable farming" equips farmers not just with tools, seeds, and instruction, but also invests them with more expansive knowledge of agriculture and long-term planning, sustainable assessment invests students with the full spectrum of skills necessary to self-assess. We have to use strategies of feedback that are independent of our grade to empower our students and prepare them for "learning through life":

> [L]earners as far as possible undertake their own formative assessment processes using whatever resources they can identify—in most learning through life this is all there is. It is impossible to overestimate the importance of this point. It is rare to find outside an educational institution ready-made formative assessment processes available. The learner has normally to construct them for themselves in situ using colleagues, peers, and friends and drawing on technical and informational sources that are found in workplaces or society more generally. . . . If [students] are not engaged in the construction and reconstruction of criteria for judging work, they will not be able to effectively establish criteria for work when a teacher is absent. (pp. 7, 12)

We start by expanding what feedback is, and who can give it.

Creating a Community of Feedback

As we addressed in chapter 5, traditional grading places the teacher in the role of judge, as the sole arbiter of quality, and the only person in the classroom qualified to give feedback. We know that students often do not understand the feedback they're given (Chance, 2000; Hyland 2000), such as "this essay needs to be better organized," and therefore are unable to improve. Our goal, introduced with the previous chapter's discussion of "lifting the veil," is that equitable grading democratizes evaluation and feedback so the capacity and authority to evaluate is shared among the teacher and her students. When students are knowledgeable and empowered to be resources of feedback for each other, students build a greater sense of self-control over learning. Nicol and Macfarlane-Dick (2006) explain:

> Firstly, students who have just learned something are often better able than teachers to explain it to their classmates in a language and in a way that is accessible. Secondly, peer discussion exposes students to alternative perspectives on problems and to alternative tactics and strategies. Alternative perspectives enable students to revise or reject their initial hypothesis and construct new knowledge and meaning through negotiation. Thirdly, by commenting on the work of peers, students develop detachment of judgment (about work in relation to standards) which is transferred to the assessment of their own work (e.g., "I didn't do that either"). Fourthly, peer discussion can be motivational in that it encourages students to persist (see, Boyle & Nicol, 2003). Finally, it is sometimes easier for students to accept critiques of their work from peers rather than tutors. (p. 11)

Giving helpful feedback to others, being able to hear and reflect on that feedback, and feeling comfortable giving yourself feedback to measure progress on a goal are soft skills rarely taught explicitly in schools. We can explicitly build a classroom community where feedback—from peers and even from oneself—is so ubiquitous that it becomes integrated into the learning process.

To create a community of feedback, the teacher's first step is to explicitly describe what a student needs to know and do, and what meeting, exceeding, and falling short of those expectations looks like. As we saw in the previous chapter, rubrics and standards scales are an ideal tool to communicate these expectations and, when they are well-constructed, provide each student with a road map of how to earn the grade she wants. As mentioned in the previous chapter, the power of rubrics and standards scales is not just in their explicitness and transparency, but in how they empower students to judge the quality of a student's performance—their own or their peers.

When students are qualified to give accurate feedback, the teacher's role can dramatically shift. Instead of being the sole arbiter of quality, each student can become empowered to assess student work and identify weaknesses, strengths, and specific avenues for improvement. Students can assess their own or any other student's work with as much authority as the teacher. Along with calibration exercises (described in the previous chapter), teachers also find that to build a community of feedback they must scaffold for students how to be less judgmental and instead to give constructive feedback. The specific language of a rubric can be tremendously helpful to equip students with a nonjudgmental and specific vocabulary (instead of "This wasn't so good," it's "Your topic sentence didn't include all parts of your argument."). Students still may need other feedback tools, including sentence starters ("One criteria where you met the standard was . . .," "You could achieve the next level of performance if you . . .") and role plays, not only to be more aware of tone and build empathy toward the person receiving the feedback, but also to be able to receive feedback without being defensive or argumentative, to inquire and listen to fully understand their peer's assessment. Some students may also bring a style to their feedback that reflects their cultural backgrounds, and teachers can use that diversity to build classroom feedback norms. Teachers can even scaffold for students what to do after they hear feedback—how to sift through the feedback and identify next steps and goals to improve their performance—a crucially important soft skill. Bernardo, a high school history teacher for five years, wants to strengthen students' self- and peer-assessment skills so that the quality of work improves *before* he evaluates it:

> "I thought that they were going to inflate their grades of each other, but they didn't. If anything, they were mostly spot on. If it was off at all, it was probably them grading themselves harder than I would grade them. The next step for me is not allowing them to turn in something unless it's been scored by a peer, and then having a conversation when they think they have a four but their peer would give them a three. The peers could tell them what they can do before it gets turned in to me."

We've seen how increased transparency of expectations through rubrics can make better use of the teacher's time, empower students, and strengthen the trusting relationship between teacher and students. Just as the rubrics in chapter 12 are used to help students to internalize and meet high expectations for academic performance, rubrics for soft skills can be just as powerful. They give students a clarity of what skills teachers believe are important—behaviors such as "staying on-task" or "collaborating effectively." Rather than making students feel disempowered and dependent entirely on the judgment of the teacher (particularly with the discretionary elements of soft skills such as Participation), teachers can identify and explicitly describe what levels of proficiency in those soft skills look like. They make the teacher's expectations for behavior explicit and transparent and introduce a language and vocabulary to talk about those expectations. For example, the Windsor Locks Middle School in Connecticut developed a rubric for its schoolwide Habits of Scholarship.

Windsor Locks Middle School Habits of Scholarship Rubric

	MODEL STUDENT 4.00–3.50 — *I consistently (4)*	GOOD STANDING 3.49–2.75 — *I often (3)*	AT RISK 2.74–2.00 — *I sometimes (2)*	INELIGIBLE 1.99–0.00 — *I rarely (1)*
CLASS PARTICIPATION *I am a thoughtful, inquisitive member of the classroom community.*	• Listen to all contributions. • Contribute positively. • Collaborate actively. • Ask questions that help myself and others.	• Listen to all contributions. • Contribute positively. • Collaborate actively. • Ask questions that help myself and others.	• Listen to all contributions. • Contribute positively. • Collaborate actively. • Ask questions that help myself and others.	• Listen to all contributions. • Contribute positively. • Collaborate actively. • Ask questions that help myself and others.
APPROPRIATE CONDUCT *My behavior allows me—and others—to learn constantly.*	• Use appropriate volume and tone. • Respect all people, space, and property. • Allow all others to participate, think, and learn. • Demonstrate positive relationships and citizenship.	• Use appropriate volume and tone. • Respect all people, space, and property. • Allow all others to participate, think, and learn. • Demonstrate positive relationships and citizenship.	• Use appropriate volume and tone. • Respect all people, space, and property. • Allow all others to participate, think, and learn. • Demonstrate positive relationships and citizenship.	• Use appropriate volume and tone. • Respect all people, space, and property. • Allow all others to participate, think, and learn. • Demonstrate positive relationships and citizenship.
TIME MAXIMIZATION *My time and energy are spent on learning.*	• Come to class on time and with all required materials. • Start my work immediately and without reminders. • Use given time for work and learning. • Complete assignments and submit them on time.	• Come to class on time and with all required materials. • Start my work immediately and without reminders. • Use given time for work and learning. • Complete assignments and submit them on time.	• Come to class on time and with all required materials. • Start my work immediately and without reminders. • Use given time for work and learning. • Complete assignments and submit them on time.	• Come to class on time and with all required materials. • Start my work immediately and without reminders. • Use given time for work and learning. • Complete assignments and submit them on time.

This district created a vocabulary and a framework to answer the questions: What are the behaviors that demonstrate high quality Participation? What is the relationship between Time Maximization and academic success?

And just as a classroom can calibrate expectations for a lab report, we can do the same thing for behaviors. Students and teachers can share examples of different behaviors and identify where those behaviors fall on the rubric. As teachers walk around the room during work time on an assignment, they can let students know where they are on the rubric, modeling effective feedback and applying the soft-skills rubric's expectations. Students during group work can use the rubric to assess their own group's collective behavior and calibrate it against the teacher's assessment. Students can give feedback on a soft-skills rubric to each other using the rubric's nomenclature. Feedback can be compared and calibrated—a student's self-assessment against either a peer's or the teacher's—to resolve discrepancies and expectations. Was the student's behavior using her time effectively or not? As with the academic rubrics, the more frequently a classroom uses a rubric and the more varied its uses and application, the stronger the culture of ongoing feedback on performance becomes, and the less feedback becomes freighted with judgment. And as we saw with academic rubrics, when a classroom community has a shared understanding of soft skills, students are empowered, the teacher can reallocate her time and expertise to other classroom needs, and trusting relationships—both between teachers and students, and among students—are strengthened.

We'll continue to expand our thinking about how equitable grading can build students' soft skills and self-regulation by learning about one more set of grading practices: student performance trackers.

Student Trackers and Goal-Setting

Student trackers create a formalized process that teaches students to record their performance over time as well as to build the student's soft skills. Student trackers benefit students' development of soft skills by (1) assigning responsibility to the student to record and become fully aware of their performance; (2) teaching students to reflect on that performance and to make connections between their actions and their performance outcomes; and (3) empowering students through a formalized cycle of setting goals, taking actions, and seeing results. Trackers promote a sense of ownership and agency.

No longer does the teacher need to be the only caretaker of student achievement data. Students keep a log of their performance over time to identify trends, strengths, and areas of struggle and for improvement. Trackers redefine the grade from being arbitrary and owned by the teacher to being within a student's power to affect through self-assessment, planning, actions, and reflection.

For example, Karina, a high school English teacher, has her students identify goals for their performance on each element of a writing rubric and compare their targets to their actual performance:

Writing Performance Tracker

DOCUMENT	PURPOSE	ORGANIZATION	ELABORATION OF EVIDENCE	LANGUAGE AND VOCABULARY	CONVENTIONS	COMMENTS/OBSERVATIONS
Goal for Document A						I believe I earned a(n) _____ in _____ because _____ _____ _____ _____.
Score for Document A						I understand/don't understand why I earned a(n) _____ in _____ because _____ _____.
Goal for Document B						I believe I earned a(n) _____ in _____ because _____ _____ _____.
Score for Document B						I understand/don't understand why I earned a(n) _____ in _____ because _____ _____.

Through this tracker, Karina builds students' soft skills of goal-setting, self-assessment, reflection, and future goal-setting: What are they working on? Are they meeting their goal? Why did they fall short, and what are concrete ways to move closer to their goals next time? Students might identify that they need to spend time practicing a particular writing skill—such as checking for misplaced apostrophes or incomplete sentences—or a soft skill—such as spending more time proofreading or finding a less distracting environment to write. Karina also uses student trackers to structure differentiated writing instruction (students self-organize into small groups based on the element they are focused on improving), and to strengthen students' internalized understanding of high-quality writing.

In a variation on this model, a student can identify her current level of performance, what specifically she will do to improve, record that subsequent performance, and reflect on how or whether her efforts resulted in a change in performance. For example, a student could record the homework assignments she completes, the number of times she comes to tutoring, and her score on the assessment, and then reflect on the relationship between those three pieces of data. The teacher could help her decide what she will change as she approaches the next unit or the retake of the assessment, and the student could record the next unit's assessment, and reflect on the impact of those changes on her academic performance. In both this and Karina's design, students are developing self-regulation and other soft skills: reflecting on progress and goal-setting, as well as adjusting behaviors such as how to study or reprioritizing to complete more homework. These activities reinforce the real purpose of homework and soft skills, obviating the need to include either in the academic grade.

Student trackers can also help students to build their metacognitive thinking, to be more aware of how they study, how they behave, what they struggle with that impedes their academic performance, and the habits that will sustain and support their improvement. Trackers can help students to reflect on the connection between soft skills and academic achievement even more explicitly by having students record academic progress along with their place on a soft-skills rubric. Teachers ask students to reflect on those cause-effect relationships: How did their behavior on soft skills each day this week correlate with their academic performance on the quiz? Which aspect of their performance on the soft-skills rubric seemed to have the strongest impact on their academic achievement? What change in behavior is likely to have the greatest impact on the next assessment?

Students can recognize what strengths they have that help their academic performance, which ones impede their academic performance, and how the improvement of those weaknesses in specific, observable ways results in more academic success. Trackers reinforce a growth mindset and are motivating: Capacity is not fixed, and students can control their fate through deliberate and specific steps.

We might doubt that our students can handle the responsibility of trackers, or that even if they can record their progress, they aren't capable of deep reflection and self-improvement. We might also worry (and fear) that our students don't have the maturation and intellectual capacity to be internally motivated by seeing the connection between their behaviors and their academic outcomes, and that including soft skills in a grade is the only way students will learn them. The good news is that the research is very clear: Teachers can structure learning environments that build students' learning processes and soft skills through meta-cognitive training (reflections), self-monitoring (trackers), and by providing opportunities to practice self-regulation (goal-setting and planning) (Nicol & Macfarlane-Dick, 2006). Any student, even those historically at risk of academic failure, can become skilled at self-regulation (Pintrich & Zusho, 2002). Middle and high school teachers, even elementary teachers, report the benefits of replacing teacher-dominated grading with formalizing meta-cognitive activities and providing students with opportunities to connect their actions to their outcomes.

Student trackers don't exempt the teacher from collecting soft-skills data, but which information the teacher selects to collect and how it is used changes. For example, many teachers who use student trackers of soft skills choose to collect this data in their grade book within a category weighted at 0 percent. Having this data helps teachers communicate the story of a student's performance in a class: to the student, a caregiver, or an administrator who wants to know why a student has the grade she has. When a student did poorly on an assessment, what about her study-skills data helps us understand why she did poorly, and even more importantly, how does this story inform what to do that can change the academic performance?

No longer including soft-skills data in the academic grade makes our grades more accurate and bias-resistant and means that we delegate responsibility and ownership for that data—the collection, reflection, and goal-setting based on it—to the students. They can diagnose and make sense of their own data—what did or didn't they do that was causally connected to their performance on an assessment? When we give feedback on soft skills not through the grade, but through activities and tools that build self-regulation, the long-term benefit is that our students will become self-regulating and won't be dependent on others to motivate them, to tell them how to improve, or to tell them if they're good enough. It's self-sustaining assessment. After all, if students graduate with a dependency on other people to tell them when they are adequate, good, or excellent, and to set goals for them and tell them when they've reached them, then we're perpetuating the disempowerment of our students, particularly those from most underserved communities. And if teachers needed a selfish reason to promote peer and self-feedback, just think of how our workload can be decreased when students are knowledgeable enough to judge the quality of their own performance and identify their own next steps!

Summary of Concepts

1. Soft skills are critical for students' success in the adult, professional world, but including the evaluation of soft skills in a grade makes grades inequitable. These practices warp the grade's accuracy, inject subjectivity and implicit biases, make the grade less transparent and clear, and falsely represent what soft-skills feedback is in the professional world.

2. Even though soft skills are the means by which students can have more successful academic outcomes, traditional grading disconnects the means of success from its ends by evaluating and reporting soft skills independently of academic performance and reduces the performance of soft skills to a measure of student compliance. When we reestablish the causal relationship between soft skills and academic performance and no longer include soft skills in the grade, we increase students' intrinsic motivation to develop those soft skills as a direct means to greater academic performance.

3. As opposed to many twentieth century soft skills valued in schools—following directions, promptness, and others important to success in blue-collar jobs and which preserve many historical stratifications—self-regulation is the skill of setting goals based on an external standard, seeking out feedback and resources for improvement, and obtaining frequent self- and external feedback. We best teach self-regulation not by assigning points for soft skills, but instead by lifting the veil by defining soft skills, reducing biases through rubrics, delegating to students the responsibility to record soft skills and academic performance, and facilitating processes for reflection and goal-setting: "sustainable assessment."

Questions to Consider

1. Do you believe each soft skill has an equal impact on a student's academic performance, or do some soft skills have more impact than others? Does it depend on the industry or the context? Might this mean that part of teaching soft skills is teaching students how to assess a context? How might we scaffold the teaching of this skill?

2. How student specific is the connection between any given soft skill and an academic performance? How much does it change depending on the academic subject or skill to be performed? What implications does this have on how to give feedback on a student's soft skills competence, or the use of a student tracker?

3. For Teachers: Some schools use "student-led grade conferences" in which students, alongside their teacher, explain their performance to their caregivers. They share academic and study skills data, identify strengths and weaknesses, and identify goals and plans for improvement. It's the use of multiple soft skills; students not only reflect on their performance and set goals, they learn how to present information cogently and well-organized to an audience. How might you pilot this in your classroom for a specific project or performance?

....

CHAPTER 14

Putting It All Together

Nick and Cathy

In this chapter, we will answer the following questions:

1. How can an array of equitable grading practices be mutually supporting and reinforcing, working in tandem to promote greater success for all students, particularly those historically underserved?

I n Part I of this book, we explored the complexities of teachers' relationship with grading. In Part II, we examined the history of traditional grading practices and how their continued use, premised on debunked beliefs about our students, thwarts effective teaching and learning and perpetuates inequitable outcomes in our classrooms and schools. We established a new vision with three pillars: Equitable grading is Accurate, Bias-Resistant, and Motivational for all students, particularly those historically underserved—African American and Latino, from low-income families, with special needs, and nonnative English speakers. In Part III, we identified equitable practices that move us toward our vision guided by those pillars and our Driving Principles:

We've examined five sets of equitable grading practices that flow from these Driving Principles—grading practices that are *Mathematically Accurate*, that *Value Knowledge Over Behavior*, that *Support Hope and a Growth Mindset*, that *Lift the Veil*, and that *Build "Soft Skills."* It's now time to look at the whole picture.

Although some equitable grading practices in this book can be used in isolation (e.g., minimum percentages or not offering extra credit), they build on and support the introduction of other equitable grading practices. For example, once you begin using

PILLAR	DRIVING PRINCIPLE	CHAPTER	GRADING PRACTICES
Accurate	Our grading must use calculations that are mathematically sound, easy to understand, and correctly describe a student's level of academic performance.	7	• Avoiding zeros • Minimum grading • 0–4 scale
		8	• Weight more recent performance • Grades based on an individual's achievement, not the group's
Bias-Resistant	Grades should be based on valid evidence of a student's content knowledge, and not based on evidence that is likely to be corrupted by a teacher's implicit bias or reflect a student's environment.	9	• Grades based on required content, not extra credit • Grades based on student work, not the timing of work • Alternative (non-grade) consequences for cheating • Excluding Participation and Effort
		10	• Grades based entirely on summative assessments, not formative assessments (such as homework)
Motivational	The way we grade should motivate students to achieve academic success, support a growth mindset, and give students opportunities for redemption.	11	• Minimum grading and 0–4 scale • Renaming grades • Retakes and redos
	The way we grade should be so transparent and understandable that every student can know their grade at any time and know how to get the grade she wants.	12	• Rubrics • Standards scales • Tests without points • Standards-based grade books
	Equitable grading distinguishes and connects the means for learning effectively the "soft skills," the practice, the mistakes, from its ends—academic success, and utilizes the broad and diverse universe of feedback and consequences, of which only one part is a grade.	13	• Emphasizing self-regulation • Creating a community of feedback • Student trackers

rubrics, you'll see how valuable and helpful the 0–4 scale becomes. When retakes start to increase motivation and hope in your classroom, you'll find it necessary to stop averaging performance over time. Driving Principles drive equitable practices, and the equitable practices implicate other Driving Principles, which in turn create the need for additional practices. Offering retakes in which more current and accurate scores replace earlier scores creates more mathematically sound calculations of grades, promotes a growth mindset, makes the process of earning a grade more transparent, and doesn't penalize students for fewer support resources, and these stem from Driving Principles that also encourage student trackers and reflections as a logical extension for the retake process. Teachers find that when these grading practices are implemented in conjunction with each other, they collectively transform a classroom or school to be a more equitable and caring learning community.

To witness some of these interconnections and their potential cumulative impact, we'll profile two teachers who have taken on this work.

Nick: Rethinking Assessments: Getting Away From the Games, and Focusing on Learning

Nick, a fourth-year physics teacher at a comprehensive high school, was concerned that the grade students earned didn't accurately reflect what they knew. "I always felt tests and quizzes were the best indicators of what students actually knew, and if somebody didn't show something on the test, then they wouldn't get those specific points. The problem was that people could do pretty well in my class without doing very well on the assessments. I had a lot of students who would get Cs on the test but end up with Bs or sometimes As in the class because they do all of their homework, their classwork, and their projects. A lot of students, many 'good students'—the ones that do all their homework and behave well in class—a lot of them rely on those points to maintain their grades." As an initial step to make his grades more equitable, Nick significantly increased the weight of summative assessments in a student's grade, and soon realized that this change required him to rethink his entire approach to summative assessments.

First, while he previously created tests that were traditional, with point values for each question, Nick now designs exams by identifying how students will need to prove mastery on each standard: "I figure out what would be the most straightforward way for students to demonstrate that they have achieved the standards, and that's where I start. Then I create multiple choice or free response or other types of questions—it works differently for different topics. I'm very well aware now of the most common misconceptions that students have that keep them from meeting the standard, and so those are the answers that I look for to indicate that maybe there's something missing from their understanding, that they've got a C-level understanding of a certain topic instead of B-level understanding."

But what has revolutionized his classroom was how he corrects his assessments. He no longer assigns a grade by a ratio of points earned over points possible: "I used to look at each question and determine how many points I thought it would be worth and what percentage of the test I wanted to make each question. Answers were either right or wrong and I would just count up whatever percentage they got right on that test and that would give them their grade." Now, Nick identifies errors and correct responses, and writes feedback notes for the student on the test but returns the tests with no points. When he returns a test to a student, he attaches a "Standards Mastered Checklist" that lists for each student the standards or substandards that she has mastered based on the test. Because Nick has changed his assessments, he's been able to reimagine how assessments can be a differentiated learning tool.

Congratulations! You have demonstrated mastery of the following skills:

- ☐ Representing an object with a square or dot

- ☐ Showing forces acting on an object by having vectors coming from the center or sides of the free-body diagram

- ☐ Identifying the presence of the following forces: gravity, air resistance, normal, friction, tension, applied in simple situations

- ☐ Identifying the presence of the following forces: gravity, air resistance, normal, friction, tension, applied in complex situations

- ☐ Determining the correct directions of the following forces: gravity, air resistance, normal, friction, tension, applied in simple situations

- ☐ Determining the correct directions of the following forces: gravity, air resistance, normal, friction, tension, applied in complex situations

- ☐ Determining the correct magnitudes of the following forces: friction, normal, tension, air resistance

- ☐ Determining the net force from a given free-body diagram

- ☐ Determining the net force from a given situation

- ☐ Using information from a free-body diagram and a given situation to determine the direction of acceleration

- ☐ Using the acceleration of an object to predict the relative magnitudes of the forces

- ☐ Using Newton's third law to determine the reaction force for a given force

- ☐ Applying Newton's third law to determine the relative magnitude of a reaction force

---

There's no calculation of points at all. Instead, he assigns a letter grade based on what the student's responses indicate about her level of mastery of the unit's standards. "It's really a different way of looking at things. It's looking more at what does this student understand and what is missing from their understanding. Are they missing the really tough questions? Or are they missing questions that they really ought to know? Sometimes students will have some strange issues where they're missing the B answers, but they are getting the A answers. It can be tricky to figure out what is the grade. They may have some gaps in their knowledge which should drop them to a C, but they're showing great things in other questions."

Because Nick's only goal in assigning grades is to correctly indicate a student's level of understanding, if a student doesn't perform well on an assessment he can look for alternate assessment strategies. "I told students, 'If you don't test well, there are certainly other ways that you can demonstrate your understanding. Why don't you come in and we'll talk about them?' And so, they come in, and we'll have a conversation." In fact, this new insight into the purpose of assessment and grades has given him the freedom to evaluate student understanding using *any evidence that the student has presented*. "Now the grade is entirely based on demonstrations of understanding, which are primarily quizzes and tests, but I realize too that I can include things like kids coming in for help and what I see there. When I'm working one-on-one with the student, I can take that into account. When they ask questions or raise their hand to answer questions in class, I can look back on that when it comes time for grading and remember, 'Oh, okay, yeah, this person does kind of know something about this because they said that smart thing in class about this.'"

This freedom to exercise professional judgment transforms grading from a tabulation of points into something more complex. "Grading takes a little bit more thinking. It takes a little more thoughtfulness. It can be difficult for me to figure out what they do need to show me to have a B-level understanding, C-level understanding, A-level understanding, etc. It takes a little bit more of a looking back at what students have said and done in class. Sometimes it is more difficult to grade this way, and it might take a little more time, but it makes sense to me. There's none of that concern that my grades might be ambiguous, that they might not be truly reflective of what students are doing. I understand what my grades mean. I feel that they are accurate and fair. I feel very confident in my grading system now, and I really believe grades reflect the student's actual understanding of the content."

With all this attention to getting the most accurate information about student knowledge, Nick comfortably and confidently excludes homework, classwork, and labs from the grade. His own thinking, and his conversations with students about it, illuminates how the idea of "learning" has been transformed in his classroom:

"The students and I had a number of conversations about how homework, classwork and labs are a means to learning the materials, which they will then demonstrate on the quiz and tests. I was surprised at how positive students were. They're well aware that a lot of classes are almost like a game, where you accumulate points by doing the right things, and you figure out what you need to do to get a certain grade. It's much more straightforward in my class. Your grade is based on your understanding of the content. We can get away from all those games and we can focus on learning. We can

(Continued)

(Continued)

focus on improving our understanding of the material. When I said that, one student just blurted out, 'I like this way of grading.' And I said, 'Me, too.'

"It was a difficult shift for some students because it's so different from what they're used to and what they've been doing their entire academic careers, but they're surprisingly adaptable. Now they see that the purpose of the homework is actually to learn the material. It's not about going through the motions of class activities or finding ways of copying the homework which really is doing nobody any good—and it's no longer worth points anyway. I've told students that the homework is your opportunity to practice and to see how well you understand these things. Homework completion at first took a dip when I stopped counting it for points, but then they realized that 'Oh, I want to get a good grade in this class. I need to understand the material,' and then homework completion has shot up. It's the opposite of what I feared would happen."

But the test isn't the end of the learning in Nick's classroom; It's where new learning begins. When Nick returns the tests, every student must identify her incorrect or incomplete responses on the test and, for each mistake, use a conversation protocol with peers to find what led to that mistake:

Part 1 (1 min.): Only person A speaks—explain the mistake they made and why they thought to answer the question that way.

Part 2 (2 min.): Only persons B and C speak—have a conversation about what might be causing person A's mistake.

Part 3 (4 min.): Person A explains what they think their misconception is, persons B and C ask clarifying questions, and the group comes to an agreement as to what the misconception was. Then determine the truth about the misconception and create a question that would test whether someone understands that truth.

The students work together to diagnose the underlying misconception that each student's wrong answer reflects and correct the misconception. Then, on a "Misconception Identification Form," the student shows her new (and corrected) understanding of the content by creating a question designed to trip up someone who continues to have the misconception. After completing the form, a student gets an opportunity to retake the exam with new questions, and the new scores replace the previous ones. What Nick has found is that through a focus on standards mastery, the increased emphasis on summative assessments, and the postassessment diagnosis and reflections, his students are becoming more attuned to what they don't know:

Students tell me that they recognize that there are certain gaps they have in their understanding. And they usually ask if they can get help with those things and then try to demonstrate their understanding later, and that's what we do. "I coach runners, and every day I want my runners to know what the purpose is of our workout that day. Having that understanding and that focus helps them to do the workout the right way. Similarly, with homework and classwork and the labs, students are recognizing that 'Okay. I'm supposed to be learning something from this.' Not, 'I need to do this a certain way to get points.'" Some students are asking me for extra problems and more practice that they can do on their own, and I don't think I ever had that before.

Nick finds it so professionally rewarding to grade in this way—beholden not to an antiquated system of points, stuck in a dynamic of controlling students, and dependent on grading software calculations, but being able to fully utilize his expertise, authentically partnering with his students, and focusing entirely on learning. "I especially appreciate the empowerment that comes with recognizing that I am the best judge of what my students know, not some number generated by a carefully devised system, even if that system was designed by me."

Nick combines a number of equitable grading practices:

Mathematically Accurate

- Replacing summative assessment performance with retake performance

Support Hope and a Growth Mindset

- Not including homework in the grade
- Not including Participation or classwork in the grade
- Normalizing mistakes through "Misconception Identification Form" and peer discussions
- Allowing retakes

Value Knowledge, Not Environment or Behavior

- Not including homework in the grade
- Not including behaviors in the grade
- Allowing multiple ways for students to demonstrate understanding
- Considering any and all evidence that would inform the correct description of a student's level of content mastery

Build Soft Skills

- Using the "Misconception Identification Form" to build students' capacity to self-identify weaknesses
- Establish clearer purpose for "means" of homework and classwork

Perhaps most profoundly, this work has magnified Nick's passion for providing students with the dignity of truthful feedback about their academic proficiency:

"I told them: They deserve better from their education than making learning just a game of getting points. They deserve to get accurate reflections of where their understanding is so that they can see where they need to improve and be able to focus on that to improve their understanding of the content material and actually learn the material that they should be learning. We place more of the focus on actually learning, and students are more confident that their work will pay off. Students appreciate it, and I feel a lot more confident that my grades are meaningful and accurate."

Cathy: A Clearer Vision of Excellence

In Cathy's middle school humanities class, she and her fellow sixth-grade humanities teachers develop and confirm rubrics for each standard they'll be addressing in the upcoming term. Several skills "spiral" over the year—standards for writing, for example—so rather than create a unique rubric for each assessment or project, some rubrics have common criteria (rows) for writing but with different content criteria. Her team recognize that rubrics are tools for both teachers and students, so the rubrics' descriptions for each performance level on each criterion balance the use of academic vocabulary with "student-friendly" language. For Cathy, a fourth year teacher, the transparency of rubrics are critically important for student learning:

"The rubrics help students to better understand what goes into their grade: What is expected of a good piece of writing? How they can improve their own writing? How they can improve their own grade? Using academic vocabulary pushes them, but then you also want every student to understand the rubric and be able to use it—not just those kids who are really quick and at a higher level, but you want the kid who's at the lowest end to say, 'OK, I get this.'"

Cathy helps her students understand and internalize the expectations of rubrics by asking them to evaluate models, to peer edit, and to self-assess. She has found that rubrics empower students with clear guidance on what it takes to succeed. "In previous years, peer evaluations were almost a waste of time. Now students are actually using them and they're productive. It's really easy for me to write comments and refer to the rubric, and students understand what they need to do to improve. Students used to think, 'I'm going to try really hard and write a good essay.' Now the rubric really helps them know exactly what they need to do, describing aspects of writing by using actual language from the rubric. They are saying the vocabulary in the rubric: 'I have to provide textual evidence.'"

Cathy's rubrics, and all of her grade book entries, are on a 0–4 scale which, in contrast to the point accumulation and percentage ratios, allows students to overcome intermittent failures. "Before we started using the 0–4 scale, I feel like a lot of students would give up if they had a low grade because it was just point based: the deficit would be so big. Now in my class there's always an opportunity to do well. It has really helped to motivate students and has definitely changed the culture of the whole school."

Cathy and her team found that even though they developed the rubrics collaboratively, they weren't scoring students consistently across classrooms. They realized that the only way to ensure consistent grading among them—so that a student's performance on the assessment, regardless of her teacher, earns the same score on the rubric—is that her team needed to periodically calibrate their application of the rubrics by scoring samples individually and comparing scores. But rather than collectively score when students submit the final assessments, the teachers calibrate *before* beginning the project or unit. They do this so that the shared interpretation and expectations of the rubric guides them and their students during the entire learning process. Early calibration ensures consistent expectations for the student performance "target" and consistent formative feedback to the students before the summative assessment scoring.

The team wanted to make sure their grading was consistent with the external measures of their statewide assessment. They found that although they were calibrated as a team, the grades they gave for student work had been higher than their students' scores on the external measure. As Cathy's colleague, Kelly, shared: "We looked at the SBAC data and almost had simultaneous heart attacks. There's no reason that they should be getting an A in English if they're getting a two on the SBAC."

This calibration, both among her colleagues and using an external standardized assessment, was eye-opening for Cathy:

"I was giving far too many students higher grades. If they had a good essay, or they answered the question, I had been giving them a four. The [sixth-grade humanities] teachers graded some essays together and most of them were like threes or twos. It really now actually makes me see who really is a four, you know? I also found that I needed to be a little bit more aware that there are some students that score a one. Even when I want them to be successful, it's a disservice to give them a two."

With this combination of a 0–4 scale and calibrated rubrics, the number of students receiving Ds and Fs has dramatically dropped in Cathy's and her teaching team's classes, and at the same time, the percentage of their students receiving As has decreased as well.

To Cathy, her grades are more equitable because they are accurate and she can be more honest with her students. No matter the challenges of our most vulnerable students, and how desperately we want them to persevere and succeed, Cathy recognizes that to give them an inaccurate grade in the name of motivation and empathy is a "disservice." All our students, whether they struggle or not, and whether they have every advantage or none, deserve the dignity of knowing their accurate level of academic performance.

Because Cathy and her team have also determined performance levels on each standard on a scale of 0–4, her grade book has changed dramatically. All standards are listed as the first assignments of the term, and they are all tagged as a category called "Standards" that is worth 100 percent of the grade. All other data she collects, whether it be a student's homework completion or the score on an essay (or if an essay assesses multiple standards, each of the scores is entered), are weighted at 0 percent of the grade. Cathy enters scores for each standard as students demonstrate their knowledge on assessments, and she updates those scores manually when more current assessments give her more up-to-date information about a student's level of content mastery. Her manual entry, based on updated information, overcomes the problem of averaging performance over time and ensures that her grades are mathematically accurate. Below is a portion of Cathy's gradebook.

Reporting Term: S2		Standards			Assignments						
Students	S2 Final Grade	Language / Grammar	Text Structure	Central Idea	Rosa Parks Writing: Language / Grammar 1/27/2017 pts: 4	Rosa Parks Writing: Text Structure 1/27/2017 pts: 4	Rosa Parks Writing: Central Idea 1/27/2017 pts: 4	Freedom Walk Essay: Language / Grammar 2/8/2017 pts: 4	Freedom Walk Essay: Text Structure 2/8/2017 pts: 4	Freedom Walk Essay: Central Idea 2/8/2017 pts: 4
Student 1	C+	2	2.7	3	2	2	3	2	2.7	3
Student 2	A–	3	4	4	4	4	4	3	4	4
Student 3	C+	2	2	3	2	3	2.3	2	2	3
Student 4	B	3	3	3	3	4	4	3	3	3
Student 5	D+	1	1.3	2	1	1.3	1	1	1.3	2
Student 6	C+	2.3	2	2.7	2	2	2	2.3	2	3
Student 7	C–	1	2	2	1	2	2	1	2	2
Student 8	B–	2	3	4	2	4	4	2	3	3
Student 9	B+	3	3	4	3	3	3	3	3	4

In contrast to Cathy's previous grade book design (and the traditional design) in which points are calculated and generate a final grade, the scores of assessments—both formative (light blue) and summative (medium blue) have no weight in a grade book formula; they are just data points that Cathy considers when she enters scores for each standard. Instead of ceding her authority to a grade book formula that connects scores on assessments to a calculated grade, Cathy utilizes her professional judgment, calibrated against her colleagues' and external measures, to determine a student's level of standards mastery based on the evidence. While there are a number of different approaches to standards-based grading, this is one of the purest implementations of this reporting strategy—grades are only based on standards and are accurate in real time as students progress in their learning.

By using 0–4 descriptions of the performance levels for each standard, and having the grade represent only a student's performance on standards in real time, Cathy finds that the language of standards, and what constitutes different levels of performance, drive the discourse of the classroom. The use of rubrics and scales has cut her grading time significantly, and students better recognize their own strengths, areas for growth, and what it takes to improve. All of these changes to her grading have shifted how Cathy approaches the core of her day-to-day work. "Now that I have a better understanding of what I'm grading students on, it's helped me to understand what to expect of students, which has helped me to understand what to teach them, which has given me a better understanding of what I want to focus on in every class."

Cathy's equitable grading practices include the following:

Mathematically Accurate

- No averaging of performance

Support Hope and a Growth Mindset

- Not including homework in the grade
- Not including Participation or classwork in the grade
- 0–4 scale
- Allowing retakes
- 100 percent weight on performance on standards

Value Knowledge, Not Environment or Behavior

- Not including homework in the grade
- Not including behaviors in the grade

(Continued)

(Continued)

- No group grade
- Performance on standards as only ingredients of grade

Lift the Veil on What It Takes to Succeed

- Rubrics (peer assessment and teaching students the rubric through samples)
- Performance-level descriptions for each standard
- Standards-based grade book

Build Soft Skills

- Rubrics used for self-assessment
- Community of feedback

Cathy and Nick are grading and assessing in radically different ways than our inherited system and are witnessing different student behaviors toward their learning. How is it that these teachers were able to stop grading homework and classwork but students continue to do the assignments? How did they figure out how to manage retakes and design assessments? How did they decide how to design rubrics and reorganize their grade book? They accomplished their success—and are still striving to improve, by the way—through all the habits we want in our students: hard work, risk-taking, and reflection.

Neither Nick nor Cathy simply decided to implement an entire set of equitable practices in one fell swoop. Instead, each began with a single equitable practice that paved the way for more; each equitable grading practice, because of its positive impact on students and teachers, facilitated, revealed, supported, and created the need for others. They each, like all of us, brought to this work their own web of beliefs, identity, experiences, and dedication to equity, and ultimately constructed their own more equitable combination of practices. Through trial, error, reflection, and persistence, they weaved a new web of belief about what students are capable of, how they learn, and what motivates and empowers them.

The most successful teachers in this work recognize the damage that our antiquated system of grading has, and continues to exact, on their students and on their teaching. They know that improvements to teaching occur gradually, with mistakes as well as surprises, and are more likely to happen with colleagues than alone. They are open to new possibilities, to accept the "red pill" (a la *The Matrix*) and explore how to make grading more equitable. Finally, and crucially, they are deeply committed to implementing more equitable grading practices, feeling a moral imperative to improve the education structures, systems, and possibilities for our most historically underserved and vulnerable.

Summary of Concepts

1. Some constellations of equitable practices lend themselves to be mutually supportive and reinforcing. Nick integrated retakes, weighting more recent performance, and student trackers. Cathy integrated rubrics, 0–4 scoring, standards scales, and standards-based grade books. Both weigh performance on standards at 100 percent.

2. While sets of practice support each other, it is not easy to implement them all at once. Teachers should try these practices in smaller bites, adjusting their design to fit within the teacher's individual style and other practices. Allow them to naturally lead to each other.

Questions to Consider: For Teachers

1. Which equitable practice will you try first? How will you know whether it was successful?

2. As you try these practices, how will you apply a growth mindset and an embrace of mistakes to your own learning?

3. Will you let students know about the new grading practices you are trying and why, or will you conceal that information from them? How might they benefit if you explain not just what you're trying, but why? If, as we've seen, lifting the veil and being transparent in grading can empower students and build intrinsic motivation, could we apply that transparency to our own journey to improve grading?

4. What would a partnership with students to make grading more equitable look like?

Epilogue

A Return to Mallory's School

Jesicah, a principal of a middle school in Southern California, was one of a packed room of teachers and principals attending Mallory's presentation at a statewide education conference. Mallory shared how she and I had worked together for two years to introduce her teachers to more equitable grading practices and to support them through their skepticism and stumblings. The final PowerPoint slides of Mallory's presentation showed not just how student performance had improved, but how much the teachers valued the opportunity to examine traditional grading and explore more equitable approaches. "She and her school were light years ahead of all of us. They were actually doing what we all know is right but don't know how to do it," confessed Jesicah. After the presentation she approached Mallory to learn more, asking her "to teach me everything you know." They spoke for a while and scheduled a time to continue the conversation later by phone.

When they spoke a week later, Jesicah was surprised to learn that Mallory was transitioning to a different role, but she encouraged Jesicah to apply for her position. Jesicah had been principal of her school for seven years, but the opportunity was too good to pass up. "I was going to leave my school only if I really felt like I was walking into a place that understood what equity is about. Hearing Mallory and seeing the work that was started, I knew I could jump there." Jesicah was selected to be the new principal of Centennial College Prep Middle School, and she continued Mallory's efforts to improve grading over the next three years.

Today, five years after Mallory first decided that equitable grading needed to be a priority, and now under Jesicah's leadership, these are the school's "agreements" for grading—policies that the entire faculty affirmed by consensus two years ago and have continued to affirm annually:

CCPA's Grading Agreements

- All assignments, assessments, and final grades are on the 0–4 scale.
- No extra credit is available or awarded.

(Continued)

- Student grades are not affected if work is submitted late.

- Retakes are available to any students when they have received support and demonstrated that they have a stronger understanding. Those grades replace earlier scores.

- Summative assessments are weighted between 90 percent–100 percent of a student's grade.

- All assignments in a grade book are explicitly linked to a standard.

- All nonacademic performance ("soft skills," timeliness of work, etc.) is not included in the grade. Students are instead given feedback verbally, with written notes, or through an online feedback program which students and caregivers can access.

THE EQUITABLE GRADING POLICIES AGREED UPON BY CONSENSUS AT JESICAH'S (AND MALLORY'S) SCHOOL.

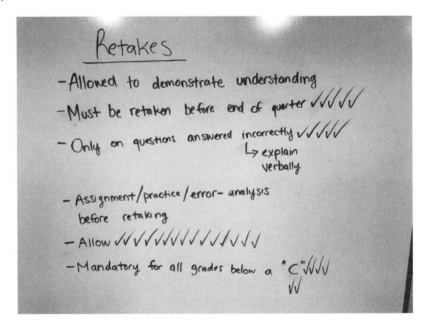

In addition, most teachers have organized their grade book to be standards based (see chapter 12).

Mallory's belief that improving the equity of grading would be a powerful lever, not just to raise student achievement but to improve teaching and learning schoolwide, has proven true under Jesicah's leadership. Teachers design assessments specifically to determine a student's level of standards mastery. With grades based entirely on performance on the standards, plus standards-based grade books, teachers can easily analyze their classes and determine for each student which standards haven't yet been mastered. As Jesicah explains,

"The buzzword nowadays is 'differentiation.' but how do you actually do that when you have a whole bunch of fluff in the grade books, and all you're really doing is differentiating for the compliant and the noncompliant child, rather than the child who has learned the standard and who hasn't?"

Jesicah's teachers also appreciate that their grading practices don't mandate that every assignment get a grade and be inputted into the grade book; they can instead use the time to make informed decisions about the next day's lesson.

Students' experiences have changed just as markedly. With the expectations so transparent, caregiver–teacher conferences have been transformed into student-led conferences. Instead of teachers telling caregivers, "Your child has a B. They need to make up some work," students lead a thirty-minute conversation with their caregiver, walking them through portfolios and sharing how that work earned them their grade. Every teacher has weekly office hours when students can receive support and do retakes. Students at the school continue to increase their scores on California's standardized assessment each year, and at faster rates than the state's average.

The school's commitment to equitable grading has even affected the process for hiring teachers. Teacher candidates are asked in a panel interview to respond to a scenario:

A student enters your class without a pencil, hadn't done the homework, and doesn't complete the classwork. When you ask the student to go to the board and solve a problem, the student does it entirely correctly. What do you do?

The panel—comprised of Jesicah, other administrators, and teachers—listens to whether the candidate focuses on the student's noncompliance for not bringing a pencil or not submitting homework, or instead identifies that the student has mastered the content and needs to be challenged.

Though many schools speak the language of equity, Jesicah describes how the school's grading practices put equity into action:

"Our grading policies recognize that when students are coming into sixth grade, where they are academically is really based on the quality of their last three teachers and not anything else. To have a grading system that penalizes students based on whether they had a strong teacher or not seems very unfair. Everybody has a different starting point and we need to recognize that.

(Continued)

"Kids really appreciate and recognize that we see learning as a continued process and not an end-all, be-all. If a kid has a really horrible first quarter, they can still pull themselves out. There is no teacher who is saying, 'Sorry, you have an F, there's no chance for you at this point.' Do we have any kids like that? Oh my gosh. That's half our students!"

Jesicah still has concerns: Despite the consensus on grading policies each year, there remains variance among teachers (for example, some teachers weight summative assessments at 100 percent, while others keep it at 90 percent—a very slight variance, but still a variance). Jesicah and her staff impress upon their students that their school's grading policies aren't the norm yet in high schools, and she isn't sure if their grading practices affect students in high school (she's planning some alumni panels to find out). Despite the inevitable transition in grading that students will face entering high school, Jesicah is resolute: "At the end of the day, grades need to be about course content mastery. That's going to set them up for success more than being able to understand how to work a grading scale. Grade scales and policies are going to come and go, but I'm more focused on: 'Do you actually know the content you need in order to be successful in high school?'" In fact, in Jesicah's vision, her middle school students are learning how to advocate for equitable grading in whatever high schools they attend—to ask for the opportunity to continue learning and to retake an assessment, to persuade teachers to grade them based on where they end up, not average their performance over time—in other words, to be graded accurately, without bias, and in ways that motivate them to learn intrinsically.

To make our classrooms and schools more equitable is to challenge some of the fundamental designs and purposes of our Industrial Revolution–era schools. Our century-old grading policies were never meant to accurately describe student performance, to be resistant to our implicit biases, or to motivate students intrinsically. Those schools and their grading systems were designed to assimilate students into the needs of the factory, to manage their behavior, and to sort them efficiently to replicate existing hierarchies. To change our grading to be more equitable is to align our schools, our teaching, and our students' learning experiences with what we now believe: that students must never be privileged or punished based on their environment and histories, that every child can meet expectations and that we truly empower students when we intrinsically motivate them to learn.

There are lots of reasons to avoid the practices in this book. We don't have the energy, the time, the resources, the support. It will never work; the pushback will be too great. It will be too confusing. Caregivers will never allow it. It's pushing a boulder uphill; I'm the only one who is trying this. Other schools won't understand it; it will put our students at a disadvantage. The traditional system is too powerful.

All this may be true. All initiatives, particularly those that promote equity, are too frequently sidelined. It's certainly easier to not push against the way things are, even when we know that by not pushing, we tacitly perpetuate a status quo that is unacceptable. If we truly want to reduce the achievement and opportunity gaps, we have to pursue equitable grading in spite of the challenges. I am reminded of a quote by Edward Everett Hale, a Unitarian minister of the nineteenth century:

> *I am only one, but I am still one.*
>
> *I cannot do everything, but still I can do something; and because I cannot do everything, I will not refuse to do something I can do.*

Hopefully this book fortifies you, provides you with the language, the research, the arguments, and some ideas that equip you to take the first step, to broach the conversation with colleagues, to reach out to school and district leadership, to expand your web of belief, and to try a new grading practice—to not refuse to do something that you can do.

I conclude with a quote by Zac, a high school social studies teacher: "I've moved away from thinking of grading as a carrot or a stick; grades should be a mirror." The equitable practices of this book have helped Zac and other teachers understand that grades shouldn't be used as a behavior management system; grades should clearly reflect what students know, accurately and without bias. I would take his metaphor one step further: Grading practices are a mirror not just to students, but to us, their teachers. Each teacher's grading choices—whether to offer students redemption or a single chance, whether to reward students or punish them based on prior educational experiences or environment, to invite biases or restrain them, to describe in a grade only what students know or to include how they behave, to make students dependent on our judgments or empower them to self-assess and connect their behavior to their achievement—all of these choices reflect who that teacher is and what she believes. At the end of this book's Prologue, Lucy, an eighteen-year teacher, confesses after learning about these equitable grading practices, "*I look at what I have been doing and I have to do things differently.*"

When you look at how you grade, what does it reflect about who you are and what you believe? And what do you have to do differently?

Bibliography

Prologue

Elementary and Secondary Education Act, California Education Code §49066(a) (enacted 1976, amended 1980).

Erickson, J. (2010). Grading practices: The third rail. *Principal Leadership*, *10*(7), 22–26.

Guskey, T. (2013). The case against percentage grades. *Education Leadership*, *71*(1), 68–72.

O'Connor, K. (2010). *A repair kit for grading: 15 fixes for broken grades* (2nd ed.). New York, NY: Pearson.

Reeves, D. (2004). The case against the zero. *Phi Delta Kappan*, *86*(4), 324–325.

Chapter 1

Bonner, M. W. (2016). Grading rigor in counselor education: A specifications grading framework. *Educational Research Quarterly*, *39*(4).

Brackett, M. A., Floman, J. L., Ashton-James, C., Cherkasskiya, L., & Salovey, P. (2013). The influence of teacher emotion on grading practices: A preliminary look at the evaluation of student writing. *Teachers and Teaching*, *19*(6), 634–646.

Brookhart, S. M., Guskey, T. R., Bowers, A. J., McMillan, J. H., Smith, J. K., Smith, L. F., . . . & Welsh, M. E. (2016). A century of grading research: Meaning and value in the most common educational measure. *Review of Educational Research*, *86*(4), 803–848.

Carroll, L. (2011). *Alice's adventures in wonderland* (2nd ed.). Peterborough, Ontario, Canada: Broadview Press.

Frary, R. B., Cross, L. H., & Weber, L. J. (1993). Testing and grading practices and opinions of secondary teachers of academic subjects: Implications for instruction in measurement. *Educational Measurement: Issues and Practice*, *12*(3), 23–30.

Guskey, T. R. (2009). Bound by tradition: Teachers' views of crucial grading and reporting issues. *Online submission*.

Guskey, T. R., & Bailey, J. M. (2001). *Developing grading and reporting systems for student learning*. Thousand Oaks, CA: Corwin.

Quine, W. V. O., & Ullian, J. S. (1978). *The web of belief* (Vol. 2). New York, NY: Random House.

Randall, J., & Engelhard, G. (2010). Examining the grading practices of teachers. *Teaching and Teacher Education*, *26*(7), 1372–1380.

Chapter 2

Bowles, S., & Gintis, H. (1976). *Schooling in capitalist America* (Vol. 57). New York, NY: Basic Books.

Brookhart, S. M., Guskey, T. R., Bowers, A. J., McMillan, J. H., Smith, J. K., Smith, L. F., . . . & Welsh, M. E. (2016). A century of grading research: Meaning and value in the most common educational measure. *Review of Educational Research, 86*(4), 803–848.

Craig, T. A. (2011). *Effects of standards-based report cards on student learning.* Boston, MA: Northeastern University.

Cubberley, E. P. (1909). *Changing conceptions of education.* Boston, MA: Houghton Mifflin.

Dewey, J. (1922/1983). *Individuality, equality and superiority.* In J. Boydston, (Ed.), *John Dewey: The middle works* (Vol. 13). Carbondale: Southern Illinois University Press

Dickson, V. E. (1922). Classification of school children according to mental ability. In L. M. Terman, V. E. Dickson, A. H. Sutherland, R. H. Franzen, C. R. Tupper, & G. Fernald (Eds.), *Intelligence tests and school reorganization* (pp. 32–52). Yonkers-on-Hudson, NY: World Book.

Guskey, T. R., & Bailey, J. M. (2001). *Developing grading and reporting systems for student learning.* Thousand Oaks, CA: Corwin.

Schneider, J., & Hutt, E. (2014). Making the grade: a history of the A–F marking scheme. *Journal of Curriculum Studies, 46*(2), 201–224.

Snyder, T. D. (Ed.). (1993). *120 years of American education: A statistical portrait.* Washington, DC: National Center for Education Statistics.

Tyack, D. B. (1974). *The one best system: A history of American urban education* (Vol. 95). Cambridge MA: Harvard University Press.

Tyack, D. B., & Cuban, L. (1995). *Tinkering toward utopia.* Cambridge MA: Harvard University Press.

Chapter 3

Delpit, L. (2006). *Other people's children: Cultural conflict in the classroom.* New York, NY: The New Press.

Ennis, C. D., & McCauley, M. T. (2002). Creating urban classroom communities worthy of trust. *Journal of Curriculum Studies, 34*(2), 149–172.

Hattie, J. (2008). *Visible learning: A synthesis of over 800 meta-analyses relating to achievement.* New York, NY: Routledge.

Hattie, J. (2012). *Visible learning for teachers: Maximizing impact on learning.* New York, NY: Routledge.

Heath, S. B., & McLaughlin, M. W. (1993). *Identity and inner-city youth: Beyond ethnicity and gender.* New York, NY: Teachers College Press.

Kohn, A. (1999). *Punished by rewards: The trouble with gold stars, incentive plans, A's, praise, and other bribes.* Boston, MA: Houghton Mifflin Harcourt.

Marzano, R. J. (2000). *Transforming classroom grading.* Alexandria, VA: Association for Supervision and Curriculum Development.

Noddings, N. (1996). The caring professional. In S. Gordon, P. Benner, & N. Noddings (Eds.), *Caregiving: Readings in knowledge, practice, ethics, and politics* (pp. 160–172). Philadelphia: University of Pennsylvania Press.

Noddings, N. (2015). *The challenge to care in schools* (2nd ed.). New York, NY: Teachers College Press.

Payne, R. K. (1998). *A framework for understanding poverty.* Highlands, TX: Aha! Process.

Pianta, R. C. (1999). *Enhancing relationships between children and teachers.* Washington, DC: American Psychological Association.

Pink, D. H. (2011). *Drive: The surprising truth about what motivates us.* New York, NY: Penguin.

Wentzel, K. R. (1997). Student motivation in middle school: The role of perceived pedagogical caring. *Journal of Educational Psychology, 89*(3), 411.

Yeager, D. S., Purdie-Vaughns, V., Garcia, J., Apfel, N., Brzustoski, P., Master, A., . . . & Cohen, G. L. (2014). Breaking the cycle of mistrust: Wise interventions to provide critical feedback across the racial divide. *Journal of Experimental Psychology: General, 143*(2), 804.

Chapter 4

Beattie, G., Cohen, D., & McGuire, L. (2013). An exploration of possible unconscious ethnic biases in higher education: The role of implicit attitudes on selection for university posts. *Semiotica, 2013*(197), 171–201.

Brookhart, S. M. (1991). Grading practices and validity. *Educational Measurement: Issues and Practice, 10*(1), 35–36.

Codrington, J., & Fairchild, H. H. (2012). *Special education and the mis-education of African American children: A call to action.* Washington, DC: The Association of Black Psychologists.

Downey, D. B., & Pribesh, S. (2004). When race matters: Teachers' evaluations of students' classroom behavior. *Sociology of Education, 77*(4), 267–282.

Epstein, R., Blake, J., & González, T. (2017). *Girlhood interrupted: The erasure of Black girls' childhood.* Washington, DC: Georgetown Center on Poverty and Inequality.

Gershenson, S., Holt, S. B., & Papageorge, N. W. (2016). Who believes in me? The effect of student–teacher demographic match on teacher expectations. *Economics of Education Review, 52*, 209–224.

Greenwald, A. G., & Krieger, L. H. (2006). Implicit bias: Scientific foundations. *California Law Review, 94*, 945.

Greenwald, A. G., McGhee, D. E., & Schwartz, J. L. (1998). Measuring individual differences in implicit cognition: The implicit association test. *Journal of Personality and Social Psychology, 74*(6), 1464.

Kang, J., Bennett, M., Carbado, D., & Casey, P. (2011). Implicit bias in the courtroom. *UCLA Law Review, 59*, 1124.

Kang, J., & Lane, K. (2010). Seeing through colorblindness: Implicit bias and the law. *UCLA Law Review, 58*, 465.

Lhamon, C. E., & Samuels, J. (2014). *Dear colleague letter on the nondiscriminatory administration of school discipline.* Washington, DC: U.S. Department of Education, Office of Civil Rights & US Department of Justice, Civil Rights Division.

Nosek, B. A., Smyth, F. L., Hansen, J. J., Devos, T., Lindner, N. M., Ranganath, K. A., . . . & Banaji, M. R. (2007). Pervasiveness and correlates of implicit attitudes and stereotypes. *European Review of Social Psychology, 18*(1), 36–88.

Rachlinski, J. J., Johnson, S. L., Wistrich, A. J., & Guthrie, C. (2008). Does unconscious racial bias affect trial judges. *Notre Dame Law Review, 84*, 1195.

Reskin, B. F. (2005). Including mechanisms in our models of ascriptive inequality. In *Handbook of employment discrimination research* (pp. 75–97). Dordrecht, Netherlands: Springer.

Staats, C. (2014). *Implicit racial bias and school discipline disparities* (Kirwan Institute Special Report). Columbus: Ohio State University.

U.S. Department of Education, Office of Special Education and Rehabilitative Services. (2015). *37th Annual Report to Congress on the Implementation of the Individuals with Disabilities Education Act, 2015.* Washington, DC: Author. Retrieved from https://files .eric.ed.gov/fulltext/ED572022.pdf

Chapter 5

Anderman, E. M., & Midgley, C. (1997). Changes in achievement goal orientations, perceived academic competence, and grades across the transition to middle-level schools. *Contemporary Educational Psychology, 22*(3), 269–298.

Barron, K. E., & Harackiewicz, J. M. (2001). Achievement goals and optimal motivation: Testing multiple goal models. *Journal of Personality and Social Psychology, 80*(5), 706.

Darnon, C., Harackiewicz, J. M., Butera, F., Mugny, G., & Quiamzade, A. (2007). Performance-approach and performance-avoidance goals: When uncertainty makes a difference. *Personality and Social Psychology Bulletin, 33*(6), 813–827.

Dweck, C. S. (2006). *Mindset: The new psychology of success.* New York, NY: Random House.

Elliot, A. J., & Church, M. A. (1997). A hierarchical model of approach and avoidance achievement motivation. *Journal of Personality and Social Psychology, 72*(1), 218.

Elliot, A. J., & McGregor, H. A. (2001). A 2 × 2 achievement goal framework. *Journal of Personality and Social Psychology, 80*(3), 501.

Elliot, A. J., McGregor, H. A., & Gable, S. (1999). Achievement goals, study strategies, and exam performance: A mediational analysis. *Journal of Educational Psychology, 91*(3), 549.

Grant, H., & Dweck, C. S. (2003). Clarifying achievement goals and their impact. *Journal of Personality and Social Psychology, 85*(3), 541.

Kaplan, A., & Maehr, M. L. (1999). Achievement goals and student well-being. *Contemporary Educational Psychology, 24*(4), 330–358.

Kaplan, A., & Midgley, C. (1999). The relationship between perceptions of the classroom goal structure and early adolescents' affect in school: The mediating role of coping strategies. *Learning and Individual Differences, 11*(2), 187–212.

La Guardia, J., & Ryan, R. (2002). What adolescents need. *Academic Motivation of Adolescents, 2,* 193.

Lay, R., & Wakstein, J. (1985). Race, academic achievement, and self-concept of ability. *Research in Higher Education, 22*(1), 43–64.

Osborne, J. W. (1995). Academics, self-esteem, and race: A look at the underlying assumptions of the disidentification hypothesis. *Personality and Social Psychology Bulletin, 21*(5), 449–455.

Osborne, J. W., & Walker, C. (2006). Stereotype threat, identification with academics, and withdrawal from school: Why the most successful students of colour might be most likely to withdraw. *Educational Psychology, 26*(4), 563–577.

Patrick, H., Anderman, L. H., Ryan, A. M., Edelin, K. C., & Midgley, C. (2001). Teachers' communication of goal orientations in four fifth-grade classrooms. *The Elementary School Journal, 102*(1), 35–58.

Roeser, R. W., Midgley, C., & Urdan, T. C. (1996). Perceptions of the school psychological environment and early adolescents' psychological and behavioral functioning in
school: The mediating role of goals and belonging. *Journal of Educational Psychology,*
88(3), 408.

Ryan, A. M., Alfeld-Lire, C., & Pintrich, P. R. (1996, April). *A longitudinal study of the impact of*
classroom achievement goals on student motivation and cognition. Paper presented at the meetings of the American Educational Research Association, New York, NY.

Skaalvik, E. M. (1997). Self-enhancing and self-defeating ego orientation: Relations with
task and avoidance orientation, achievement, self-perceptions, and anxiety. *Journal of*
Educational Psychology, 89(1), 71.

Steele, C. M. (1992). Race and the schooling of Black Americans. *The Atlantic Monthly,*
269(4), 68–78.

Steele, C. M. (1997). A threat in the air: How stereotypes shape intellectual identity and
performance. *American Psychologist, 52*(6), 613.

Wolters, C. A. (2004). Advancing achievement goal theory: Using goal structures and goal
orientations to predict students' motivation, cognition, and achievement. *Journal of*
Educational Psychology, 96(2), 236.

Chapter 7

Carifio, J., & Carey, T. (2013). The arguments and data in favor of minimum grading. *Mid-*
Western Educational Researcher, 25(4).

Carifio, J., & Carey, T. (2015). Further findings on the positive effects of minimum grading.
Journal of Education and Social Policy, 2(4), 130–136.

Dueck, M. (2014). *Grading smarter, not harder: Assessment strategies that motivate kids and help*
them learn. Alexandria, VA: ASCD.

Guskey, T. R. (2009). *Bound by tradition: Teachers' views of crucial grading and reporting issues.*
Online Submission.

Guskey, T. R., & Jung, L. A. (2016). GRADING: Why you should trust your judgment.
Educational Leadership, 73(7), 50.

O'Connor, K. (2009). Reforming grading practices in secondary schools. *Principal's Research*
Review, 4(1), 1–7.

Reeves, D. B. (2004). The case against the zero. *Phi Delta Kappan, 86*(4), 324–325.

Reeves, D. B. (2008). Leading to change/Effective grading practices. *Educational Leadership,*
65(5), 85.

Smallwood, M. L. (1935). *An historical study of examinations and grading systems in early American*
universities: A critical study of the original records of Harvard, William and Mary, Yale, Mount
Holyoke, and Michigan from their founding to 1900 (Vol. 24). Cambridge, MA: Harvard
University Press.

Starch, D. (1913). Reliability and distribution of grades. *Science, 38*(983), 630–636.

Starch, D. (1915). Can the variability of marks be reduced? *School and Society, 2*(33), 242–243.

Chapter 8

Close, D. (2009). Fair grades. *Teaching Philosophy, 32*(4), 361–398.

Chapter 9

Close, D. (2009). Fair grades. *Teaching Philosophy*, *32*(4), 361–398.

Fried, R. L. (2005). *The game of school: Why we all play it, how it hurts kids, and what it will take to change it*. San Francisco, CA: Jossey-Bass.

Hardy, M. S. (2002). Extra credit: Gifts for the gifted? *Teaching of Psychology*, *29*(3), 233–234.

Kelly, S. (2008). What types of students' effort are rewarded with high marks? *Sociology of Education*, *81*(1), 32–52.

Padilla-Walker, L. M. (2006). The impact of daily extra credit quizzes on exam performance. *Teaching of Psychology*, *33*(4), 236–239.

Padilla-Walker, L. M., Thompson, R. A., Zamboanga, B. L., & Schmersal, L. A. (2005). Extra credit as incentive for voluntary research participation. *Teaching of Psychology*, *32*(3), 150–153.

Powell, J. A., Heller, C. C., & Bundalli, F. (2011). *Systems thinking and race: Workshop summary*. Los Angeles: The California Endowment. Retrieved from http://www.racialequity tools.org/resourcefiles/Powell_Systems_Thinking_Structural_Race_Overview.pdf

Skiba, R. J., Michael, R. S., Nardo, A. C., & Peterson, R. L. (2002). The color of discipline: Sources of racial and gender disproportionality in school punishment. *The Urban Review*, *34*(4), 317–342.

Chapter 10

Blakemore, S. J., & Choudhury, S. (2006). Development of the adolescent brain: Implications for executive function and social cognition. *Journal of Child Psychology and Psychiatry*, *47*(3/4), 296–312.

Butler, R., & Nisan, M. (1986). Effects of no feedback, task-related comments, and grades on intrinsic motivation and performance. *Journal of Educational Psychology*, *78*(3), 210.

Fisher, B. L., Allen, R., & Kose, G. (1996). The relationship between anxiety and problem-solving skills in children with and without learning disabilities. *Journal of Learning Disabilities*, *29*(4), 439–446.

Gillock, K. L., & Reyes, O. (1999). Stress, support, and academic performance of urban, low-income, Mexican-American adolescents. *Journal of Youth and Adolescence*, *28*(2), 259–282.

Goldstein, S. E., Boxer, P., & Rudolph, E. (2015). Middle school transition stress: Links with academic performance, motivation, and school experiences. *Contemporary School Psychology*, *19*(1), 21–29.

Josephson Institute. (2010). *Josephson Institute's 2010 Report Card on the Ethics of American Youth*. Los Angeles, CA: Author. Retrieved from http://charactercounts.org/pdf/report card/2010/ReportCard2010_data-tables.pdf

Kaplan, D. S., Liu, R. X., & Kaplan, H. B. (2005). School related stress in early adolescence and academic performance three years later: The conditional influence of self-expectations. *Social Psychology of Education*, *8*(1), 3–17.

Mangione, L. (2008). Is homework working? *Phi Delta Kappan*, *89*(8), 614–615.

Papay, J. P., Costello, R. J., Hedl, J. J., & Spielberger, C. D. (1975). Effects of trait and state anxiety on the performance of elementary school children in traditional and individualized multiage classrooms. *Journal of Educational Psychology*, *67*(6), 840.

Solano-Flores, G. (2008). Who is given tests in what language by whom, when, and where? The need for probabilistic views of language in the testing of English language learners. *Educational Researcher, 37*(4), 189–199.

Stewart, S. M., Lam, T. H., Betson, C. L., Wong, C. M., & Wong, A. M. P. (1999). A prospective analysis of stress and academic performance in the first two years of medical school. *Medical Education-Oxford, 33*(4), 243–250.

Chapter 11

Alexander, M. (2012). *The new Jim Crow: Mass incarceration in the age of colorblindness.* New York, NY: The New Press.

Amabile, T. M. (1996). *Creativity in context: Update to the social psychology of creativity.* Hachette, England: Routledge.

Brandt, R. (1995). Punished by rewards. *Educational Leadership, 53*(1), 13–16.

Covington, M. V. (1992). *Making the grade: A self-worth perspective on motivation and school reform.* New York, NY: Cambridge University Press.

De Castella, K., Byrne, D., & Covington, M. (2013). Unmotivated or motivated to fail? A cross-cultural study of achievement motivation, fear of failure, and student disengagement. *Journal of Educational Psychology, 105*(3), 861.

Deci, E. L., Koestner, R., & Ryan, R. M. (1999). A meta-analytic review of experiments examining the effects of extrinsic rewards on intrinsic motivation. *Psychological Bulletin, 125*(6), 627.

Docan, T. N. (2006). Positive and negative incentives in the classroom: An analysis of grading systems and student motivation. *Journal of Scholarship of Teaching and Learning, 6*(2), 21–40.

Dueck, M. (2014). *Grading smarter, not harder: Assessment strategies that motivate kids and help them learn.* Alexandria, VA: ASCD.

Gay, G. (2010). *Culturally responsive teaching: Theory, research, and practice.* New York, NY: Teachers College Press.

Greenhaus, J. H., Parasuraman, S., & Wormley, W. M. (1990). Effects of race on organizational experiences, job performance evaluations, and career outcomes. *Academy of Management Journal, 33*(1), 64–86.

Guskey, T. R. (2000). Grading policies that work against standards . . . and how to fix them. *NASSP Bulletin, 84*(620), 20–29.

Guskey, T. R. (2008). *Practical solutions for serious problems in standards-based grading.* Thousand Oaks, CA: Corwin.

Guskey, T. R., & Bailey, J. M. (2001). *Developing grading and reporting systems for student learning.* Thousand Oaks, CA: Corwin.

Haladyna, T. M. (1999). *A complete guide to student grading.* Boston, MA: Allyn & Bacon.

Hammond, Z. (2014). *Culturally responsive teaching and the brain: Promoting authentic engagement and rigor among culturally and linguistically diverse students.* Thousand Oaks, CA: Corwin.

Kaufman, J. C., & Sternberg, R. J. (Eds.). (2006). *The international handbook of creativity.* New York, NY: Cambridge University Press.

Kohn, A. (1999). *Punished by rewards: The trouble with gold stars, incentive plans, A's, praise, and other bribes.* Boston, MA: Houghton Mifflin Harcourt.

Kohn, A. (2011). The case against grades. *Educational Leadership, 69*(3), 28–33.

Lepper, M. R., Greene, D., & Nisbett, R. E. (1973). Undermining children's intrinsic interest with extrinsic reward: A test of the "overjustification" hypothesis. *Journal of Personality and Social Psychology, 28*(1), 129.

Lhamon, C. E., & Samuels, J. (2014). *Dear colleague letter on the nondiscriminatory administration of school discipline.* Washington, DC: U.S. Department of Education, Office of Civil Rights & US Department of Justice, Civil Rights Division.

Marzano, R. J. (2000). *Transforming classroom grading.* Alexandria, VA: Association for Supervision and Curriculum Development.

Moore, R. (2008). Who's helped by help-sessions in introductory science courses? *The American Biology Teacher, 70*(5), 269–273.

Pink, D. H. (2011). *Drive: The surprising truth about what motivates us.* New York, NY: Penguin.

Stiggins, R. (2005). Assessment for learning: Building a culture of confident learners. In R. DuFour, & R. DuFour (Eds.), *On common ground: The power of professional learning communities* (pp. 65–83). Bloomington, IN: National Educational Service.

Urdan, T., & Schoenfelder, E. (2006). Classroom effects on student motivation: Goal structures, social relationships, and competence beliefs. *Journal of School Psychology, 44*(5), 331–349.

Wormeli, R. (2011). Redos and retakes done right. *Educational Leadership, 69*(3), 22–26.

Chapter 12

Boud, D. (1995). Assessment and learning: Contradictory or complementary. *Assessment for Learning in Higher Education*, 35–48.

Marzano, R. J. (2011). *Formative assessment & standards-based grading.* Bloomington, IN: Solution Tree Press.

Staats, C. (2014). *Implicit racial bias and school discipline disparities* (Kirwan Institute Special Report). Columbus: Ohio State University.

Stiggins, R. J., Arter, J. A., Chappuis, J., & Chappuis, S. (2004). *Classroom assessment for student learning: Doing it right—using it well.* Boston, MA: Pearson, Assessment Training Institute.

Tyler, R. W. (2004). *Basic principles of curriculum and instruction.* Chicago, IL: University of Chicago Press.

Yeager, D. S., Purdie-Vaughns, V., Garcia, J., Apfel, N., Brzustoski, P., Master, A., . . . & Cohen, G. L. (2014). Breaking the cycle of mistrust: Wise interventions to provide critical feedback across the racial divide. *Journal of Experimental Psychology: General, 143*(2), 804.

Chapter 13

Alexander, M. (2012). *The new Jim Crow: Mass incarceration in the age of colorblindness.* New York, NY: The New Press.

Black, P. (2013). Formative and summative aspects of assessment: Theoretical and research foundations in the context of pedagogy. In J. H. McMillan (Ed.), *SAGE handbook of research on classroom assessment* (pp. 167–178). Thousand Oaks, CA: Sage.

Black, P., Harrison, C., Lee, C., Marshall, B., & Wiliam, D. (2004). Working inside the black box: Assessment for learning in the classroom. *Phi Delta Kappan, 86*(1), 8–21.

Butler, R., & Nisan, M. (1986). Effects of no feedback, task-related comments, and grades on intrinsic motivation and performance. *Journal of Educational Psychology, 78*(3), 210.

Greenhaus, J. H., Parasuraman, S., & Wormley, W. M. (1990). Effects of race on organizational experiences, job performance evaluations, and career outcomes. *Academy of Management Journal, 33*(1), 64–86.

Kanfer, R., Ackerman, P. L., & Sternberg, R. J. (1989). Dynamics of skill acquisition: Building a bridge between intelligence and motivation. *Advances in the Psychology of Human Intelligence, 5*, 83–134.

Kluger, A. N., & DeNisi, A. (1996). The effects of feedback interventions on performance: A historical review, a meta-analysis, and a preliminary feedback intervention theory. *Psychological Bulletin, 119*(2), 254.

Kohn, M. L. (1963). Social class and parent–child relationships: An interpretation. *American Journal of Sociology, 68*(4), 471–480.

Lipnevich, A. A., & Smith, J. K. (2008). Response to assessment feedback: The effects of grades, praise, and source of information. *ETS Research Report Series, 2008*(1).

Nicol, D. J., & Macfarlane-Dick, D. (2006). Formative assessment and self-regulated learning: A model and seven principles of good feedback practice. *Studies in Higher Education, 31*(2), 199–218.

Pintrich, P. R., & Zusho, A. (2002). The development of academic self-regulation: The role of cognitive and motivational factors. In A. Wigfield & J. S. Eccles (Eds.), *Development of achievement motivation* (pp. 249–284). New York, NY: Elsevier.

Index

A SAGE Publishing Company

Helping educators make the greatest impact

CORWIN HAS ONE MISSION: to enhance education through intentional professional learning.

We build long-term relationships with our authors, educators, clients, and associations who partner with us to develop and continuously improve the best evidence-based practices that establish and support lifelong learning.

Solutions you want. Experts you trust. Results you need.

AUTHOR CONSULTING

Author Consulting

On-site professional learning with sustainable results! Let us help you design a professional learning plan to meet the unique needs of your school or district. www.corwin.com/pd

INSTITUTES

Institutes

Corwin Institutes provide collaborative learning experiences that equip your team with tools and action plans ready for immediate implementation. www.corwin.com/institutes

ECOURSES

eCourses

Practical, flexible online professional learning designed to let you go at your own pace. www.corwin.com/ecourses

READ2EARN

Read2Earn

Did you know you can earn graduate credit for reading this book? Find out how: www.corwin.com/read2earn

Contact an account manager at (800) 831-6640 or visit **www.corwin.com** for more information.